D0710664

MARIE~ANNE

MAGGIE SIGGINS

MARIE~ANNE

The Extraordinary Life of Louis Riel's Grandmother

McClelland & Stewart

LIBRARY AND ARCHIVES CANADA CATALOGUING IN PUBLICATION

Siggins, Maggie, 1942–
Marie-Anne : the extraordinary life of Louis Riel's grandmother / Maggie Siggins.

ISBN 978-0-7710-8029-6

1. Lagimodière, Marie-Anne, 1780–1875. 2. Frontier and pioneer life – Prairie Provinces. 3. Fur trade – Canada, Western – History – 19th century. 4. Northwest, Canadian – History – To 1870. 5. Women pioneers – Canada, Western – Biography. I. Title.

FC3213.1.L34S44 2008   971.2'01092   C2008-900942-8

We acknowledge the financial support of the Government of Canada through the Book Publishing Industry Development Program and that of the Government of Ontario through the Ontario Media Development Corporation's Ontario Book Initiative. We further acknowledge the support of the Canada Council for the Arts and the Ontario Arts Council for our publishing program.

Typeset in Janson by M&S, Toronto

Printed and bound in Canada

This book is printed on acid-free paper that is 100% recycled, ancient-forest friendly (100% post-consumer recycled).

McClelland & Stewart Ltd.
75 Sherbourne Street
Toronto, Ontario
M5A 2P9
www.mcclelland.com

1 2 3 4 5   12 11 10 09 08

For my beloved husband, Gerry Sperling
whose help and inspiration has been a gift.

CONTENTS

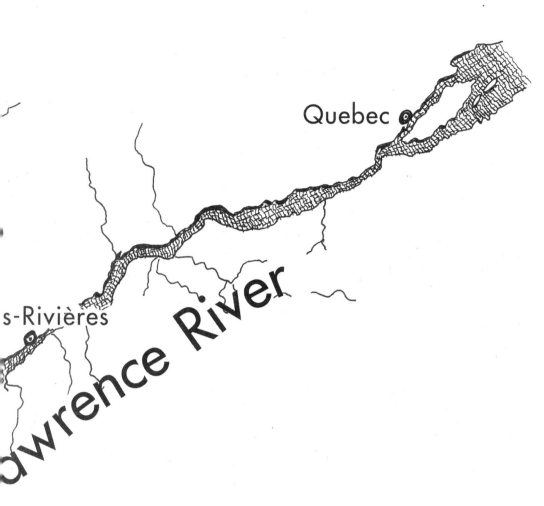

Quebec

s-Rivières

Lawrence River

The Trois Rivières area, where Marie-Anne was born and lived until she left for the North West in 1807

—

WHILE WRITING A BIOGRAPHY of Louis Riel, I became aware of a figure lurking in the background who, I came to realize, had a profound influence on the great Canadian reformer and martyr. This was Riel's grandmother, Marie-Anne Lagimodière, *née* Gaboury. As my research progressed, I came to regard her as the most exceptional Canadian woman of the nineteenth century. The achievements of Laura Secord, Susanna Moodie, and Frances Ann Hopkins pale in comparison. She was the first woman of European extraction to live in Canada's far west, by about forty years. In 1807, she left her birthplace in Quebec to make her home first in the Red River Valley and then in the North West. In 1812 she, her husband, and their five children (three more would arrive later) travelled east again and became embroiled in the chaos and tragedy that marked the establishment of Lord Selkirk's Red River Settlement.

A biography of this brave and endearing woman was obviously in order, but because there are so few documents and letters relating to her life, it seemed a daunting task. There do, however, exist several accounts of Marie-Anne's life. The one written closest to the time she live is by Father Georges Dugast, and was published in 1902 by the Historical and Scientific Society of Manitoba, twenty-eight years after her death. This thirty-two-page pamphlet bears this weighty title: *The First Canadian Woman in the Northwest, or the Story of Marie Anne Gaboury, Wife of John Baptiste Lajimoniere Who Arrived in the Northwest in 1807, and Died at St. Boniface at the Age of 96 Years.* It and other accounts provide a skeleton chronology of Marie-Anne's travels and adventures, just enough to set her in her time and place.

My husband, Gerry Sperling, and I set out to follow in this incredible woman's footsteps. We tracked her along the Ottawa River and across Georgian Bay to Sault Ste. Marie. (She travelled by canoe, we by motor launch.) We visited Pembina, North Dakota, where she gave birth to her first child; made our way to Fort William, now a Disney-style reconstruction at Thunder Bay, Ontario; followed her route along the North Saskatchewan River; and spent days at Fort Edmonton, where she lived for three years. Visiting museums, archives, and libraries, and delving into family lore were part of this voyage. As a result, I've been able to correct some of the factual errors in Father Dugast's manuscript and add considerable material to Marie-Anne's story. I used original documents whenever I could – censuses and wills, fur traders' journals, oral histories, the eyewitness accounts of the Selkirk Settlers, and witnesses' statements about the tragic Seven Oaks incident. From these, I've attempted to recreate her life in Quebec and the North West, and at Red River.

As my investigation proceeded, I became more and more skeptical of Father Dugast's biography, where he fashioned a Marie-Anne who is entirely obedient, docile, straitlaced, and above all religiously devout. Common sense dictates that she would not have survived her adventures unless she had been one tough cookie.

It's been said that in Marie-Anne's latter years she and her favourite grandchild, Louis Riel, were very close. No wonder. They were kindred spirits.

PROLOGUE

—

JULY, 1868

So, my Louis, you are finally home. What a commotion you've created, all of St. Boniface clasping you to its heaving bosom. Your mother made a spectacle of herself as usual, cackling with glee one minute, and sobbing stupid tears the next. But yes, you are a sight for sore eyes, especially ancient ones like mine. So handsome, though in a refined sort of way. Nothing like the robust, raw-boned man your grandfather was. And cultured! You wear your fine education like a Joseph's coat. My sitting room has been transformed into a regular Paris salon, everybody wanting to see for themselves what so many years of high-class education have wrought. Thank the Lord you didn't quote Latin at Father Barnard. He has a hard time comprehending the language. But I was pleased you spoke English with the government inspector, Mr. Whitewood. His foxhound face turned scarlet, so I guess you made him understand how lamentable our situation is here in Red River.

For all that, it's the Indian language that will be most useful to you, if it is here in this crude place that you hope to make your mark.

It was I who taught you the language of the sauvages. *I remember you as a small boy with that head of curly hair belting out* Chuk-chuk-a-thu, Chuk-chuk-a-thu, *blackbird, blackbird. You learned Cree quickly, amazingly so, and I knew, even then, that you were exceptional, destined for a life almost as remarkable as mine has been.*

Please, Louis, don't think this decrepit old biddy you see before you now, encased in this dowdy gown and with a cross of penance around her neck, bears any resemblance to the young woman who ran the rapids on the French River and who rode horses bareback on the open prairies like a daredevil. You and I, we have the same impetuous soul, the same reckless spirit, the same fervour.

MARIE~ANNE

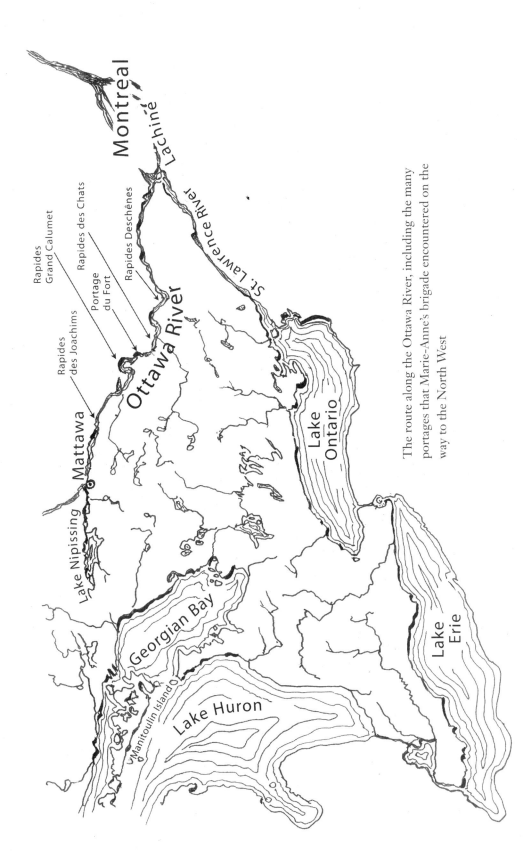

The route along the Ottawa River, including the many portages that Marie-Anne's brigade encountered on the way to the North West

Montréal

Lachine

St. Lawrence River

Rapides Grand Calumet

Rapides des Chats

Portage du Fort

Rapides Deschênes

Rapides des Joachims

Ottawa River

Mattawa

Lake Nipissing

Lake Ontario

Georgian Bay

Manitoulin Island

Lake Huron

Lake Erie

PART ONE

—

THE JOURNEY

CHAPTER ONE

—

How MARIE-ANNE GABOURY grew into such a hardy, fearless, even reckless young woman is hard to fathom. She was brought up to be obedient, nondescript, and always willing – eager even – to stifle her own desires for the good of her family. Young women in Quebec in the late eighteenth century did what was expected of them: biennial child bearing, morning-to-night farm work, care and comfort of husbands and, of course, earnest God worship. They did so without question, without complaint. Father Bertrand was to be honoured no matter how foul his breath as he mumbled admonitions from behind the confessional curtain. Hateful Madame Grignon was to be kowtowed to only because she was the sister of the seigneur. And a father was to be obeyed even if he picked out the ugliest boy in the village as his daughter's future husband. Rebellion was unheard of – yet Marie-Anne did indeed rebel.

Marie-Anne Gaboury was born near the village of Rivière-du-Loup (now Louiseville), Quebec, on August 15, 1780, the sixth child of Charles Gaboury and Marie-Anne Tessier.[1] There are conflicting accounts of her birth date, but parish records confirm her birth in Rivière-du-Loup. (Marie-Anne was the third most popular name given to eldest daughters in French Canada, after Marie and Marie-Madeleine.)[2] In 1786, an older brother, Augustin, died at age eleven, whether by accident or disease is not known. This was a tragedy for the family, of course, and the next son, born in 1788, was also called Augustin. Six years separated this child and Marie-Anne; she probably often looked after him. In later years she revealed how close the two had been; it was Augustin whom she missed the most when she left Quebec.

The family farm was situated in the fertile St. Lawrence basin on a plateau in the Trompe-Souris range near the village of Maskinongé, in the parish of St-Joseph-de-Maskinongé, on the Rivière de Maskinongé, alongside the Baie de Maskinongé (the early settlers were very fond of netting the mighty muskellunge that populated the nearby river). There, on narrow strips of land running from the river to the forest behind, wheat, barley, hay, and (because the habitants loved pancakes so much) lowly buckwheat were grown. For years only a small portion of this yield was sold, but from the 1790s onward wheat futures played a part in Lower Canada's increasingly sophisticated farming economy. By 1802 a record one million bushels of wheat were shipped from the port of Quebec City to countries throughout the British Empire.[3] Life for families like the Gabourys became more prosperous and comfortable.

The family garden, supervised sternly by Marie-Anne's mother, produced an abundance of carrots, cabbages, onions, tomatoes, squash, strawberries, apples, and pears. There was usually a milk cow, and a half-dozen hens and a rooster. The Gabourys may not have been rich but they were never hungry.

The family's roots lay deep in New France. Ancestors on the paternal side emigrated from Normandy during the 1690s and had been farming in Maskinongé ever since. Another branch of the family were descendants of the *filles du roi*, or "daughters of the king," who, under the auspices of Louis XIV, had been swept off the streets of Paris and Rouen and shipped to New France. Fifty percent of the eight hundred *filles* came from the Hospice de la Salpêtrière, a huge institution that forcibly housed the underbelly of Parisian society, including orphans and abandoned children, pregnant and sick women, and prostitutes.[4] In New France of the 1660s, there were six men, mostly indentured servants, for every woman. How was the young colony to thrive with so few mothers? The French monarch had the answer: provide healthy young ladies with money for ocean passages, dowries of thirty sterling livres, room and board once they reached New France, and a trousseau.

Seated in the convent parlour of the Congrégation de Notre-Dame in Ville-Marie (present-day Montreal), these royal wards were allowed to inspect potential husbands, carefully, one at a time. Did he still have all his teeth? That was the first clue as to how strong and healthy a potential mate might be. Had he built a house? If the answer was yes, he was probably hard working and organized. With six-to-one odds, most *filles du roi* found husbands soon after arriving, and they quickly did what the king wanted them to – reproduce. By 1671, seven hundred babies had been born, and the balance of the sexes had evened out. The result was a self-contained, although not exactly booming, colony.

Charles Gaboury and his wife Marie-Anne (*née* Tessier) did not own their land but were *censitaires*, tenant farmers, working their *rotures*, narrow strips of between one and six hectares ceded to

them by the seigneur. The seigneurial system had been trans-
planted to New France in the seventeenth century as a way of
promoting immigration. The French monarchy awarded large
tracts of riverfront land to members of the aristocracy and to the
Roman Catholic Church. These landowners were required to live
on or near their property, to bear the cost of recruiting and settling
peasant colonists, and to construct a gristmill for general use.[5] In
turn, the habitants paid an annual rent called the *cens et rentes*, as
well as taxes that included the *banalités* levied on grain, licences for
hunting, fishing, and woodcutting and, most hated of all, the
corvée, a certain number of days every year that the habitant was
required to work for the seigneur, fixing roads or helping bring in
the harvest.

Maskinongé was first conceded as a seigneurie in 1672 to
two brothers, Pierre-Noël Legardeur de Tilly and Jean-Baptiste
Legardeur de Saint-Michel. The Legardeurs were one of five families who had been allotted some nineteen seigneuries around
Trois-Rivières, including Maskinongé.[6] These people were the
kingpins, the governors, the administrators, the moral arbiters of
the new society. Arranged marriages strengthened this family
compact. Pierre-Noël Legardeur, for example, married Madeleine,
daughter of Pierre Boucher, for decades the most influential man
in the Trois-Rivières region. Boucher was a prosperous fur trader,
governor, head of the feudal court, authority on agriculture production, and organizer of the local militia. By the eighteenth
century, the Bouchers had taken over the Legardeurs' property. It
was the Bouchers, with their lordly privileges, who dominated the
life of the Gabourys during Marie-Anne's time. Every Sunday
morning the habitants of St-Joseph-de-Maskinongé stood at attention as the Boucher clan swept into their seats at the front of the
church and they stood again as the nobility filed out.

Yet Lower Canada's seigneurial class, which was stoutly maintained by the British after the Conquest, was not by any means at the top of the social heap. This exalted position was occupied by government officials and military personnel, English speakers all, with close ties to Great Britain. Of course, these people would have played little if any role in Marie-Anne Gaboury's life. It was just as well. This was the era when the Victorian poem "The Angel in the House," was beginning to hold sway, with its celebration of womanly submissiveness that was even more stultifying for nonconforming women than the restricted role the Catholic Church allowed them.

The class structure in Quebec at the turn of the nineteenth century was as rigid as St. Macrina's iron cross. Growing up in the hidebound village of Maskinongé, Marie-Anne Gaboury was destined to be the wife of a habitant. All her chroniclers agree that she was a remarkable beauty. And she was known to be smart, personable, and hard working. Yet so fixed was the pecking order of her society that, even with her advantages, she could not dream of marrying into the merchant class, never mind the aristocracy.

Members of the gentry were not the only ones dedicated to keeping Quebec's hierarchy firmly in place; the well-being of the Roman Catholic Church depended on securing the status quo. Religious orders controlled huge seigneuries; the Sulpicians at one point owned the entire island of Montreal. The *censitaires* handed over one-twenty-sixth of the harvest to the church each year, and paid pew rentals and fees for special masses, baptisms, marriages, and burials.

With the defeat of the French at the Battle of the Plains of Abraham in 1759, many Québécois feared that the Catholic religion and the French language would be suppressed by the British authorities. Quite the opposite happened. The *Quebec Act* of 1774 legitimized and strengthened the Catholic Church, which imposed a rigid, authoritarian governance. Father Joseph-Octave Plessis summed up the church's attitude in a funeral oration in 1794: "Every soul must submit to the established authority and anyone resisting this power is resisting God." Sixteen years later he added, "Fear God and honour the King!"[7] Imprinted on children – Marie-Anne Gaboury would have been twelve at the time – was the message that conformity was next to godliness, especially for girls.

Like almost everyone else in Quebec at the time, the Gaboury and Tessier clans were piously devout. An uncle who had taken orders and taught at the seminary of St-Sulpice for many years was the guardian and role model for the young set. His guiding principle was simple: Nothing about the Catholic faith was ever to be questioned.

In 1792, tragedy struck the Gaboury family. Marie-Anne's father, Charles, died. Perhaps he was a victim of one of the epidemics that raged during that time – cholera, typhus, smallpox, scarlet and yellow fever, and measles, as well as dysentery, diarrhea, gastritis, all caused by the polluted waters of the St. Lawrence River.[8] Or perhaps he was simply worn out from the hard work of farming. Charles Gaboury was forty-nine years old and his youngest child, Joseph Isaac, had been born only a year and a half earlier.

The history of the family farm remains confusing. Marie-Anne Tessier, with her brood in tow, moved to a smaller acreage further north, in the Ormière range. Eventually the eldest son, Pierre, worked the original farm on the Trompe-Souris range, but it was not until six years after his father's death, when Pierre was twenty-four, that his occupation changed from labourer to farmer in the parish records. By that time he had married Madeleine Gonneville; a child was born two months later – these things happened even in church-dominated Quebec.

Four years after her husband's death, on September 5, 1797, Marie-Anne Tessier married Jean-Baptiste Mainguy, a bachelor sixteen years younger than her first husband. There is no record of Marie-Anne Tessier's exact age – at the time she was probably a few years older than Mainguy – but no offspring were born from this union. Mainguy operated a small but busy canteen on the one good "highway" in the colony, the King's Road.[9] Mainguy was a landowner, and the marriage was a step up for the widow Tessier.

Their house was located directly down the hill from St. Joseph's Church. When Marie-Anne was fifteen, her mother arranged for her to become the housekeeper for the parish priest, Father Ignace Prudent Vinet. She would work in the rectory for ten years, receiving very little pay, perhaps only her meals.

Father Vinet was born in Longue Point, northeast of Montreal, on August 30, 1762. He studied at the Séminaire du Québec, a training ground for priests established by Monsignor de Laval in 1663, to preach an evangelical Catholic message throughout North America. Vinet was ordained in March 1792. After serving as an assistant curé for four years, he was assigned to be head priest at St. Joseph's. The Maskinongé faithful considered themselves lucky to have him; at that time men of the cloth were hard to come by. The British, fearful of powerful religious orders, forbade the Jesuits and Récollets from enrolling novitiates, which resulted in a sharp decline in religious recruiting. In 1759 there was one priest for every 350 parishioners in Quebec; by 1805 there was one curé for every 1,075 faithful.[10]

A priest in Lower Canada ruled supreme in his parish; he was usually the only person who was literate, the only link to the outside world, the guardian of the French language and culture. "Love the land, the land of your fathers and your ancestors," preached the curés, by which they meant don't fool around with the money-grubbing, worldly Protestant *anglais*, and don't hunger after greater opportunities or social and economic egalitarianism.

Father Vinet's worldly goods, auctioned off after his death in 1818, paint an interesting picture of his domestic world. He kept a small farm on the rectory's property: he owned six piglets and four hogs, and a number of chicken coops. There were the usual implements – scythes, saws, axes, shovels, hatchets and scrapers, pitchforks, watering cans, winnowing sieves, large and small carts, harnesses. Strewn about were piles of wood, scrap iron, poles and posts, rails, vats of lard and quicklime, and bags of grain. He owned a sleigh as well as a large four-wheeled carriage. The kitchen, where Marie-Anne would have spent most of her time, was equally well equipped. Besides the usual cauldrons, saucepans, pots, kettles, and frying pans, there was a waffle iron, a turnspit, a coffee grinder, and several flasks, as well as a variety of cutlery, plates, casseroles, pitchers, and fine crockery objects. Indeed, the priest possessed luxurious items that most habitants could not afford in a lifetime: a fine grandfather clock, feather beds, soft mattresses, several chandeliers, nice linen curtains, a mahogany bureau, tables made of rosewood – a pedestal, a semicircular, and a large rectangular – two chairs beautifully upholstered in a deep blue fabric, woven wall hangings, several impressive glass carafes for serving water or wine, a picture of Saint Francis Xavier, and several very expensive and very good cast iron stoves. Marie-Anne must have had to take special care with these valuable objects; in the process she may have acquired a taste for refinement.

One can only speculate about Father Vinet's relationship with his beautiful seventeen-year-old housekeeper. Records indicate that Marie-Anne knew the rudiments of reading and writing, a most unusual accomplishment, since at the time 85 percent of the population was illiterate; one scholar estimates that at the end of the eighteenth century more than 90 percent of the habitants signed their marriage documents with an X. Typically, a priest's library would not have been large. It probably included texts of Christian morality; Abbé Cernay's, *Le pédagogue des familles chrestiennes*, Laurent Durand's hymnbook, *Cantiques de l'âme dévote*, and the prayer book *L'Office de la semaine sainte* were fashionable at the time.[11] So were the adventures of various explorers, the writings of Samuel de Champlain and Jacques Cartier, for example. But another kind of literature was greatly admired by the literate class, the grisly accounts of various Jesuits martyred by the ferocious natives dwelling in Canada's interior. The murder of Jean de Brébeuf in 1649 as described by Christophe Regnault, the *donné* who was sent to retrieve Brébeuf's mutilated body, was particularly popular: "Father de Brébeuf had his legs, thighs, and arms stripped of flesh to the very bone. I saw a large number of great blisters, which he had on several places on his body from the boiling water, which these barbarians had poured over him in a mockery of Holy Baptism."

Marie-Anne once admitted to her children that she had been terrified of Aboriginal people before she left Quebec. It's something of a mystery why this should have been; the Iroquois wars had ended in 1701 and they, as well as the Huron, Algonquin, and Mi'kmaq, had been tamed for years, living in lands set aside for them during the French regime.[12] Might she have read these grisly accounts in Father Vinet's library?

Marie-Anne also knew a smattering of Latin and a bit of arithmetic. Who else but the worthy priest would have taught her these things? Her illiterate mother might well have been upset, admonishing him: "Why, Father, do you put ideas in the girl's head? My daughter will think our farm boys not good enough for her." And she was dead right.

Her unusual education and her beauty must have given Marie-
Anne a certain self-assurance, because she rebelled in the only way
a young woman of the time could. As she reached her late teens, the
usual age for marriage, suitors lined up. M. Bérubé owned his own
land, ninety square *arpents*, and didn't have to pay one cent in
seigneurial dues. On his farm M. Rivard could count seven chickens,
twelve cows, three oxen, four horses, ten sheep, and a half-dozen
swine. But with terrier-like determination, Marie-Anne turned away
each and every one. Years went by until, at age twenty-six, she was
still single and her family despaired that she would remain a spin-
ster forever.

In December of 1806 the parish of St-Joseph-de-Maskinongé was
all abuzz. After serving in the northwest fur trade, a native son had
returned home. It wasn't an unusual occurrence for men working
the fur trade to come back each fall in time for harvesting, but this
young man had been away for seven long years. When Jean-
Baptiste Lagimodière had set out as a voyageur, he had been a
scrawny kid. Now here he was a strapping, good-looking fellow.
Money jingled in his pocket, everyone praised his nice manners and
religious devotion and, most importantly, he was single. One can
imagine that the mademoiselles of Maskinongé were all atwitter.

While the citizenry of the parish were fascinated with this
romantic woodsman, Jean-Baptiste must have been impressed with
the progress that had been made in his native village. In 1806 the
county of Maskinongé was enjoying an economic growth spurt, primarily because of the burgeoning production of milk and cheese,
which had increased 47 percent in ten years. The village now numbered one thousand souls; just ten years earlier only 581 people had
lived there. A general store, well stocked by the standard of the day,
had just been built on the King's Road about three kilometres west

of St. Joseph's Church. And perhaps because there were finally enough landowners (including Marie-Anne's stepfather) who were paying taxes, an elementary school had been constructed across the street from the store. It was here that "the entire world," as Marie-Anne's biographer, Father Dugast, puts it, gathered in great excitement to enjoy the exploits of the returning prodigal.

It was a blustery night. According to the fashion, Marie-Anne would have wrapped herself in her large wool capote and either walked or been driven to the school in the family's horse-pulled sled. Because her housekeeping duties required that she remain at the rectory until well after the supper hour, she was late. The seats had all been taken by the time she arrived, but several men offered her theirs. She shook her head, *non, merci,* and stood at the back. Wood stoves in those days were notorious for giving off too much heat, and the vapour rising from sodden wool garments produced a rank smell. Everyone waited in lively anticipation for the arrival of Father Vinet. As the most prominent citizen at the gathering, he had the honour of introducing the speaker.

Jean-Baptiste Lagimodière was dressed in a fur trapper's costume: a jacket of deerskin fringed with dark brown horsehair; moccasins beautifully beaded with porcupine quills dyed red, blue, and yellow; a capote of caribou skin – all set off by a jaunty cap of otter skin that he snatched off his head as he began his talk. (Georges Dugast would write: "He had many wonderful tales to recount! What marvellous facts fell from his lips. They were not always strictly true, but what did that matter? They were interesting. What more could one desire?"[13])

His long-winded stories about attacking bears and menacing Indians were nothing new to Marie-Anne; such exploits were scattered throughout the accounts of Jacques Cartier and Samuel de Champlain found on the rectory's bookshelves. But there must have been something fascinating about his delivery for she was eager to meet him afterwards.

When Jean-Baptiste caught sight of Marie-Anne, he was entranced. By everyone's account she was gorgeous, with the fair skin of her Norman ancestors – the cold that evening would have given her a high colour – large, intelligent eyes of turquoise blue, and hair the colour of burnished copper. He couldn't take his eyes off her.

After his presentation, the villagers crowded around the adventurer, shaking his hand, kissing his cheeks, squeezing his shoulders. He probably didn't get to talk to Marie-Anne before she left, but later he asked his friends, "Is she Mademoiselle or Madame Gaboury?" and was relieved to learn that she was single.

There would have been many opportunities for Jean-Baptiste to get to know the beautiful Marie-Anne. A visit to Father Vinet at St. Joseph's rectory was a necessary social courtesy and, as housekeeper, she would have served the tea. He saw her in church not only for Sunday services but, since it was Christmas time, for carol singing, a pageant of the birth of Christ, and three masses on the day itself. And he might have accompanied her on the myriad of charity missions that were demanded of the priest's housekeeper – delivering a pot of soup to poor families, nursing the ill, chatting with the elderly.

In only a few weeks it was time to think of marriage. Parental permission was needed only if the bride was a minor, but out of courtesy Jean-Baptiste probably requested a meeting with Marie-Anne's mother and stepfather.

Theirs was a typical petit bourgeois house. Squat and small, its main room was dominated by a black stove and a rough wooden table with four straight-backed chairs. Beside the huge stone fireplace, a black frying pan hung on the wall. In one corner sat the ubiquitous wooden bucket with a dipper attached, containing fresh drinking water from the well. Nearby was a well-used wooden butter churn with its accompanying stool; Marie-Anne would have spent hours at the task of separating butterfat from buttermilk. On a commode were placed ordinary objects – eggs, tomatoes, freshly baked bread. And some treasures collected over time would have been on display: typically, a chest made of pine and embellished with inlaid cherrywood; a set of dishes decorated in a willow pattern featuring fat cows and an equally plump dairy-maid; a lantern made of antelope antlers; a statue of the popular St. Roch, the French nobleman who spent his life administering to the poor and sick and who was born with an image of a red cross on his breast; a children's painted wooden horse mounted on wheels; wooden figures of every kind of animal, especially dogs and moose; a crucifix carved so intricately that drops of blood seemed to ooze from the crown of thorns onto the dying Christ's forehead. But what really mattered to Jean-Baptiste was the condition of the domicile: was it neat and clean, had the floor been swept, had the fireplace been emptied of soot? All of this reflected on Marie-Anne's skills at tending house.

One can be sure that Marie-Anne's mother and stepfather encouraged Jean-Baptiste. To be single and female in French Canada at the turn of the eighteenth century was to be considered a pariah. And Madam Tessier knew Jean-Baptiste's family as hard-working people, devout and respectable. Almost certainly she tried to persuade her stubborn daughter to accept his offer.

And as etiquette dictated, Jean-Baptiste had to ask the permission of her employer, Father Vinet. The priest was likely more than willing. Having preached Sunday after Sunday on the value of motherhood, the sanctity of the family, he hardly could do otherwise than give his consent.

Local legend has it that Jean-Baptiste got down on his knees in the March slush of the rectory garden and proposed to Marie-Anne. What was her reaction? Was she overjoyed or apprehensive? Single for so long, perhaps she had reservations. A husband was legally the head of the household with close to absolute power; as one scholar puts it, "This position allowed him to pass off his personal interests as family interests."[14] A wife could not start a business, take legal action, or sell her property without her husband's approval. The one advantage French-Canadian women had over their Anglo counterparts was fairly important given the number of widows in Lower Canada: after the death of the husband, the wife and children were given priority over creditors and had the right to buy back certain assets that had been sold outside the family.[15]

But Marie-Anne might well have asked herself what freedom she had as a single woman. If she wanted to go for a walk, she had to ask permission of the priest, or her stepfather, or her brothers. Indeed, the twenty-five-year-old housekeeper had had to plead with Father Vinet for permission to attend Jean-Baptiste's fête the night she met her future husband. A single woman was barred from all the professions, and she could not hold any official position; about the only job open to her was the one Marie-Anne already held – servant. And cleaning up after a self-centred, messy priest could not have been anybody's idea of a glorious future.

Marie-Anne was old enough to know the value of her own sharp intelligence and that she could play a role in Jean-Baptiste's future success; in Lower Canada there were plenty of examples of clever women who were the brains behind their husbands' businesses. Perhaps she and Jean-Baptiste could establish a dealership in lumber, wheat, or furs. She might even have pictured an elderly Monsieur Lagimodière, all jowls and paunch, snoozing in an overstuffed armchair at Montreal's famous Beaver Club, where rich fur traders had been drinking and partying the winters away since 1785.

It's doubtful that Marie-Anne would have had a large dowry; her family was not wealthy enough for that. But a fine trousseau would have been carefully assembled. We don't know what Marie-Anne brought to the marriage, but there is a record of the personal belongings of another young woman of roughly the same social stature. These consisted of three headdresses, four taffeta handkerchiefs, two pairs of shoe ribbons, one hundred sewing needles, one comb, one spool of white thread, three pairs of stockings, two pairs of gloves, one pair of scissors, two knives, one thousand pins, one bonnet, four lace braids, three fine cotton chemises, and a pink garter.[16]

A few weeks before the wedding, Marie-Anne and Jean-Baptiste went to a notary to finalize their marriage contract. Jean-Baptiste marked the document with an X, Marie-Anne signed her name. If theirs was similar to 90 percent of the marriage arrangements in Lower Canada, they agreed that all moveable goods and real estate purchased after the marriage would be jointly owned, although only the husband had the legal right to manage this property. He could sell, give away, or use joint possessions as collateral without his wife's knowledge or permission. Only an inheritance received by the wife was hers to control, and even then the husband could do what he liked with the profits on these assets – for example, the rent on property or the proceeds from a harvest.[17] Probably Marie-Anne and Jean-Baptiste didn't think much about the contract; neither owned any property, nor could they foresee getting their hands on much in the near future.

The couple was married on April 21, 1807. Marie-Anne Tessier would have wanted to signal to her peers that, with her own marriage to the landowner Jean-Baptiste Mainguy, she and her family had moved up in the world, so her daughter was dressed in the typical wedding outfit of the day: silk stockings, an embroidered chemise with whalebone stays, perhaps a gown of cream silk muslin tied under the bosom with a pink ribbon embroidered with roses and with double-layer ruffles at the sleeves, a lovely lace shawl, and a pretty headdress.[18] The groom showed up proudly wearing his coureur de bois costume, made of fur and hides and cinched with a cherry-red *l'Assomption* sash. Handsome was too tame a word for him, stupendous might do, but Marie-Anne might have been a little embarrassed, a little disappointed. She had hoped that Jean-Baptiste now saw his future self as a respectable merchant or farmer, not as a renegade buffalo hunter.

Weddings were big events in small-town Quebec, a chance for major celebration, eating, drinking, and dancing, often lasting for days. These parties were so disorderly that at one point the Monseigneur de Saint-Vallier tried to put at stop to them by issuing the following ordinance:

> So that Priests can more effectively deal with scandalous acts of disrespect and profanation that occur very frequently during the celebration of Marriage, We have deemed it appropriate to order them to inform all those wishing to marry that they have received an order from Us not to admit into Nuptial Benediction any ladies who are immodestly dressed, whose head is not covered, whose breasts are exposed or only covered with transparent material. We order them also to ensure . . . that there is no impiety, jesting or insolence in the Church.[19]

Almost the entire parish of St-Joseph-de-Maskinongé crowded into the pretty stone church, its bell tower and sweeping roof surprisingly elegant for so small a sanctuary, to hear Marie-Anne

Gaboury and Jean-Baptiste Lagimodière exchange marriage vows. We don't know how rowdy their wedding feast was, but a favourite topic of conversation was surely the successes and failures of the outsiders in their midst – the Lagimodière family. Was Jean-Baptiste a worthy catch for the beautiful Marie-Anne Gaboury?

CHAPTER TWO

—

THE FIRST LAGIMODIÈRE ANCESTOR to arrive in New France in the mid-seventeenth century *was* somewhat exceptional. Samuel Lecompte, Sieur de La Vimaudière (over the years the family name somehow metamorphosed into Lagimodière) was a surgeon and prosperous merchant.[1] Few of his descendants achieved the same exalted standing, however. Most were ordinary habitants farming *rotures* in the St. Lawrence lowlands.

Jean-Baptiste's mother, Marie-Josèphe Jared, and his father, Jean-Baptiste Lagimodière, came from the same parish, St-Antoine-sur-Richelieu, about 220 kilometres north of Montreal. According to church records, they were married in 1776. Two years later, Jean-Baptiste was born, and in March 1786 his brother Joseph arrived. (Given the times, there probably were several miscarriages and still-births in the intervening eight years.) Nine months after Joseph's birth, Marie-Josèphe died while delivering her third child. She was only thirty-three. The two young brothers were taken in by an aunt who lived in the Maskinongé area, and their father rented farmland on the east side of the Maskinongé River, about six hundred metres north of the village's bridge. They were not the most prosperous family in the area by any means.

At the age of twenty-one Jean-Baptiste did what countless young Québécois men had done before him; he signed up with the North West Company, the fur enterprise based in Montreal that was the lifeblood of Quebec's economy. He worked his way west as one of six middlemen, paddling a huge *canot de maître*, the freighter of the fur trade (named after Louis Maître of Trois-Rivières, who was a master canoe builder). When he reached the Red River Valley, he stayed to work as a general labourer at the Pembina River post in what is now North Dakota. Soon his skills as a hunter became evident and he was assigned to track down game for food. Eventually he became an independent hunter, one of the *gens libres*, the tough "freemen" who supplied the fur traders with their staple food, pemmican, which is dried buffalo meat laced with lard. After seven years in the west, he finally headed home, on the lookout for a wife.

Needless to say, only Marie-Anne and Jean-Baptiste could judge if their wedding night was a success. Probably Father Vinet blessed their honeymoon, although the standard benediction was something of a downer: "Remember that your Nuptial bed will one day be your death bed, from which your souls will be taken on high before the Judgment Seat of God, to receive terrible punishment of the Seven Husbands of Sara, if you become slaves to your body, your passions and your lust."[2] But at least it was acknowledged that Catholic women in Lower Canada got pleasure from sex, which was fine as long as their husbands were involved. Marie-Anne was not afflicted by the Victorian priggishness of the British among whom "the word 'pregnant' was never spoken in mixed company; expectant mothers had 'interesting' conditions; legs were forbidden – women never revealed theirs, and if for some reason they had to mention them, they were called 'limbs' – and books authored by males and females were carefully separated on shelves."[3]

By all accounts Jean-Baptiste had every intention of farming in the Maskinongé area after his marriage, but he was quickly stymied by a severe land shortage. Two interrelated phenomena had led to this dilemma. First, timber had become so valuable that the seigneurs no longer wanted to cede their acreage. One widow who lived near the Gabourys had been left a huge tract of land when her husband died, yet in six years she had conceded not one *arpent*. The religious organizations were not much better; in 1806 the number of people on the waiting list for Jesuit land grants in the Trois-Rivières area was over three hundred. To add to the problem, the government-controlled freehold land that was available was located deep in the bush, making it almost impossible to get to, never mind that it took five years to clear enough hardwood forest before a family could build a profitable farm.[4] Second, the population in the St. Lawrence lowlands had ballooned. More and more habitant families had to subdivide their holdings to provide some means of living for their heirs. Their farms became smaller and smaller. At the same time, the well-to-do had the resources to cut roads through the bush and get their hands on this Crown land, thereby creating larger and larger farms for themselves. These circumstances created a proletariat of young men desperate to find a foothold in society. In certain locations they made up as much as 40 percent of heads of households.[5]

There was employment other than farming but nothing suitable for Jean-Baptiste. He was too old to apprentice to a craftsman, and jobs in commercial enterprises were few and far between – the Forges-du-Saint-Maurice, an ironworks near Trois-Rivières, was the only industry in the entire Lower Canada. He might have thought of forestry – it was certainly booming. In just a few years, Lower Canada's entire financial base shifted from fur to lumber. And with this industry came all kinds of new businesses – shipbuilding, construction, logging, sawmills, the manufacture of barrels and hoops. But none of these occupations appealed to Lagimodière. As spring approached he told his friends that in his dreams he could actually sniff the balsam branches that covered the floor of the wigwams he had slept in. He longed to head for the North West. But he faced a terrible dilemma: the one promise he had made to his bride was that he would not return to the fur trade.

After their wedding, the Lagimodières moved in with Jean-Baptiste's younger brother, Joseph, and his wife, Marguerite. Their home was a typical habitant house, constructed of stone and timber with a wood-shingle roof, with a kitchen, bedroom/parlour, and a storage attic in which the newlyweds likely camped alongside bags of grain and farm tools.

It was supposed to be a temporary arrangement. Jean-Baptiste was expected to build a house, work a small portion of his father's rented land, and perhaps over the years acquire acreage of his own. Yet as the days went by, nothing happened: building materials weren't collected, the land allotted to Jean-Baptiste remained untilled, seed grew mouldy.

During his sojourn in the North West, Jean-Baptiste had been introduced to an independent trader, George Montague, an adventurer from Belfast.[6] Some time after his wedding, Jean-Baptiste met with Montague to carry on business discussions. On their agenda were lucrative fur-bearing animals – beaver, wolf, otter, marten, mink, fisher, raccoon, wolverine, lynx – and how Jean-Baptiste could trap and Montague market them.

Most of the English-speaking bourgeoisie who had grown rich from international trade and government patronage (which were closed to their French-Canadian counterparts) lived in Quebec City, but a few had seized on business opportunities in the growing towns. George Montague was one of these. He had retired to Trois-Rivières, about eighty kilometres east of Maskinongé. Out of courtesy, he invited Jean-Baptiste's bride to meet his family. They lived in a typical merchant's dwelling, an elegant house with whitewashed walls and polished pine floors. There would have been an ample entrance hall, a sitting room with an enormous fieldstone fireplace (to provide warmth; cooking went on in a kitchen separated from the main building so that if a fire occurred there was a fighting chance to save the house), and a staircase leading to a full second floor of sleeping chambers. These were comfortable – Turkish rugs, gold-framed mirrors, and porcelain chamber pots decorated with daisies. Marie-Anne, who had never ventured further than a few kilometres from the village where she was born, must have been overwhelmed.

If the lavishness of this residence excited her so must have Trois-Rivières, then a bustling town just beginning to feel its muscle. The famous Ursuline Convent, located down the road from the Montague house, was particularly impressive. Marie-Anne might have experienced a shiver of anxiety walking by it; time after time, as she refused marriage suitors, her mother had threatened that she would end up a cloistered nun. And there was St. James Anglican Church, attended by the Montague family; Marie-Anne must have been curious, and a little frightened: she had never met a Protestant before. The town's grime, the mud, the foul smells, especially from the outdoor butchers' market, the chaotic jangle were all unnerving. Still, one can imagine her saying to herself, "I could get used to this place. As the wife of a well-to-do merchant, I could live here."

Family legend has it that Marie-Anne seldom lost her temper, but that when she did white-hot fury was the result. Jean-Baptiste had his first taste of this on the trip home from Trois-Rivières. He confessed that he wanted to return to the North West – Montague had agreed to finance the trip and Jean-Baptiste planned to leave in eight days. He explained that he saw no possibility of making a go of farming. Bribery – the seigneurs, the overseers, the lawyers, even the priests, all held their hands palm side up – was the only way to obtain land and, at eighty livres for only forty *arpents*, this was highway robbery. Not only that, he longed for the freedom of the frontier. There are some indications that a week before his wedding Jean-Baptiste signed a contract that specified that a space be reserved for Marie-Anne for the journey out west. If this is true, then according to her biographer and family legend, he never told his bride-to-be about it.

There were many "fur widows" living in Maskinongé. Typically, after their marriage to voyageurs, they moved in with their in-laws, waiting for their husbands to show up every four years or so. After a month or two at home, these men left again for the North West, and soon another baby arrived. The wives were left alone once again to care for the children – with the church and their mothers-in-law overseeing their every move. Tradition dictated that it was the wife's duty to maintain her husband's tie to civilization and the Catholic Church. It was not exactly a destiny that appealed to someone of Marie-Anne's ambitions. Her biographer, Georges Dugast, writes of the dilemma that faced her: "Either she must allow her husband to go by himself without the hope of seeing him again for many long years, perhaps never, or accompany him into a barbarous country to share during the remainder of her days his fatigues, discomforts and dangers."[7]

Marie-Anne didn't ponder this enormous decision for too long. When she had vowed that she would share Jean-Baptiste's fate no matter what, she meant it. She would go to the North West with him.

No white woman had attempted such a foolhardy journey before. The black flies and mosquitoes alone would make life unbearable. And what about the Indians among whom they would live? Since childhood Marie-Anne had been told that the *sauvages* were pagans, barbarians, vastly inferior to the civilized white man. Dugast writes that the "missionaries had not then penetrated that land to carry into it the light of faith, and the tribes in these immense territories [the North West] were living in darkness."[8] Fortunately Marie-Anne's deep-rooted fear of natives would, over time, profoundly change. She would even become "Indianized."

Dugast describes a meeting with Father Vinet: "After having examined every point well, without making a flattering picture of it, M. Vinet counseled Madame Lajimoniere [sic] that if in spite of all considerations she felt herself courageous and strong enough to go to the North West she should follow her husband rather than let him depart alone."[9] Actually there was another reason for the priest's encouragement. He had already heard a confession from Jean-Baptiste so lascivious that he had squirmed in discomfort. If Jean-Baptiste's soul was to be saved, his wife must go with him.

It was such a bizarre turn of events – in the two hundred or so years that young Quebec men headed to the North West, not once had a wife found the courage to follow (never mind become a player in the fur trade on her own). Marie-Anne's mother must have carefully probed her daughter's motives. Was she being forced into this dangerous life by her husband? Apparently Marie-Anne convinced her that it was entirely her decision.

As the time of her departure approached, Marie-Anne travelled around the Maskinongé district, saying goodbye. Her brother and sister-in-law and their children still lived on the family farm located in the Trompe-Souris range. A well-off widowed aunt resided on the range called Pied-de-la-Côte. One cousin lived in the village of St-Juste. In spring this was pleasant, hilly countryside studded with fields of black earth just seeded for wheat, copses of Gray birch and hemlock trees, thick patches of budding wildflowers. Cows and sheep grazed in the greening fields and drank from the winding Maskinongé River. It was a gentle landscape soon to be forever lost to Marie-Anne, replaced by a wild, forbidding, frightening place. Although she would live to be ninety-six, she would never see her birthplace, or her relatives, again.

Marie-Anne had only one week to prepare for an undertaking that would change her life forever. She must have agonized over what to bring. What do you pack for a 2,800-kilometre voyage by canoe that would take a month and a half, especially since each passenger was allowed only eighteen kilograms of personal luggage, including food supplies? The only items available were the clothes she wore each day, typically a corset with whalebone stays, a muslin travelling dress, plus three chemises, a petticoat, two pairs of sturdy shoes, her one good dress of silk and muslin, three day dresses, several aprons, a variety of stockings, and a cotton and a wool shawl. Jean-Baptiste must have been aghast when he inspected her luggage. How on earth could someone survive in the bush wearing dainty shoes and skirts flapping about her ankles?

For generations the Lagimodière family have laughed over what became known as "Marie-Anne's folly." Unbeknownst to Jean-Baptiste, she snuck into the baggage a flatiron, which when heated on the stove was used to smooth wrinkles out of clothing. In itself it weighed over one kilogram. It was a tell-tale signal, and an unnerving one, that she had no idea what kind of life lay ahead.

Every spring, in the villages along the St. Lawrence, the towns-folk gathered to say goodbye to their voyageurs. Given the aston-ishing occasion of the *daughter* of two old families going off with the men, all of Maskinongé assembled to bid the Lagimodières farewell. As tradition dictated, small gifts were offered. Father Vinet might have given Marie-Anne a breviary. After all, where she was going there were no priests and therefore no sacraments – and there wouldn't be any for years. Perhaps now and then, for the good of the "savage" soul, she could recite the psalms, hymns, lessons, and prayers, the heart of the Catholic daily worship, although whether a woman performing this ritual was acceptable to God was questionable indeed. As her gift to her daughter, Marie-Anne Tessier had carefully stitched a sunbonnet, made of stiff, pale grey muslin, the sides of which all but covered Marie-Anne face, like a visor set in a suit of armour. It was ugly but it would literally save her life on the voyage west.

The Lagimodières' immediate destination was the embarkation point for all canoes heading west, the village of Lachine, located at the exact point where the rapids boiled around the Island of Montreal. Here freight was hauled by horse and cart from Montreal and loaded onto the canoes.* Like everyone else Jean-Baptiste and

---

* How Lachine got its name tells a lot about the aspirations of the early fur trade. On one of his explorations to the North West, the adventurer and fur trader Jean Nicollet (1598–1642) brought along a capote (cloak) made of Chinese material, red with embroidered blue dragons and yellow peonies, with which he planned to impress the emperor when he reached the China Sea. He never got there, of course, but he did show off his outfit to some Indian chiefs along the way. He named the point from where his trip began Lachine – an indication that he was sure he'd find the Orient on the west coast of Canada.[10]

Marie-Anne made the trip to Lachine by horse and buggy. They would have had lots of company along the way; in 1807 North West Company employed 1,500 people, most of them voyageurs who set off every spring after crops had been planted and returned in the fall in time to harvest. Most travelled along the Chemin du Roi, or King's Highway, the first transportation artery to join Quebec City and Montreal.

The north shore of the St. Lawrence had been subdivided among family members for so many years that the farms were now narrow strips about 1.5 kilometres long, and not much wider than an ordinary roadway. The houses, outhouses, and barns were so close together along the winding highway that it was more like one continuous village than separate farms. The relatives of the Gabourys, Mainguys, and Lagimodières who lived along this route numbered in the hundreds, if not thousands. Time and again the travellers would have been invited to stop and offered tea, a meal, a bed for the night – and gossip, so much gossip. One can imagine that the same question was asked over and over again: How could someone so refined, pretty, and well-spoken as Marie-Anne even think of facing the fierce wilderness? Wasn't Jean-Baptiste daft and maybe even cruel to force his delicate wife to accompany him? Apparently nothing Marie-Anne said convinced them that she was the one who insisted on going. The Lagimodières must have been relieved when they reached the Island of Montreal.

There were few inns where respectable women travellers could feel comfortable. One such safe haven was the Maison Saint-Gabriel, where Marie-Anne probably lodged for the night. Situated near Fort Pointe-à-Callière, the magnificent three-storey stone house had been built by Marguerite Bourgeoys in 1668 for the Sisters of the Congregation of Notre Dame. It was here that the *filles du roy* were sheltered on their arrival from France, where the bachelors came to court them, and where the marriage contracts were arranged. Marie-Anne would have joined the others in the attic dormitory, where the nuns and travellers slept all in a row.

Marie-Anne must have known the tragic story of one of the most unfortunate of the "king's daughters," for it was a legend in Lower Canada at the time. Élizabeth Migeon, having met her husband at the Maison Saint-Gabriel, went to live with him on his farm on the Île d'Orléans. Not long afterward she was kidnapped by the Iroquois. Whether she was murdered or held captive, perhaps as a sex slave, was never discovered. She was never heard from again. It would have been understandable if Marie-Anne, perhaps sleeping in the very bed that Élizabeth Migeon had occupied, suffered nightmares that night.

By the time the Lagimodières arrived at the Lachine docks, the *canots de maître*, 10 metres long, and two metres across the beam, and carrying a three-tonne load, would have been piled high, with not a speck of their white cedar floor boards visible. It was very unusual for the North West Company to accommodate passengers, who not only took up cargo space but the seats of two paddlers. It remains a mystery how the Lagimodières managed their passage, although they might have been aided by Montague's connections and money or by Jean-Baptiste's reputation as one of the best hunters and trappers among the French Canadians. Rivalry with the Hudson's Bay Company was heating up, and the Nor'Westers would have wanted him on their side.

Jean-Baptiste had spent his childhood listening to the stories about the *pays d'en haut* and had longed for the dangerous but exciting life of the voyageur. There are hints that he might have been too big physically for the job – the paddlers could not be taller than 1.65 metres – for he never worked as a traditional voyageur travelling each year to the North West and back. He was hired on as a labourer, working for the *hiverants* (wintering clerks), those tough North West Company men who did the actual trading onsite with the Indians. Jean-Baptiste had spent five years in the Red River Valley, sorting and packing beaver pelts and trading goods, cutting and stacking firewood – a never-ending job – repairing the various fort buildings, fashioning crude furniture, cleaning the grounds (particularly the latrines), and fishing and hunting buffalo – skills that he was particularly good at. Eventually he learned the fine art of trapping, especially of beaver, the "black gold" of Canada from the seventeenth through the nineteenth century.

It's difficult today to comprehend how huge the fur trade was for three hundred years in the northern part of North America. Indeed, it moulded Canada into a sea-to-sea country. Historian Frits Pannekoek writes:

> Such noted scholars as Harold Adam Innis and Donald Creighton have asserted that Canada exists in its present form *because* of the fur trade. Fur was the single product or "staple" – like cod fish earlier in the Maritimes or wheat on the prairies in a later period – that was so dominant as to set the tone for the nation's economic and social development. The settlements, transportation routes, and financial structures created in support of the fur trade, in this view, moulded the east-west geographical unity of Canada.[11]

Another historian, J.M.S. Careless, puts the theory more succinctly: "To a great extent Canada was built on the back of the beaver."[12]

Actually it wasn't so much the beaver as the top hat. As early as the Middle Ages, European hat makers had known that the beaver's soft undercoat, in particular the long barbs at the tip of each hair, was wonderful material to make felt headgear. But it wasn't until the North American variety – black and glossy, "the most wonderful beaver wool" in the world, as Baron de La Hontan put it – came on the market that top hats really became popular. Felt made from beaver was remarkably water resistant – hardly anybody carried umbrellas in the eighteenth century – and it was supple. Brims could be moulded into all sorts of fantastic shapes; the Wellington, the d'Orsay, the Regent, and the Paris Beau were a few of the astonishing number of styles in vogue at one time or another. And despite the enduring and endearing image of the gallant sporting his elegant topper and cloak as he sashayed to the opera, the wide-brimmed beaver felt hat was worn by men of all economic circumstances.

Almost immediately after the white man showed up in the valley of the St. Lawrence River, fur became the impetus for the creation of the Canadian nation. The first documented trade in beaver occurred in the summer of 1534, when Jacques Cartier encountered fifty Mi'kmaq enjoying a picnic on a beach in the Baie de Chaleur. "They made frequent signs to us to come on shore, holding up some furs on a stick," the explorer wrote in his log. The Indians eagerly traded the beaver robes right off their backs for beads and other shiny objects. In 1608, Samuel de Champlain founded a warehouse-fort at Québec (now the site of Quebec City), for the express purpose of revving up the fur trade. Each spring, in late May or early June, Indians decked out in their brightest finery would bring their winter catch of ermine, marten, wolf, lynx, fisher, red fox (to be made into coats, muffs, collars), and of course beaver, to Québec, or eventually to the more popular Ville-Marie (now Montreal). Stalls were set up by the Europeans to display all sorts of trade goods – pots, kettles, knives, guns, brightly coloured cloth, and of course, beads. The native people would sort through all this until they had just enough – conspicuous consumption was not an Indian trait. The Montagnais and Algonquin trapped in the St. Lawrence Valley and transported their loot to the French merchants, but the Huron became the most important dealers. They hunted few furs themselves but were enterprising middlemen, using their vast network to expand the trade of the Indian peoples in the interior Great Lakes region. Eventually, though, all the First Nations that dealt directly with the French paid dearly for their folly.

Measles and smallpox decimated the Montagnais and Algonquin in 1634, and two years later the Hurons were afflicted by the same epidemics. Their long-time enemies, the Iroquois, quickly closed in for the kill. As historians John Dickinson and Brian Young write, "Ravaged by disease, divided by missionary propaganda, and unable to obtain firearms unless they turned their back on traditional customs, such as feasts that maintained solidarity, the aboriginal allies of the French fell victim to the numerically and militarily superior Iroquois."[13]

These calamities completely transformed New France's fur trade. From the mid-seventeenth century on, the white man had to make his way into the wild boreal forest to bargain with Indians on their home turf. Thus was born the gutsy, reckless, tough coureur de bois, out to make money, possibly even a fortune, which he certainly couldn't do by laboriously ploughing the land. By 1672 there were three to four hundred of these "wood-runners"; in the next eight years their numbers doubled, and by 1750 there were thousands. Historian Georges-Hébert Germain notes they were nicknamed "coureurs de risques" and describes the life thus: "They could easily be drowned or be injured during a portage or might well be tortured or killed if they ever fell into the hands of the Iroquois. But they also risked fines or a flogging, possibly even the galleys, if they engaged in the fur trade without a license [as many did] or, worse still, tried to sell their furs on the black market instead of through the trading companies."[14]

By shipping beaver pelts from Quebec to Europe, the traders grew wealthy enough to form a colonial aristocracy, at least until New France fell to the British in 1759–60. After the Conquest, Anglo-Saxon merchants showed up in Quebec to supply the troops and newly arrived civil servants. These capitalists were, as one scholar writes, "loyal to the British crown, but maintained many linkages to the Scottish highlands . . . [They] maintained the control of the business by utilizing clan and marital ties to solidify their relationships with colleagues, and to introduce sons, nephews and cousins (many from the Scottish homeland) into the company service."[15] Names like McGillivray, McTavish, Mackenzie, and McGill became a permanent part of the Canadian landscape. With their connections to British firms and lines of credit, these were formidable competitors, driving out smaller enterprises and eventually taking over the fur trade.

This "Montreal mafia" were engaged in a daunting undertaking. The transportation system was complex and expensive. Trade goods from European suppliers were shipped from London to Quebec City and then on to Montreal. There they were sorted, organized, and repackaged before being transported to remote outposts in the North West. Then the whole process started over again, with beaver pelts and other skins travelling in the opposite direction. It took several years of financial credit to carry this operation before a profit was seen. In an attempt to mitigate these difficulties, individual merchants banded together in short-term partnerships, pooling their resources and easing competition. These partnerships gradually coalesced into a larger entity called the North West Company, which became an astonishingly profitable enterprise.[16] In 1791 only sixteen thousand pounds was expended to earn eighty-eight thousand pounds on the London fur exchange.[17]

If these businessmen were anything, they were independent minded, cantankerous, and pig-headed. In fifteen years, the coalition had frayed and a new outfit, the XY Company, had been formed in opposition to the Nor'Westers. The merchant aristocracy of Montreal proceeded to engage in cutthroat competition that featured theft, murder, and the free flow of liquor to Indian trappers. This brawl resulted in one advantage to the Québécois: more workers were required – one reason Jean-Baptiste had landed his job.

By 1804 a truce had been negotiated between the North West and the XY companies, the enterprises merged and new efficiencies were introduced. Jean-Baptiste was one of hundreds of North West Company *engagés* who were cut loose. He then became what was termed a "freeman," an independent operator who was under no obligation to anyone and signed no contract with a fur company. Freemen acted as individual agents, living on the fringes of both Indian and fur trade societies. Historian Ruth Swan writes that

French Canadian descendants married Native women and lived separate from the fur trade posts. They adopted Indian clothing, technology and languages. They became the great horsemen and buffalo hunters, fluent in Cree and using Indian expertise to survive on the plains and parkland. They were economically and psychologically independent. They provided an entrepreneurial service and had a relationship of mutual dependency with the posts that they served. It was the best of both worlds. They did not have to take orders from a boss, they could hunt and provide a living for the families, and there were enough of them to provide military protection from the Sioux.[18]

They and their families lived off the land, hunting buffalo and other big game, snaring grouse and small animals, and fishing. But they were also businessmen, serving as guides and translators, selling provisions, particularly pemmican, to the company fur traders, trapping furs on their own and trading them with whoever or whatever outfit gave them the best price. They were successful because they formed close alliances with the First Nations people they encountered. As the historian Marcel Giraud writes: "The Canadians [freemen] have great influence over the natives by adopting all their customs and making them companions. They drink, sing, conjure, scold with them like one of themselves and the Indians are never kept out of their houses whether drunk or sober, night or day."[19]

When Jean-Baptiste returned to Quebec in late 1806, he realized at once that he detested the fineries of so-called civilization. In the North West there was no government, no priest, no police, and this appealed to his independent spirit. So he decided that he would return to buffalo hunting and fur trapping. This time, he was doing something entirely unheard of – taking along his wife, a white woman, a woman of European traditions. If only she could survive the journey.

CHAPTER THREE

—

WHEN THE LAGIMODIÈRES ARRIVED at the Lachine docks
before dawn, they saw, through the gloom, a frenzy of activity – a
jig with purpose. Workers danced back and forth from warehouse*
to loading station carrying huge bundles of goods – guns, hatchets,
kettles, blankets, pots, red and yellow calico, glass beads. All these
items would be traded to the Indians for furs. A mountain of kegs
full of rum also stood ready to be loaded.

Voyageurs strutted about, smoking their long clay pipes, greeting
each other with a slap on the back. They put on a high-and-mighty
air, but in reality they were ordinary farm workers who, once the
seeding was done, hauled their paddles from the barn and puffed
their chests out, full of bravado. They were as physically tough as
work mules and they were cocky: they knew there'd be no Montreal

---

* The stone warehouse used to store trading goods and furs was built in
1803. It still stands at Lachine and is a National Historic Site.

fur trade without them. Each sported his best shirt, mostly bright-red plaid, a hat – stocking caps, headbands, fedoras – and "carraboo" leggings made of animal skins.[1] Worn around the waist was that badge of honour, the *ceinture fléchée*, of red wool woven in an arrowhead design, in which the essentials – several knives, a tobacco pouch and a wooden drinking cup – were nested. A Tulle *fusil de chasse* – a light flintlock musket – and a tightly sealed powder horn were hooked onto the sash and slung around the shoulder.

The bosses – the partners, or *bourgeois*, as they were called in the North West Company – and their underlings, the tough wintering clerks (*hivernants*), were huddled together on the wharf, where they had been since three in the morning, discussing last-minute plans. On hand to bid everyone adieu were the mothers and fathers, wives and girlfriends, and children, all gaily dressed, all making a frightful noise.

Like everyone else, the Lagimodières strolled about, Jean-Baptiste calling out greetings to old acquaintances, listening to friends congratulate him on his beautiful bride. Most people probably assumed that Marie-Anne was there to bid farewell, and it would have been a shock when they discovered that this petite, fragile-looking woman was about to do the unthinkable – travel to the North West. But Jean-Baptiste found himself in an awkward position for reasons other than Marie-Anne's presence.

Having firmly established himself as an independent, one of the *gens libres*, or freemen, he was no longer regarded as a common voyageur. Yet he was not a member of the gentry, either. He had not been invited, for example, to the farewell banquet of sturgeon, venison, bear steak and many bottles of the finest Madeira laid on the day before for the clerks and partners. (One guest later admitted, "By six or seven o'clock I had, in common with many others, fallen from my seat and curled up in the fire-place.") Marie-Anne and Jean-Baptiste probably supped at a little roadside inn on tourtière or some other inexpensive dish.

The Lagimodières were already assigned to a *canot de maître*. These canoes held between sixty and sixty-five carefully wrapped packs, each weighing forty kilograms. About 70 percent of this cargo was made up of trade items, 30 percent provisions – 500 weight of biscuit, 200 weight of pork and three bushels of peas.[2] Other baggage included two oilcloths to cover the goods, a sail, an axe, a towing line, a kettle, and a sponge to soak up water, as well as a supply of gum, bark, and wattape (spruce root) used to repair the boat.[3] Cargo was placed on poles laid along the bottom of the canoe so that nothing touched the fragile birchbark skin.

The bow of the *canot de maître* was usually painted white and displayed the filigreed North West Company coat of arms; on the stern, ornamented by a flower design or a drawing of a beaver, was printed the name of the man who owned the canoe, or that of his wife or patron saint – St. Gertrude the Great, intervener to souls awaiting escape from purgatory, was particularly popular. There were usually eight to twelve crew members. At the bow sat the *avant*, who wore a top hat decorated with tinselled ribbons, and at the stern was the *gouvernail* (steersman) with his long "sweep" paddle and finally the *milieux*, the middle paddlers, seated through-out the rest of the canoe.

When the crew members shook hands with Marie-Anne, they no doubt were astonished. Not only had no white woman ever travelled with them before, but passengers of any kind were seldom accommodated on these journeys. To take up precious space intended for cargo was simply too expensive. The voyageurs must have wondered how the Lagimodières had managed it. For Marie-Anne, the ten men gathered around her were a blur of faces. She knew right away, though, who the expedition's bosses were. While everyone else sported red feathers in their hats, only the bowman and steersman were allowed to embellish theirs with two glorious plumes, a mark of their experience, expertise, and confidence.

Although he put it rather awkwardly, the fur trader McKenny captured the importance of such symbols. "The voyageurs are engaged, on the spot, each with a red feather in his hat, and two other [feathers] in possession of the steersman, one for the bow, and the other for the stern of the canoe. These plumes in the canoe are intended to indicate that [the canoe] has been tried and found worthy."[4]

The Lagimodières travelled in a flotilla consisting of some ten to thirty canoes. The *bourgeois* was in charge, but he seldom contradicted the guide or, as he was sometimes called, the pilot, whom all others were expected to obey and who was paid far more than an ordinary *engagé*. As one writer described him: "He stood in the bow of the leading canoe; he had gone over and over the course to take for each rapid, as he had risen over the years from common voyageur or 'milieu,' through the ranks to his present position."[5]

At last it was time to depart. The crowd gathered at the water's edge made a fearful hullabaloo cheering the brigade off. The eight oarsmen set their paddles, the steersman and bowman half knelt, half stood, tense and waiting. Then the order rang out: *Allez!* Slowly, steadily, each bright paddle dipped into the water. The low-lying canoes shot forward. Soon the crowd's au revoirs and God-be-with-yous faded away. As part of the ceremony, the clerks and the *bourgeois* hung on to their top hats against the wind and Marie-Anne probably did the same with her bonnet.[6]

Sitting on a blanket in the middle of the craft beside her husband, she had barely enough time to squirm her way to comfort before the flotilla lurched across the swelling waves and, as tradition dictated, they turned toward land. The water close to shore was shallow and strewn with sharp rocks; canoe bottoms could be punctured easily. To avoid accident, the voyageurs jumped out and waded onto the beach. Jean-Baptiste carried Marie-Anne in his arms. She might have been embarrassed about this, but clerks and *bourgeois* also caught rides on the backs of voyageurs. They didn't want to get their shoes wet either.

The group hurried along a pleasant walkway and made for a rough wooden structure with a pointed steeple. This was the Church of St. Ann, the last vestige of the voyageurs' Catholic religion until they returned to Quebec. The explorer Peter Pond described the significance of the place in 1770 (spellings and punctuation have been altered): "This Church is Dedicated to St Ann who Protects all Voyageurs. Here is a Small Box with a Hole in the top for the Reception of a Little money for the Holy father to Say a Small Mass for those who Put a small Sum in the Box. Scarce a Voyageur but Stops here and puts in his mite and By that Means they Suppose they are Protected."[7]

Just three years before the Lagimodières journeyed west, a young Irishman, Thomas Moore, travelled with a fur brigade from Niagara Falls to Montreal. He wrote a poem entitled "Canadian Boat Song," which included this reference to the Church of Ste. Ann:

> Faintly as tolls the evening chime
> Our voices keep tune and our oars keep time.
> Soon as the woods on shore look dim,
> We'll sing at St Ann's our parting hymn,
> Row, brothers, row, the stream runs fast,
> The rapids are near and the daylight's past.[8]

Since Marie-Anne was named after both the Virgin and her mother, she would have felt a special affinity for the voyageurs' patron saint. But, at that moment, with all of the oarsmen crammed into the little building, and with the sharp reek of human sweat hanging in the air, she faced for the first time the totally masculine world she was now part of, a domain without a touch of comfort, softness or subtlety, a tough, uncompromising territory. She probably put her coin in the box along with the others.

The mouth of the Ottawa River was located at Ste. Anne-de-Bellevue, west of Montreal. After that the river churned into whitewater, aggressive, wild, tormented, as it raged through three rapids. Here Marie-Anne was initiated into the perils of wilderness travel.

There were trails through the woods, but the bush was so thick and the pathway so narrow that the heavy canoes could not be carried over the portage, and anyway the crew tried to avoid this burden as much as they could. Fortunately, there was an alternative. After the cargo was unloaded and the passengers had disembarked, the voyageurs on shore pulled the craft by rope through the spinning water. The bowman and steersman remained in the canoe, navigating it through the boil. It was not an easy manoeuvre. Samuel de Champlain almost died at this place. His journal describes how his canoe was turned broadside and sucked into a whirlpool. His hand got caught in the rope and was nearly cut off. Luckily, he fell between two rocks, which gave him enough leverage to save himself and the boat.

There were eighteen major portages along the Ottawa River and trekking them was strenuous, exhausting work. Fortunately for Marie-Anne, despite her small-boned physique, she was strong and healthy; she had always been a great walker, tramping all over the Maskinongé countryside.

This first portage was just 1,500 metres long, winding up and down through deep forest. The Jesuit Joseph Le Caron travelled the same route in the mid-seventeenth century and, although 150 years later the pathways were more clearly etched, Marie-Anne's experience would have been similar to his: "We often came upon rocks, mud holes, and fallen trees, which we had to scramble over, and sometimes we must force our way with head and hands through dense woods and thickets."[9] Marie-Anne's neck-to-toe dress would have caught on the rocks and branches, her shoes, so inadequate, caused her to slip and stumble, her heavy outer garments made her perspire profusely. But all this discomfort was minor compared with what she was about to face.

Swarming clouds of ravenous insects descended. The black flies delighted in moist skin. The huge mosquitoes joined in. In an instant, the flesh of Marie-Anne's forehead, cheeks, neck, and hands was punctured into a mess of bloody, swollen, itching sores. Jean-Baptiste grabbed the light crocheted shawl she was wearing around her shoulders and covered her head. She couldn't see through the material; her eyes were swollen shut from the bites. Her husband had to lead her, like a blind refugee, along the portage trail. The buzzing crescendo remained in her ears for years to come. (After that first horrible experience, likely netting was found for Marie-Anne. The voyageurs wore it draped over their heads whenever the insects were particularly bad.)

Father Le Caron had this to say of the insects: "If I had not kept my face wrapped in a cloth, I am almost sure they [the mosquitoes] would have blinded me, so pestiferous and poisonous are the bites of these little demons . . . I confess that this is the worst martyrdom I suffered in this country; hunger, thirst, weariness, and fever are nothing to it."[10]

The brigade spent their first night at the upper end of the Lake of Two Mountains. Everything and everyone came ashore, the cargo was stacked, the canoes were tipped over. The paddlers slept with only their heads underneath the vessel, a poor refuge when it rained or snowed (it was, after all, still April). Jean-Baptiste had brought an oilskin, which he threw over tree branches to create a makeshift tent as protection against the elements and the bugs. It was set apart away from the main group, but there was still little privacy for the newlyweds.

Sometimes in the evenings rum was passed around, a dram for each man, the voyageurs' one solace on the long, hard trip. A fire was lit, the usual meal of salt pork, corn gruel, and buckwheat biscuits prepared. The voyageurs ate so much pork that they were called *mangeurs du lard*. Now and then they added variety to their diet by catching fish, particularly sturgeon. These were cut up (the tail was removed but not the head; the eyes were considered particularly succulent) and distributed to the crew, who baked the pieces over the fire for about an hour. Thanks to Montague's advance, the Lagimodières probably brought their own food packets, which might have been similar to the rations of smoked beef, tongue, sausage, barley, cheese, figs, and prunes enjoyed by the *bourgeois*.

At three in the morning came the call, "Levez, levez!" and immediately everyone jumped into motion. With only five or six hours' rest, Marie-Anne must have been exhausted. How could she have slept soundly on the hard ground, in the freezing cold, with only a piece of oilskin to protect her from insects and weather? There was barely enough time to make a cup of tea.

Before the departure the canoes were carefully examined for damage. If one of the birchbark shells has been punctured, the men set to work patching it with spruce gum and wattape, using a needle-nosed awl. The job completed, they were on their way.

At daybreak they went ashore for breakfast at Chute-à-Blondeau, at the end of the Long Sault, where ruins of stockades poked up in the bush. It was at this place in May 1660 that Adam Dollard des Ormeaux, an ordinary colonist, had led sixteen French volunteers and forty-four Huron and Algonquin to intercept an army of Iroquois warriors who were on their way to attack Montreal. After a ten-day journey by canoe, Dollard's camp was discovered by an advance party of three hundred Iroquois, who lay siege for days. In the end, Dollard was slain and nine of his comrades were captured, and later tortured and eaten. Most of French-Canadian society, and especially the Church, viewed Dollard des Ormeaux as a great hero, possibly a saint. The man's judgment was never questioned, although it should have been. His men had never fought in an Indian war before, yet he and his cohorts arrogantly thought they could trounce seven hundred – four hundred more had joined the advance party – skilled Indian warriors. The colonists hung in there, not so much because they were brave, but because they had no other choice. The myth that Montreal was saved from attack by the courage of the French and their native allies, who frightened the Iroquois off, was perpetuated. In fact, once the warriors had collected enough scalps and prisoners, they headed home to celebrate. There was no need to press on to the French colony.

The next portion of the Ottawa River was devoid of rapids; the canoes lapped along swiftly for one hundred kilometres. This was the time for singing, and there were plenty of fine baritone, tenor, and bass voices among the voyagers. Ballads like this one became legendary:

À la claire fontaine
M'en allant promener,
J'ai trouvé l'eau si belle
Que je m'y suis baigné.
Il y a longtemps que je t'aime,
Jamais je ne t'oublierai.*

After fifteen hours on the water, the brigade stopped for the night at a favourite voyageur campground about twelve kilometres east of what is now Ottawa. There, Marie-Anne found herself face to face with Indian people for the first time, for it was at this spot that natives, primarily Northern Ojibwe, came to sell provisions to the voyageurs.

They called themselves Anishnabe, or "the people'; outsiders labelled them Ojibwe, and one interpretation of the word is "those who make pictographs," a reference to the records of the Midewinin (Grand Medicine Society) engraved on birchbark scrolls. Some scholars believe their pictographs are the closest thing to written documents found among Indians north of Mexico.[11] The Ojibwe first encountered the white man in the 1640s at their annual summer celebration near what is now Sault Ste. Marie, Ontario. Included in the party were the Ojibwes' allies, the Huron, who introduced them to their friends, the "black robes," or Jesuit missionaries. From that time on, the Ojibwe did business with the French Canadians, trading furs in exchange for European-made goods. Ojibwe women married white fur traders, and Ojibwe

---

* At the clear running fountain / Strolling by one day, / I found it so beautiful / I bathed without delay. / Long have I loved you, / Never will I forget you.

families supplied voyageurs with foods they had gathered – wild onions, plums, panbines (a fruit), and grapes. Fresh food was a welcome relief from the monotony of dry rations.

On their route the next morning, the river narrowed a little, cliffs grew more jagged, and a menacing sound, like thunder, could be heard, faintly at first and then as a roar. The canoes followed a narrow, steep-sided limestone gorge, which allowed them to ride close to the Chaudière Falls, so named by Champlain because they reminded him of an enormous cauldron – the furious water charging over the boulders, falling 15 metres and hissing like steam from a kettle. Marie-Anne must have been astonished at the sight because everyone else who had travelled there was. Nicholas Garry, deputy governor of the Hudson's Bay Company, wrote in 1821: "We had scarcely Time to admire the beautiful Scene when the Chaudière in all his Wildness and Majesty appeared before us. The imagination cannot picture anything so wild and romantic. The Ottawa dividing itself in 2 streams forms an extensive Island covered with the finest Trees (principally Oak) in a bed of Long Grass and beautiful verdure."[12] Twenty years later HBC Governor George Simpson described the falls as "a desperate struggle of the majestic Ottawa, leaping, with a roar of thunder, from ledge to ledge and from rock to rock, till at last, wearied, as it were, with its buffetings, it sinks exhausted into the placid pool below."[13]

There were two portages around the falls; at the first, crude steps had been cut into the limestone, worn smooth by centuries of traffic, so Marie-Anne wouldn't have found the trip too hard going. For the voyageurs it was a different matter. It took four of them, their muscles straining, to carry the heavy canoe along the path. As well, they had to lug the three tonnes of cargo on their backs. They wore tumplines, wide headbands connected to two strips of leather that were tied around each package. The load, weighing forty kilograms, was then hoisted up, to ensure the weight was evenly distributed. On top of the first bundle was added a second, a third, and sometimes even a fourth. Then, bent in an upside down L-shape, the men jogged over 1,500 metres, dropped their cargo at the end of the portage, and raced back for the next load, the sweat shining like oil on their bodies.

After three days of easy travel, the brigade reached another lethal barricade. The five kilometres of rapids here were so full of granite outcrops that the voyageurs were reminded of ferocious cats whose claws threatened to scratch the fragile canoe bottoms, thus the name Chute-des-Chats (Chats Falls). Everywhere large wooden crosses sat in clusters beside the steep path. These were graves of voyageurs who may have suffered drownings or heart attacks and, worst of all, those bulges protruding from the stomach or the groin, the dreaded hernia. Gangrene could set in and soon after came death. And it wasn't only the voyageurs; as one traveller wrote: "At the rapids at the head of Lac des Chats, the Indians indicated bones of many valiant canoemen who lay in the fierce waters upstream."[14]

The portage around this nightmare of whitewater was steep and rocky, and the voyageurs would do almost anything to avoid carrying their 270-kilogram canoes over such a walkaround. A *demi-charge* was the preferred method. The men unloaded half the freight, paddled madly up the churning water, dropped off the remaining cargo load, turned around, whirled down the rapids, picked up the remaining goods, and again propelled the canoe upstream. Other times they performed a *décharge*, as they had at Ste-Anne-de-Bellevue: the bowman and steersman piloted the canoe while those on shore pulled it by rope. The steersmen skilfully manoeuvred their vessels around rocks with a nonchalance that was astonishing.

From this point, the "voyageurs' highway" passed along, or close to, the Canadian Shield's southern border. There was one set of rapids after another. For Marie-Anne, the journey became a blur of scrambling up rocks, thrashing among thickets, squishing through bogs, crossing ravines by balancing on dead tree branches – all the while trying not to roll head over heels down the steep portage paths. She suffocated from the heat during the day, was chilled to the bone at night. It rained often, and she found herself slipping and sliding on the muddy trails, but she had to keep up a quick pace. Behind her, heavily laden voyageurs were running, and it was dangerous to get in the way.

By this time, Marie-Anne's neat, well-groomed appearance had deteriorated. It would have been impossible for her dress not to have ripped, although she had brought needle and thread for such repairs. But what could she do with her soaking, mud-caked shoes? Some years later, another traveller described the state of his footwear: "My shoes were still so damp that I placed them with the upper leathers toward the fire, but at such a distance as I thought beyond the range of mischief, yet the following morning I found the toes and heels drawn together, and the leather so brittle that on attempting to straighten the soles, they broke to pieces like earthen ware. I had no second pair. I was reduced to the necessity of going bare-footed."[15]

Some time during the voyage, Marie-Anne began wearing Indian clothing – moccasins embroidered with dyed porcupine quills, a pair of caribou-skin leggings – acquired one piece at a time from the Ojibwe. This was the beginning of her "Indianization," a transformation with which she was no doubt uncomfortable. Her European dress defined her femininity, denoted her Christian religion and her civilization. But she would have had no other choice.

The ordeal continued. The Portage du Grand Calumet, two kilometres long and circumventing two steep ravines, was one of the most treacherous of the long journey. The fur trader Alexander Henry the Elder described it thus: "The carrying-place is long and arduous, consisting of a high steep hill, over which the canoe cannot be carried by fewer than 12 men . . . The ascent of this carrying-place is not more fatiguing than the descent is dangerous; and, in performing it, accidents too often occur, producing strains, ruptures and injuries for life."[16] Like a mountain goat, Marie-Anne warily crossed the rocky ledges that ran high above the whirling river.

At the end of this portage there was a long sandy beach where the brigades traditionally halted for the night. The young men who were journeying for the first time on this fur trade highway were ordered to kneel in a line. Over the head of each was poured a kettle of water, an initiation into the arcane rites of the voyageur. Much laughter and ribbing accompanied the ritual.

After five weeks, the group reached the juncture of the Mattawa River. Here the brigade left the Ottawa River and travelled southwest. This involved crossing a continental divide. The Mattawa River runs into Trout Lake, situated at two hundred metres above sea level. From there lie eleven kilometres of streams and portages over the divide until one reached the other side of Lake Nipissing.

It was the roughest terrain of the voyage. Along the Ottawa River, beginning at Lachine, a distance of five hundred kilometres, there had been eighteen portages. Now the brigade was faced with same number before it reached Lake Nipissing, only eighty kilometres away. The names of these "carrying places" sound like a litany of romantic ballads: Portage Chant Plain, Portage Campion, Portage des Roches, Portage de la Cave, Portage des

Perches, Portage de Talon, Portage Pin de Musique, Portage de la Mauvaise Musique, Portage de la Tortue.

The Mattawa River was nothing but turbulence. One traveller described his encounter with the "little river" in 1854. He "met with a great many small rapids . . . very difficult going. the Bush is so thick on the Bank that it is almost impassable."[17] Twelve years earlier HBC Governor George Simpson had travelled the same route and reported in his journal:

> At one of the Rapids below Matawa [sic], the heavy canoes, which came up a few days after ourselves, lost a very valuable chest of medicines, – one of the few accidents which could be imputed to the carelessness of a voyageur during the long course of my experience. This morning, however, we were reminded that serious disasters had occurred and might occur again, for we breakfasted near two crosses, that had been placed over the bodies of two men, who were drowned while running the adjacent rapids.[18]

After picking their way over rugged, muddy trails for two days, the brigade reached Trout Lake. Sails were hauled up and the canoes sped across until the most southwesterly point at Dugas Bay was reached. From there, the course wound along a creek so narrow it could barely accommodate the six-foot beam of the canoes. Marie-Anne had to shield her face from the bulrushes that constantly slapped at her, and the water lilies grew so thick that the canoes become entwined in them. To propel the boats the voyageurs had to punt; it took great skill and balance to manipulate the long poles, tipped with an iron ferrule, and not overturn the canoe. Only a few years earlier, it had been much easier going. Beaver ponds had widened the stream; only three kilometres of portage were necessary. But the animals had been exterminated – too much trapping – and the travel route had all but dried up.

The next obstacle, Portage La Vase, could be translated as "mud portage" but *slime* or *goo* would be a more appropriate description. Jean-Baptiste probably carried Marie-Anne over the swampiest parts, but she still had to wade through much of the muck on her own. The place was full of rattlesnakes; one of the voyageurs' favourite sports was to grab them by the neck and smash their heads against the rocks.

Finally, the brigade arrived at Rivière des Vases where, after one more portage around a rocky whirlpool, the river suddenly widened. They had reached Lake Nipissing, and camped for the night.

The next day, if they were blessed with a breeze, the voyageurs would have hoisted up the sails, allowing the canoes to skim over the sparkling lake waters. The paddlers could relax; only the steersman had to stay alert. The canoes travelled diagonally across the waves, for if they weren't supported for their entire length, they would snap in two. And this lake could transform itself from a lily pond to a roiling fury in the time that it took to make tea. The landscape had also changed dramatically. Gone were the green nut-bearing trees of the south, replaced by the skinny Jack pine and huckleberry bushes of the boreal forest.

If there were no mishaps, they could cross the lake in five hours, to reach the source of the French River. Ahead lay over one hundred kilometres of treacherous water running through granite cliffs, but there was a big difference in the convoy's mode of travel. They were paddling not upriver, but down. The voyageurs, who would do anything to avoid a portage, shot the rapids whenever they could, as fast as they could, the men yelling hysterical commands at each other. As one writer puts it, "White water was the icing on the voyageurs' cake."[19] The explorer Simon Fraser was an experienced rapids runner, and he wrote that "the great difficulty consisted in keeping the canoes in the medium, or *fil d'eau*, that is to say clear of the precipice on the one side, and of the gulfs formed by the waves on the other. However, thus skimming along like lightning the crews, cool and determined, followed each other in awful silence."[20]

What did Marie-Anne think, jammed in the canoe, gripping the sides and pushing her feet against a bale for support as the white foam sprayed into the air and the little craft lurched from side to side like a wayward drunk? Was she thrilled or terrified? Probably a little of both.

Finally the last channel of rushing water was reached. Like so much flotsam, the canoes shot out of the French River into an enormous lake that Champlain called "the freshwater sea" (this part of Lake Huron was named Georgian Bay after the reigning British monarch, George IV, in 1822). To those travellers who first described it, there was something frightening about the steel-grey waters that spread like rippling jelly to the horizon. In 1761 Alexander Henry the Elder wrote: "The billows of Lake Huron . . . stretched across our horizon, like an ocean." There were "small islands, or rather rocks, either wholly bare, or very scantily covered with scrub pine-trees.'[21] With rock formations of rosy granite, yellow lichen clinging to the sides of protruding rocks, and stunted pine trees standing straight in an inch of soil, Marie-Anne encountered a landscape very different from the gentle rolling hills where she had grown up.

If the weather remained calm, the canoes would have skimmed along the vast bay. Because there were no more portages, the voyageurs were happy and relaxed. Time and again the chorus of a famous old ballad rang out: " On, roll on, my ball I roll on. On, roll on my ball, on!

It was June by this time, and the weather had turned quite hot. Her sunbonnet that had been her mother's gift protected Marie-Anne's pale face, but her arms and hands must have turned a butternut brown. With all the strenuous exercise, she had lost her feminine roundness, was now all stringy muscle.

The brigade finally arrived at the divide between lakes Huron and Superior. The connecting arm was called the St. Mary's River, and much of it was a churn of bubbling water. In the spring and summer, Ojibwe from all over gathered here; the whitefish were so plentiful that they literally jumped into waiting arms. In 1670, French missionaries had erected a tall cross on a hill overlooking the river, naming the place Sault Ste. Marie, in honour of the Virgin, and blessing the rapids. In 1751, the French established a fort on the south side of the river, which turned out to be a most strategic location. The rapids acted as a barrier east and west; whoever controlled them controlled the entire fur trade. Alexander Henry the Elder visited in 1762 and described it thus:

Here was a stockaded fort, in which, under the French government, there was kept a small garrison, commanded by an officer, who was called *the Governor*, but was in fact a clerk, who managed the Indian trade here, on government account. The houses were four in number; of which the first was the governor's, the second the interpreter's and the other two, which were the smallest, have been used for barracks.[22]

Shortly after Henry wrote this, the entire compound was destroyed by fire. In 1783, the North West Company built a trading post on the south shore of the St. Mary's River; thirteen years later, after Jay's Treaty established the border between

Canada and the United States, it was moved to the north side. As a gateway to the North West, it was the hub of the Montreal fur trade. When Marie-Anne visited, the main post consisted of a large whitewashed building with a veranda out front, a great vaulted roof, and dormer windows on the second floor; numerous store-houses and warehouses; a sawmill; and a boatyard where canoes were constructed. A Union Jack flew overhead.

The entire community gathered to greet the brigade—the Métis who worked at the post, their wives, Ojibwe trappers, kids, dogs. Never before had they seen any woman as pale as Marie-Anne with her blonde hair, dyed almost white by the sun, and fishlike blue eyes – they must have wondered whether she was a Windigo who would suck the blood from their veins.

There was one particularly lovely house at the Sault with a library, wine cellar, and large flower and vegetable garden. It belonged to John Johnston, the scion of a wealthy Irish family, and his wife, the daughter of Wabogish (White Fisher), the Ojibwe chief. Johnston was an independent fur trader, a prosperous one.[23] Jean-Baptiste had been introduced to him before, and as a freeman he could do business with him. The Lagimodières may have stayed with the Johnstons. If so, sheets on the bed, a wash bowl full of warm water, linen towels, and a porcelain chamber pot must have seemed like heaven to Marie-Anne.

In 1787 the North West Company had constructed a lock at Sault Ste Marie, the first of its kind in Canada, to ease transporta-tion over the rapids that blocked the way to Lake Superior. A lone steersman piloted a canoe, laden with cargo, into a narrow canal, and gates at one end were closed, forcing the water to rise. When the gates swung open, the water and the canoe lurched downward. An ox, walking on the pathway above the canal, was tied by rope to the prow, so that it could guide the boat.

The next morning the brigade got underway again, this time following the north shore of Lake Superior. The water was icy cold and crystalline, and it was possible to peer ten metres down to huge rock formations below. This vast landscape, with its looming, perpendicular cliffs and caves inhabited by millions of bats, was intimidating, to say the least. Thick fog, caused by the warm air meeting the cold water, often rolled in, forcing boaters to land. There was therefore always a dilemma facing travellers. Should they take a chance and shorten the distance by crossing the mouths of various bays, some of them very wide, or should they remain cautious and stick closer to shore? They often chose the time-saving route – with dire consequences.

The Lagimodières almost perished during two vicious storms that descended during the crossing. Georges Dugast writes that "Madame Lajimoniere many years afterwards told her children of the mortal fear which she had felt on this occasion, and with what fervour she had prayed not to go [perish] in the frail vessel."[24]

A dead calm descended. The sails were lowered, and the voyageurs went back to paddling. As the brigade approached St. Ignace Island, the guide pointed the lead canoe in a south-westerly direction, away from land. Soon only tiny rock islands were in sight. Then the bowman boomed out to look ahead. Demon clouds, black as ink, skittered toward them. Suddenly there was a crash of thunder, then the wail of wind. Torrents of rain ripped down. Huge waves pounded the canoes, making them roll about like wounded whales. Jean-Baptiste grabbed Marie-Anne in his arms. His deep voice and her alto joined the chorus of Hail Marys. The steersman desperately tried to turn the craft toward a small island, but the cliff was steep, the reef of rocks at its base as sharp as tomahawks. Instantly the boat changed course; they would be blown out onto the lake and perish, everyone was sure.

Many times they crossed themselves, prayers turned into moans. But miraculously the bowman managed to catch hold of a branch of a stunted tree growing amongst the rocks. He hung on for dear life. "Old woman," he bellowed at the wind, "that is enough!" In a few moments, the sun was shining and the sky was as blue as a robin's egg.

The canoes limped toward land, some of them badly taking in water, all in need of repair. The last group to arrive announced the bad news. They had spotted a canoe overturned and smashed against a rock. No survivors. The steersman yelled in rage, "Of course not. This damn lake never gives up its dead." An *hiverant* and ten voyageurs had perished.

CHAPTER FOUR

—

ONCE THE INTACT CANOES reached Fort Kaministiquia, a memorial service was held for the drowned, but it was a brief one. The summer rendezvous was in full swing. The North West brass – the *hiverants* and the Montreal agents – had gathered to conduct their annual meeting, and 1807 was very special. The newly appointed chief director of the North West Company, William McGillivray, was to be honoured by having the fort renamed Fort William. Every ounce of energy went into making sure the event ran smoothly.

The place looked like a medieval fortress, incongruous in the midst of the dark, boreal forest. The first thing the Lagimodières spotted from their canoe was a 3.5-metre-high wooden palisade enclosing the entire fort and reinforced with two guardhouses. It was supposedly built as protection against marauding Indians, although there'd been no such attack for years; the natives who visited here did so only to trade. The real purpose of these imposing stockades was to discourage theft, to keep the wrong kind of people out, and above all to inspire awe. Archaeologist A. M. Taylor explains:

> Visitors to Fort William . . . would have no need to enquire where the authority resided. The signs were blatant. After pulling their canoes up a single sloped inlet on the dock, they would find themselves standing before the one and only front entrance to the main enclosure. Passing through the gate . . . they would be led naturally along a wide path through a spacious courtyard to the front steps of the Great Hall.[1]

This building was the North West Company's command centre, and it smelled of money. "You can hear the fur business's heart beat – a heart of gold, all pounds sterling," was how the working stiffs expressed it. The Great Hall stood 1.5 metres above ground level, making it the tallest building in the compound except for the watchtowers. Constructed of clapboard painted white, it was a handsome edifice, with many large, shuttered windows, a hip roof, and a wide front balcony. To emphasize its authority, two cannons faced onto a main square that was as green and trim as the royal park at Versailles.

The Great Hall was for the exclusive use of the company's partners and clerks. Indeed, the spatial arrangement of the entire fort was symbolic of the rigid hierarchy imposed by the North West Company. Its pecking order affected everyone involved in the fur trade, and was probably a major reason why Jean-Baptiste Lagimodière decided to become a freeman, rather than a salaried employee. James Scott Hamilton writes:

In the case of the North West Company, sharp distinctions based on ethnic affiliation, literacy and social role divided the officers from the labourers [voyageurs]. The shareholders and senior clerks were predominantly Anglo-Saxon, while some clerks, and most of the guides, interpreters, steersmen and labourers were French Canadian. In spite of the important work roles of these latter employees, they had little or no prospect of promotion into the senior ranks. Anglo-Scots clerks with patronage links rapidly moved into positions of responsibility and authority, even becoming shareholders over the heads of much more experienced men of both English and French background. Nepotism and rank-related economic inequalities in the North West Company coloured inter-rank relations, and created a measure of social tension.[2]

The result of this philosophy was a strict segregation: everyone was housed according to their station in life. There were in the Great Hall four elegant bedrooms, which also served as offices for the partners who had travelled from Montreal. The twelve bedrooms in the North West House were for wintering partners, and twelve similar rooms in the Bell House were for senior clerks. French-Canadian interpreters, guides, and steersmen were also accommodated within the fort's stockade, but in one-room barracks equipped with bunks and cots. Everybody else was relegated to areas outside the stockade. *Hiverants* (who remained in the *pays d'en haut* all year, manning the canoes from Fort William to fur trading posts in the interior), voyageurs, and Indians were allotted specific separate areas; the native village to the west, the voyageurs' encampments near the main gate. The French Canadians were separated because the voyageurs were thought to be rowdy and loud, the *hiverants* more serious and responsible – plus, the two groups loathed each other. Across the river were the houses and small farms of retired *engagés*, their Indian wives, and their "half-breed" children. These were permanent settlements where corn, potatoes, and wheat were grown and sold to the fort. Jean-Baptiste would have known some of these people from his previous time in the North West, and the Lagimodières may have stayed with them during their visit.

Marie-Anne must have resented being so ostracized by the North West Company's rules. At Maskinongé, she was a servant, yes, but she was nevertheless treated with respect. Her literacy might even have allowed her to become a lady's maid or governess. Now she was considered of no consequence whatsoever, at least by the people in authority. They must have known of her presence – she was beautiful enough to turn heads anywhere – but she was breaking a cardinal rule: under no circumstances were white women, even wives, to be involved in the fur trade. Of course, she was also French Canadian, and of the peasant class.

During the day the gates of the fort remained open to all. The morning after their arrival Jean-Baptiste and Marie-Anne probably took a tour. As they passed through the palisade, immediately on the right was the well-stocked apothecary where Dr. John McLoughlin carried on his practice. He prided himself on keeping up with modern medicine; bleeding, cupping, purges, emetics, enemas, and expectorants were his specialties, although he could set bones if he had to. The Lagimodières would have stocked up on ointments and tonics, because where they were going they would rarely, if ever, encounter a medical doctor.

In front of the apothecary was one of two warehouses built on stilts so the rats couldn't eat the precious supply of Indian corn inside. To the west were located the stores. One building contained no fewer than three emporiums. The first, the Equipment Shop, was where voyageurs were issued their homeward bound supplies and where they could purchase, on account, everything from wool hats, to tobacco, to kegs of maple sugar to *l'Assomption* sashes. The second store featured the items a winterer would need, from awls to gunpowder to playing cards. It was here that the Lagimodières would do their judicious shopping for their sojourn in the North West. The third was called the Little Shop and was aimed at the larger pocketbooks of the clerks and partners, although voyageurs with extra cash also shopped here for such luxuries as dimity-quilted waistcoats, ruffled shirts, under-drawers of worsted gauze, silk garters, handkerchiefs, hosiery, hatbands and hat covers, fur muffs and cloaks of fox fur, Windsor soap, razors, shaving boxes, and even violin strings. Social distinctions were marked by what clothes one wore: the "civilized" gentleman always dressed in a European frock coat, replete with clasps, buttons, and buckles, and a top hat, no matter how uncomfortable. According to one scholar, "failure to wear such clothing was perceived as a denial of social position and responsibility . . . clothing served as a visual cue of social superiority, and aided in the maintenance of authority."[3] Lowly in status a labourer might have been, but at least he wasn't uncomfortable in his practical leggings and breech-cloth shirts.

Behind the shops was situated the counting house, where clerks hunched over wooden desks combed through columns of numbers. Professional accountants from Montreal came to scrutinize the bookkeeping of the interior posts: the number of pelts taken in; the expense of canoes, voyageurs and provisions; and, most tricky, the credit or debit balances of North West Company employees and Indian fur trappers. Their books showed that almost all the *engagés* were deeply in debt and had been for years. On average, the ratio of what they spent to what they earned was five to one.[4] This was not only because they loved shopping – for themselves they bought luxury items such as silk handkerchiefs, coloured feathers, tinselled hat cords, silver crosses and, in the case of the winterers, for their wives and families, beaver bonnets, shawls, looking glasses, scissors, pins, needles, beads, fancy combs, and frilly garters – but also because the company charged exorbitant amounts for these items. And imposing high prices wasn't the only way the company swindled its lowliest workers. An historian writing in 1918 describes these financial arrangements:

> The Northwest currency standard lent itself to skilful manipulation since it was just double the value of the Canadian currency. A voyageur would thus be tempted to purchase articles at a nominal price which might be temptingly low, only to find, in settling his accounts, that one shilling in the interior was counted as two shillings at Montreal . . . The charge was also made that the North West Company encouraged extravagance and vice on the part of its employees, in order to get them in debt.[5]

There was an easy way to get *engagés* to spend money – tempt them with booze. Trollope's Tavern was where the *régal* was distributed, an award for the long journey consisting of a two-kilogram loaf of white bread, a quarter-kilo of butter, and a mug of brandy. Of course the drinking didn't stop after the downing of one dram; liquor flowed until the voyageur was too drunk to mark his X on his chit. And conveniently, not far away, was the jail, nicknamed the Butter Tub. The drunken revelry sometimes ended there.

During their month-long sojourn at Fort William, the Lagimodières would have come across many native people, mostly Ojibwe. Their encampment was located outside the palisades, but during the day they were found everywhere within the fort. The women worked in the laundry or the mess, the men laboured in the gardens or the fur stores, cleaning, airing, and weighing beaver pelts. Marie-Anne was probably beginning to lose her dread of Aboriginal people, seeing them not as an amorphous, dusky-skinned mass, but as individuals with crooked or straight noses, big or small ears, skinny or thick waistlines. Some of the women were remarkably beautiful, with their black hair parted in the middle and falling to their backsides. They wore blue cotton petticoats decorated with beads, which were tied under their armpits and draped to their ankles. Sleeves of red or blue cotton were tied from shoulder to wrist and split along the inside of the arm. Silver rings, bracelets, and necklaces, some in the shape of large crosses, jingled as they walked.[6]

Marie-Anne may have worked for wages. There were plenty of jobs – making bread at the bakery, feeding pigs and cows at the fort's small farm, joining furniture in the carpentry shop. In 1807 Claudia Goulet, a Mètisse, was in charge of the screw-press, a device that squeezed piles of beaver or marten pelts into solid packs. These were baled and stamped with the label "NWC," then loaded for the return trip to Lachine. Claudia's mother was Ojibwe, and her father was a former French-Canadian *engagé* who decided to trust his luck as an independent fur trader on Lake Superior's north shore. The North West Company considered him a deserter. They had him arrested and shipped back to Montreal, where he was found guilty of breaking his contract. He was jailed for a year but promptly returned as a freeman. Marie-Anne probably became friendly with Claudia: both women spoke French, both were married to freemen, both their futures depended on that black gold of the North West – the beaver.

Fort William, in all its glory, was a symbol of how profitable the fur industry had become, and the occasion of its rechristening was a reminder of how the history of this establishment spelled out success, achievement, enterprise.

During the French period, before the British Conquest of 1759, fur traders became aware that the farther into the interior they travelled, the more plentiful and luxurious were the beaver pelts. Rainy Lake, Lake of the Woods, and Lake Winnipeg were thought to be the trapping grounds of the future. But how to find a way through the dense bush to get to these places from Lake Superior? Native people had figured out a route centuries ago. The key was Pigeon River, which flows into the northwestern end of Lake Superior along the border between what is now Minnesota and Ontario from a web of streams and little lakes that finally link to Rainy Lake. The difficulty was that the first thirty kilometres along the Pigeon were a nightmare of rapids and rocks. Aboriginal people had simply cut a twelve-kilometre detour around this section.

The first white man to cross their portage was the intrepid explorer Pierre Gauthier, Sieur de La Vérendrye, during his 1731 excursion to find the Western Sea and thus the Orient. Fur trading paid his expenses, however, and he had noticed how glossy and thick the pelts were once the barrier was crossed. The Cree leader and guide Ochagach showed him the portage and he used it thereafter.

Forty-four years later Alexander Henry the Elder described it in his journal:

> The transportation of goods at this Grand Portage or Great Carrying-place, was a work of seven days of severe and dangerous exertion, at the end of which we encamped on the river Aux Groseilles [Pigeon River]. The Grand Portage consists in two ridges of land, between which is a deep glen or valley, with good meadow-lands, and a broad stream of water. The lowlands are covered chiefly with birch and poplar, and the high with pine.[7]

As difficult as the portage was, the route along Pigeon River became the fur traders' highway, at least for a month in the summer. This was especially true once the North West Company came to dominate the trade. The canoes from Montreal bearing trading goods and provisions landed at a little bay of Lake Superior just south of Pigeon River. The cargo was then unloaded, sorted for the interior posts, and repacked. The voyageurs carried the enormous load over a two-hundred-metre elevation until they reached the calm portion of the river. The baggage was then reloaded and eventually shipped off into the interior. At the same time, the winterers who had arrived with canoes full of beaver pelts portaged in the opposite direction. These human pack mules covered the distance of almost thirty kilometres both ways in about six hours.

The bosses of the North West Company, those from Montreal and those from the interior, along with their understudies, the clerks, found the little bay close to the portage a convenient place to meet every summer and plan the year's events. Grand Portage became the heart of the Nor'Westers' business. The only trouble was that the place was located in U.S. territory. Under Jay's Treaty, all British forts were to be moved northward by 1796. The North West Company brass ignored this decree until the Americans threatened to collect duty on all goods crossing the border. Suddenly it was time to relocate.

Fortunately the explorer Roderick Mackenzie had rediscovered that the Kaministiquia River was another link on the Canadian side:

> After a long absence in the Indian territories, I paid this year a visit to Canada. Returning the following spring, on my first trip from Grand Portage to Lac La Pluie, I met a family of Indians at the height of land from whom I accidentally learned the existence of a water communication a little way behind and parallel to this,

extending from Lake Superior to Lake La Pluie, which is navigable for large canoes and, if adopted, would avoid the Grand Portage.[8]

In 1803 Fort Kaministiquia was constructed close to the mouth of the rediscovered "water communication." As one writer put it, "Everything was to done on a grand scale, and the amount of labour and materials required was enormous. At the height of the construction between 1802 and 1804 over one thousand men were employed."[9]

Marie-Anne may have helped with the grand banquet honouring William McGillivray. After all, she had long experience as a housekeeper and had often served elaborate meals for Father Vinet's guests. And the fort's population that summer wasn't so large that the upper echelons wouldn't have noticed the attractive white woman in their midst.

The mess of the Great Hall, where the partners, clerks, guides, and interpreters dined, was truly elegant. On the great cherrywood table sat enormous silver candelabras, fine cut-glass decanters of brandy, fat tureens of the finest china. The heavy silverware was polished to perfection, the dinner service was imported from Ireland, the wine glasses of exquisite crystal were manufactured somewhere in the Hapsburg Empire. On the walls were portraits of past and present partners, who radiated prosperity and arrogance. On one of the mantels rested a bust of the North West Company's founder, the late Simon McTavish, looking like a stern schoolmaster. On display this night were two additions to the Great Hall's picture gallery, gifts of William McGillivray. The first was a full-length portrait of Admiral Lord Horatio Nelson looking pompous and self-satisfied, the second, a depiction of the Battle of Trafalgar. The British Empire was well represented deep in the boreal forest. [10]

Servants dressed in uniforms consisting of a black dress and white apron stood at attention on one side of the room. The bagpipes sounded, and the party was marched into the mess. Immediately the gentlemen were seated, their glasses filled – brandy, port, Madeira, and Teneriffe wine flowed as if a liquor-spouting fountain had somehow sprung up in the middle of the wilderness.

William McGillivray's brother Duncan was the first to speak. "Unfortunately Mr. William McGillivray cannot be present owing to legislative duties," he apologized. "Nonetheless the Partners wish me to announce that the name Kaministiquia is discontinued and abolished forever. From this day on this place will be known as Fort William, in honour of our new chief director. Let us drink to the mighty North West Company and years of prosperity."

With that the entire company turned to the portrait of William McGillivray, and in one voice cried out, "To Fort William." Glasses were quickly downed.

This was only beginning. All the leading Scotsmen, their portraits depicting smug success, and the bust of Simon McTavish were toasted again and again. While the servants ran to replenish decanters, the same traditional toast was repeated over and over:

The Mother of All Saints
The King
The Fur Trade in All Its Branches
Voyageurs, Wives, and Children
Absent Members
To you all. [11]

In between toasts, the festive meal was served – dishes of beef, ham, sausage, whitefish, and venison accompanied by peas, corn, potatoes from the fort's garden, freshly baked bread with newly churned butter, double Gloucester and American cheeses, maple sugar tarts, and all kinds of berry pies.

But it was not only the brass who were celebrating. To mark the special occasion, a considerable quantity of "spirits and shrub" had been handed out to the common labouring men and to the Indians. The uproarious laughter and lewd songs would have made a young clerk blush, never mind a well-brought-up young woman from Quebec:

> My woman's ass is as big as a horse,
> Her breasts remind me of sausage,
> Her tongue is as barbed as a porcupine
> Her eyes as red as the devil's.

The stink of alcohol, piss, and vomit was everywhere. Many men passed out, their arms wrapped around their jugs as if they were cuddling dolls. Some were crawling on their hands and knees; others had lost control of their legs and wobbled like out-of-control tops.

It was a scene Marie-Anne never forgot. She told her children that suffering through the worst portage was nothing compared to that night of debauchery. For his entire life, her grandson Louis Riel retained a prudish attitude toward alcohol. He indulged little and detested drunkenness, perhaps a reflection of his grandmother's abhorrence.[12]

As July drew to a close, the crowd at Fort William began to disperse – business was over for the season. The pork eaters loaded the *canots de maître* with furs for their return to the east. The winterers made for the North West bearing the goods to be traded to the Indians. The Lagimodières were on their way as well, travelling with a crew of winterers in a typical *canot du nord*. These were half the size of the Montreal freight canoes, more easily carried over the swamps, shallow rivers, and many rapids they would encounter.

The Lagimodières would travel 1,100 kilometres to Pembina in the Red River Valley. With twice as many portages, it would prove a journey even more strenuous than the one from Lachine to Fort William. Marie-Anne was now a seasoned traveller, but as the canoe took off she must have had mixed feelings – more tedious, dangerous portages, more uncomfortable overnight camps, more frightening storms.

Soon after the party started up the fast-flowing Kaministiquia River, they encountered the falls of the same name. The way around was called Mountain Portage and it was a long, difficult, uphill climb. From the trail, the travellers could peer into the bowels of this seething rock cauldron, and see the catapulting water, the mist twinkling sharply in the sun like fragments of broken glass.

After the falls there were another seven portages and two *décharges* along the Kaministiquia River until the south end of Dog Lake was reached. From that point there were eighty kilometres of smooth going along the marshy, winding Dog River, Jordain Creek, and Cold Water Creek. At Cold Water Lake, the group stopped for a tea break and a drink. The water was so cold it hurt their throats as they swallowed.

The next three portages across the height of land to Lac du Milieu were treacherous with so many bog patches that tree trunks and logs had been placed lengthwise in the muck. But these were not much help. It was such slippery going that everyone, including Marie-Anne, was soon covered in mud.

Once over the divide, they encountered a maze of waterways: shallow rivers, sometimes fast flowing, sometimes as still as death; swamps full of dead spruce; and marshes of bulrushes and other slimy vegetation. Finally there came relief from the gloomy land-scape: a meadow spread with white and pink water lilies, tall yellow grasses, and tangled wild rice. Many kinds of songbirds and but-terflies flitted about. Frogs croaked. Marie-Anne would tell her children that this place was a welcome bit of paradise.

Finally, after thirteen days and thirty-four portages, the group arrived at the horn-shaped Lac La Pluie (Rainy Lake). One trav-eller, writing in 1823, considered it "remarkable for the pure, smooth, porcelain whiteness of its granite hills, which are often very high, and gleam through their scanty clothing of pine in a beautiful and singular manner." Another chronicler saw something quite different: "Rainy Lake is very uninteresting, low Banks and stunted Fir Trees."[13] Whatever they thought of the landscape, the Lagimodières must have been relieved to encounter wide-open water. The canoes skimmed along, and in a day and a half they reached the North West Company's imposing Fort Lac La Pluie, located on a high bank on the north side, near one of the forts that La Vérendrye had established as places to cache provisions while he was exploring the great northern plains in the vain hope of finding the mythic Western Sea. In 1807 it was the advance depot where furs from the far north Athabasca District were brought in and supplies sent out. The distance travelled was so great that the brigades couldn't make the journey to Fort William and back in one ·season, so this post served as a substitute. Forty voyageurs, Indian fur trappers, and labourers were stationed there. It certainly was a busy place:

Coopers made the many barrels and kegs needed for the wild rice, corn, and maple sugar and the fish (principally whitefish and stur-geon) from the excellent fishery near by. Carpenters and sawyers, in addition to erecting new buildings as need demanded, had the

never-ending task of maintaining and repairing the existing structures. Logs for the buildings had to be cut, hauled to the fort, and
squared or whip-sawed into planks . . . From the early days Fort
Lac la Pluie was known for its output of canoes. The birch trees
used for their making grew abundantly in the nearby forest.[14]

As a freeman planning to sell his pemmican, Jean-Baptiste had business to do here, and Marie-Anne rested for a few days. She may
have had the good luck to stay in one of the plain, small but comfortable houses, which were made of squared logs chinked with
stones, and had large stone fireplaces, whitewashed walls, and vegetable and flower gardens. She probably assumed a similar dwelling
would be waiting for her at Pembina, but it would be another ten
years before she had a permanent home to call her own.

The Lagimodières and the winterers set out once again. The
men were deadly serious about their work – time was of the
essence; their destination had to be reached before the cold
weather set in – and the canoe clipped along, following the pleasant Rainy River across the Lake of the Woods. In 1734, on one of
the rocky islands in this lake, twenty-one Frenchmen, including a
priest, Father Aulneau, and La Vérendrye's son were massacred by
Sioux who were wreaking revenge on the friends of their long-
time enemies, the Ojibwe and Cree.

From Lake of Woods the Lagimodière party traversed the Rat
Portage and found themselves at the entry to the Winnipeg River.
Rushing past monstrous yellow and white rocks and dropping fast,
the river was an obstacle course of spectacular rapids and waterfalls
and twenty-six difficult and exhausting portages. At one point,
while riding atop some rocks, the Lagimodières' canoe was ripped
from the prow to the second bar; the crew furiously baled the
water with kettles until finally they made it to shore.

Finally they arrived at the mouth of the Winnipeg River, at Traverse Bay on Lake Winnipeg. Here was situated Fort Bas-de-la-Rivière, an old fur trading post established by La Vérendrye seventy-five years earlier. "The Post was placed in a very beautiful Situation and surrounded by cultivated Land where they grow Potatoes, Wheat and Vegetables," writes Elizabeth Losey.[15] It was a warehouse/grocery store where the brigades heading for the far north loaded up the huge amounts of pemmican brought from buffalo country. This was the tasty staple of the fur trade, a highly nutritious food that could easily be carried anywhere and, if kept dry, stored for many months. Buffalo meat was pounded and then dried in the sun. It was then packed into forty-kilogram bags, sometimes with Saskatoon berries added. To provide some moisture, melted buffalo fat was poured on top. Voyageurs and trappers ate two or three kilos every day; they sliced off pieces and nibbled it as they travelled and, for the evening meal, they made a "rubbaboo stew" by adding flour and water. As a buffalo hunter supplying pemmican, Jean-Baptiste would often do business here.

Was Marie-Anne beginning to appreciate the strange new world she found herself in? Would she be able to see the sublime, as Robert M. Ballantyne, an apprentice clerk with the Hudson's Bay Company, did in 1864?

We suddenly discovered a little Indian boy, dressed in the extreme of the Indian summer fashions– in other words, he was in a perfect state of nakedness, with the exception of a breech-cloth; and upon casting our eyes across the river we beheld his father, in a similar costume, employed in catching fish with a hand-net. He was really a wild, picturesque-looking fellow, interested in his proceedings. When I first saw him, he was standing upon a rock close to the edge of a foaming rapid, into the eddies of which he gazed intently, with the net raised in the air, and his muscular frame motionless, as if petrified in the act of striking. Suddenly the net swung through the air, and his body quivered as he strained every sinew to force it quickly through the water: in a moment it came out with a beautiful white-fish, upwards of a foot long, glittering like silver as it struggled in the mesh.[16]

At last the Lagimodières' brigade reached the Red River, and as they travelled south the landscape changed dramatically. Rocky outcrops and evergreen trees disappeared. Suddenly there was nothing but vast grasslands waving yellow and green as far as the eye could see. Above was the astonishing blueness, the vast eternal dome of the sky. Marie-Anne always said that she was overcome with the beauty of the prairies, such a relief from the dense, dark forest.

Just before they arrived at Pembina, they smelled smoke; it grew darker, until the sun was all but blotted out. Finally they spied red flames galloping in every direction. Jean-Baptiste told his wife not to be frightened, that fires happened all the time and, as it turned out, 1807 was a particularly bad year for prairie blazes. Three years earlier another traveller had encountered similar fires on his way to Pembina:

Plains burnt in every direction. Blind Buffalo to be seen wandering about every moment. The poor beasts have all their hair singed of[f] to the Skin, and even the skin in many places is shriveled up and burnt in a most terrible manner, their Eyes swollen and closed fast. It was really pitiful to see them walking about, sometimes running foul of a large stone, at other times tumbling down hill and falling into Creeks that were not yet frozen over. In one spot we found a whole herd laying all dead near each other, the Fire having passed here only yesterday. Those animals were all still good and fresh and many of them exceedingly fat . . . and good to eat.[17]

For Marie-Anne, life at Pembina would not be full of pretty houses and flower gardens; instead the brutal and unpredictable would prevail.

CHAPTER FIVE

—

THE PEMBINA was a charming little river, winding west from the mightier Red, about two kilometres south of what would become the Canadian border.* Willow trees bowed over it in supplication, long yellow grasses grew right to its banks, whitewater roiled through its twists and turns, and the bushes were thick and green. High cranberries grew along its edges – the name Pembina is a version of the Ojibwe *anepimina* (cranberry).

In 1807 the juncture of the two rivers was dominated by a singular structure, the North West Company's Fort Pembina, where the town of Pembina, North Dakota is now situated. The Lagimodières spotted it the instant they rounded one of the Red's sharp bends. The compound consisted of a whitewashed house

---

* The Pembina River originates north of La Rivière, Manitoba and flows southeast, entering the United States northeast of Langdon, North Dakota.

constructed of oak (which also served as the trading post), a stable for fifty horses, storehouses, an ice house, and dormitories for the French-Canadian workmen, all enclosed by a sturdy stockade. Blockhouses at the corners guarded against Indian attacks. A huge oak flagpole stood in the middle of the fort's square, proudly flying both the North West Company's coat of arms and the Union Jack.

This miniature kingdom was ruled over by one of the most colourful and literate fur traders ever to trek through Canada's North West. Not much is known about Alexander Henry the Younger's early life – there seems to be no record of place and date of birth – except that his uncle, Alexander Henry the Elder, was an intrepid fur trader and explorer. A record of the younger Henry first appears in 1791, when he was working for the North West Company, trading furs with the Ojibwe in the Lower Red River district. In 1800, after attending the annual rendezvous at Grand Portage, he set out with a party of twenty-eight wintering voyageurs/labourers; twenty-one-year-old Jean-Baptiste Lagimodière was part of that group.

They built a post surrounded by palisades south of the Pembina River that fall, but business was not great. This was the territory of Dakota Sioux, the ferocious enemy of the Ojibwe; for good reason the North West Company's best customers were too terrified to travel that far south. In May 1801, Henry and company upended the logs of that fort and transported them north upstream to where the Red meets the little Pembina.

Two other North West Company posts had already been established in the neighbourhood, and then abandoned. Nor'Wester Peter Grant constructed the first on the east side of the Red River opposite the mouth of the Pembina sometime in 1793. Four years later, Charles Jean-Baptiste Chaboillez, another prolific journal writer, built on the other side of the Red. This place was typical of all of the North West Company's smaller posts. A palisade, necessary to protect the inhabitants from marauding Dakota Sioux, surrounded four buildings: the "Big House" residence for ten men; a home for the Chaboillez family and one for his chief assistant, Desjardaix (first name unknown), his wife, and two children; and a "Little House" where business was done. As one scholar explains, "From the base camp, the bourgeois organized the distribution of trap lines, probably in consultation with senior Indian [Ojibwe] hunters like Le Sucre, Le Boeuf and Old Manominé and assigned his men to collect the furs."[1]

Alexander Henry the Younger considered rebuilding Chaboillez's fort, but during his investigations he "remained for the night and slept in the old fort on the S. side [of the Pembina]. Fleas and wood lice made me very uncomfortable; the former always abound in our old buildings and are very troublesome."[2] He built on the north side instead. Jean-Baptiste Lagimodière helped construct the new fort. Alexander Henry described what they were up against:

> The ground was so encumbered with large fallen trees, and the underwood so intricate, that we could not see ten yards before us; however, I drew out the place as soon as possible. Between this spot and the plains on the W. are great numbers of fine large oaks, very proper for building, and on the N. side, between this and a small rivulet, are plenty of fine large bois blancs, proper for flooring and covering. The stockades must be hauled from some distance below, where there are fine patches of poplar.[3]

During the nine years he was at Fort Pembina, Henry never stopped enlarging and improving his domain. The residences, for example, were torn down and rebuilt in 1803. "The Men began to demolish our dwelling houses, which were built of bad wood, and rebuild new ones of Oak timber. It was astonishing the numerous nest of mice we found and the swarm of fleas that were hopping in every direction. Our Clothes were covered with them."[4] Lime brought from the nearby Hair Hills (also called the Pembina Mountains) was used to whitewash these buildings. The original stockade was constructed of poplar, but it was torn down in the second year and replaced with one of oak. The ice house held fifty sleighloads of ice to store fish and meat. And Henry was a passionate gardener. Across the river, on the grounds of Grant's old fort, a half-dozen men worked the soil, and seeded and fertilized the crop. As usual in his journals, the trader took the credit for the endeavour: "I planted potatoes, turnips, carrots, beets, parsnips, onions, and cabbage-stalks for seed. Sowed cabbage seed."[5] Later he wrote: "I gathered in my Cucumbers and made a Nine Gallon Keg of Pickles, having plenty of Vinegar, made from the sap of the Maple tree, and which is most excellent, very little inferior to that imported."[6]

As well as construction work and gardening, Jean-Baptiste and the other labourers were engaged in the never-ending toil required to keep the fort running. The *engagés* had to chop and store firewood, harvest wild hay and store it for the horses and livestock, and haul corn. They made the pouches in which they packed the furs that the natives brought in. They built furniture; fashioned tools, snowshoes and sledges; and mended their own and their boss's clothes. They baked bread and made candles out of bear fat and tallow. In April 1804, Henry reported: "My men are employed, some making Wheels, others Carts, others sawing boards and squaring timber, Smith making nails, some making soap, others sturgeon netts, and smoking Tongues, and the most active and capable are gone along with the Indians to hunt Beaver, and take care of the Furs."[7] Cleaning the fort was a year-round chore. What to do with the garbage and human waste? Henry put it bluntly:

"The stench around our camp was now so great arising from the quantities of flesh and fat we had thrown away since our arrival."

Besides collecting furs, the most important work was finding enough food to keep everyone alive, especially during the winter. The *engagés* set nets to catch fish, both for their co-workers and for the dogs, which ate enormous amounts of whitefish. They hunted big game – elk, bear, buffalo. Jean-Baptiste Lagimodière's exceptional skill at this activity quickly turned him into a prized employee.

There was also a brutality, a degradation, about fort life that flared when these hard-working men took to drink and, given Jean-Baptiste's fondness for socializing, he probably joined in. Alexander Henry reported on May 6, 1804: "Engaged my men, settled their accounts, and gave them a treat of High wines Etc. They were soon merry, then quarreled and fought. I saw five battles at the same moment in the Fort, soon after nothing was to be seen, but bloody noses, Bruised faces, Black eyes, and torn Jackets and Shirts."

In 1804, when the North West and XY companies amalgamated and implemented austerity measures, Jean-Baptiste was one of the many voyageurs whose contracts were not renewed. He probably didn't mind much, because he had already developed a taste for the life of an independent, a free spirit, *un homme libre*.

In the 1790s there was an influx of wintering voyageurs from the Great Lakes region to the Red River Valley. Some, like Lagimodière, were French Canadians, others were of mixed-blood heritage, having a French-Canadian father and an Indian mother. These latter spoke both French and native languages, and understood the intricacies of the fur trade.[8] Historian Ruth Swan writes that they "learned how to hunt bison on horseback while living on the fringe of the plain and parkland at fur trade centres like the Pembina fur trade post. In the process, they made the cultural transformation to *Indianized Frenchmen*."[9]

Most of the voyageurs who lost their jobs quickly returned to Lower Canada; only those with "a mentality of independence" adopted such a precarious life. John E. Foster has studied the character traits of these men, and in his findings a portrait of Jean-Baptiste Lagimodière emerges:

> Usually he was an engagé who had established himself as a man of consequence among his fellows. Physical prowess counted for much, but not all; generosity and a penchant for an evocative song and an entertaining story were recognized as well. The man of consequence acted to become a "master" of his own affairs and circumstances. The logic of this ethos among the fur trade engagés led some to end their relationship with the trading post as engagés and become *les hommes libres*.[10]

When the Lagimodières arrived in 1807 there were, according to Alexander Henry, about forty-five freemen and their families living and working the territory around the fort, and their numbers increased each year thereafter. The geographic location had everything to do with their success. The Pembina bordered the plains where the bison flourished. Like a ghostly, wavering black blanket, vast herds of these shaggy beasts spread across the broad prairie. The freemen became expert in hunting them and at turning their flesh into pemmican. Two innovations assisted this enterprise. The first was the adoption of the horse culture by the Assiniboine and Plains Cree, and then by the freemen. On horseback, hunters could travel long distances, tracking down and shooting the bison as they roamed about the wide prairie. The second was the creation of the Red River cart. Alexander Henry has been credited for this innovation. "Men now go again for meat, with small low Carts, the wheels of which are of one solid

piece, sawed of[f] the ends of trees whose diameter is three feet.
Those carriages, we find much more convenient, and advantageous than to load our horses on the back, and the Country being
so smooth and level that we can . . . go in every direction," he
wrote in 1801.[11] By 1807 these vehicles were an essential part of
the freemen's operations.

But another dynamic of the buffalo hunt was far more valuable
than animals or wooden contraptions. Since the first coureurs de
bois arrived in Canada's North West in the seventeenth century,
white fur trappers had mated with Indian women. They had to, in
order to survive.

One of the tasks demanded of the *engagés* during the winter
was to go *en dérouine*, leaving behind the comfort of the posts to
travel to Indian lodges and trade for furs. Marcel Giraud
describes this job:

> The "*coureur de dérouine*," as such an employee-trader was called,
> became the essential cogwheel in the trading post. Many of the
> Canadians shared . . . the life of the natives, choosing to live over
> winter in their tents, next to their families, without caring about
> the rigorous cold or the uncomfortable quarters . . . such a disper-
> sion might have an added importance of conserving the fort's scanty
> resources of food.[12]

Such travels provided these *coureurs de dérouine* a wonderful opportunity to meet young women. Naturally, romance broke out, with
"marriage" as the next step. This was done according to Indian
custom (*mariage à la façon du pays*). Peter Grant, the proprietor of
the first Pembina post, who himself married a Saulteaux woman,
described how this arrangement worked:

After preliminaries . . . nothing more is wanted but the consent of the parents, which, to a good hunter or warrior, is seldom denied. He then makes them a considerable present, which, if accepted becomes his permission to sleep with his mistress and keep her as his wife. The marriage is so far consummated without further ceremony, but, to make it binding, it is necessary that he should live at least one winter with his father-in-law, during which the old man claims an indisputed right to all the product of his hunt; but so soon as the young couple have a child of their own, they are released from any further dependence on the old people, and are at liberty to go and live where they please.[13]

And what bounty the young bride brought with her! She knew how to make pemmican – essential for the family business – tap maple trees for sugar, harvest wild rice, dress hides, collect wattape to repair canoes, fish, pick berries, trap small animals, snare small game, and make snowshoes and moccasins. John Tanner, an American who was captured by the Shawnee Indians in 1789 when he was nine years old and eventually adopted by a woman chieftain of the Ottawa tribe, lived in the Red River Valley at the same time as the Lagimodières did. They may have met him. His memoir is remarkable as an unvarnished if somewhat brutal portrayal of Indian life. His adopted mother pointed out the value of marrying: "My son, you see that I am now become old; am scarce able to make you moccasins, to dress and preserve all your skins, and do all that is needful about your lodge. You are now about taking your place as a man and a hunter, and it is right you should have some one who is young and strong to look after your property and take care of your lodge."[14]

The Indian wife was not a delicate, defenceless "angel by the hearth." She worked alongside her buffalo-hunting husband and in the process developed a unique culture, the foundation of the Métis nation. The historian Ruth Swan writes:

> [Pemmican] became the staple of the Freeman culture and economy, giving them the independence to live separately from the traders and the posts, outside the hierarchical authority of Europeans and Canadians. The *gens libres* adopted a more egalitarian model of opportunity influenced by their social interactions with local Aboriginals, including their wives and kin networks, so that they came to increasingly resent snobbery, arrogance and assumption of authority.[15]

After the Lagimodières arrived in Pembina, they joined the freemen and their families living in an enclave on one side of the fort on a knoll surrounded by oak trees. Jean-Baptiste knew many of these people from his days in the North West but it must have been something of a shock to Marie-Anne. Although there was a logic to its chaos, the camp was sprawling, dishevelled, smelly, and noisy. Children and dogs roamed everywhere; elders sat smoking their pipes and gambling. Outside each lodge or wigwam were large frames for curing buffalo skins and racks where fish were dried; skeletons of large animals hung on trees, a tradition dictated by the Ojibwe and Cree religion.

The Lagimodières set up the first home of their own here – a wigwam much like those used by the Ojibwe in their own encampment not far away. Poplar saplings were peeled into poles and then driven half a metre into the ground, half a metre apart, forming the shape of an ellipse. Opposite poles were bent and brought together at the top. These were tied with twine made of soft, green basswood. This skeleton was then covered with birchbark or bulrush mats that had been stitched together to form sheets. The whole structure was held in place with cords of basswood, the ends weighted down by rocks. Inside, the walls were covered with the bark of black ash and the ceiling with cedar bark cut in a zigzag pattern. The fireplace sat in the middle, surrounded by large stones to prevent people from stepping into it. The smoke wafted upward and floated through an opening cut at the top, not a whiff invaded the interior. Sunlight flooded in through that same gap.[16]

The families of freemen often made their teepees comfy by adding European-style innovations and the Lagimodières would have done the same. Oilskin was placed over the top of the wigwam for extra protection; instead of moose hide, a heavy piece of blue brocade covered the door opening; a crucifix was pinned on one wall, a line engraving of something like the French country-side on the other; a quilt of coloured cotton patches was rolled up in the corners. The exterior of the freemen's camp might have been disorderly, but the interiors of most homes were kept immaculately clean and tidy.

Immediately after their arrival, Marie-Anne busied herself unpacking, sewing clothes that were torn during the trip, learning how to cook in a pot balanced from a tripod. There was plenty to eat: fresh buffalo meat, whitefish and pickerel, Indian corn and potatoes and carrots, beets, cucumbers, and melons from the fort's garden. The September weather remained fine and the countryside was painted with wood asters, sweet-clover and common yarrow.

Marie-Anne must have watched what was going on around her and wondered how she would ever succeed as a buffalo hunter's wife. Everything came so naturally to the Indian women who were now her neighbours. She would learn how to pound the buffalo meat into a thick flaky mass, figure out how much lard to add – twenty-two kilograms of meat mixed with eighteen kilograms of melted fat was the rule – but how to calculate the exact amount of Saskatoon berries to add that special flavour?

One of Marie-Anne's biographers claims that Marie-Anne met Alexander Henry at Fort Pembina.[17] There's no mention of the Lagimodières anywhere in Henry's journals, although this is not unusual, as he seldom, if ever, mentions the freemen individually. Still, since the fur trader knew Jean-Baptiste from earlier days, he might have entertained them at his home. Judging by journals, his fort was truly a circus. As his guests entered through Fort Pembina's gate, his favourite pet, a black bear, would come ambling over to greet them.

The front half of the main floor of the house was where the trading was done. There were few pelts in evidence here, because they had already been stored in the warehouse nearby, where the fur press was located. Mostly on display were the goods for trade: multicoloured glass beads, bright calico, axes, guns, kettles, augers, needles, knives, blankets. The Henrys occupied two rooms behind the post, the parlour and the kitchen, as well as three rooms upstairs, two bedrooms and Alexander's office, or library as he called it.

Madame Henry was a twenty-one-year-old Saulteaux princess, the daughter of Chief Old Buffalo. At his insistence, she had waged a campaign to win Alexander's heart. It was simple – she merely showed up, dressed in her finery, in his bed every night. A prude, he kept ejecting her because he was determined, as he put it, "not to be hindered with any female impediment." "The devil could not have got her out," he wrote, but finally he could resist no longer.[18] Soon two children arrived.

Pierre Bonga was Henry's personal servant and interpreter, the son of West Indian slaves, a married couple who were owned by Captain Daniel Robertson, British commandant at Fort Mackinac, located at the juncture of lakes Michigan and Superior, during the 1780s. The Bongas were manumitted after the captain's death, but remained in the west, making their living by operating a hotel. Son Pierre had a remarkable ear and had picked up all the major Indian languages. He was also a surly fellow; when Jean-Baptiste worked at Pembina, the two men were apparently at loggerheads.

Alexander Henry's visitors were always treated to a splendid meal. There were vegetables from his garden, delicious poached sturgeon, venison baked in a pastry crust, and a variety of sweet biscuits, as well as red wine. One of the fur trader's chief topics of conversation was the Indians. They were "unreasonable," "troublesome," "indolent," and "depraved." He was always battling with the very people upon whom his livelihood depended, and this entry from his journal is typical:

> I quarreled with Little Shaw and dragged him out of the Fort by the hair &c. Indians very troublesome and threaten to level my fort to the Ground. Tabishaw desirous of breeding mischief. I had a narrow escape of being stabbed by him twice, once in the hall, once in the shop. I very plainly perceived they were bent on murdering some of us and then attempting to pillage. I therefore desired all hands to keep upon their guard, and the first Indian that would be insolent, to knock him down.[19]

One wonders if any of his guests ever mentioned that it was Henry who supplied the liquor that caused much of the animosity. And he didn't much like Jean-Baptiste's type either. On November 30, 1804 he wrote, "Those freemen are a nuisance in the country, and generally scoundrels; I have never yet found one honest man amongst them." As Ruth Swan points out, "He despised them, probably because they were competent . . . he did not like their competition and independence . . . The freemen were a threat to his business because of their expertise in the fur trade."[20]

During the time the Lagimodières lived at Pembina, the freemen were hunting buffalo on horseback and using Red River carts to bring back the meat and grease from the plains, but they had not yet organized themselves into the large hunting parties romanticized in paintings and literature, with their military discipline and democratic organization, which came to dominate the plains from the 1820s onwards. Nevertheless, the twice-yearly excursion in 1807 was a full family affair. Jean-Baptiste and Marie-Anne would have been part of it.

Alexander Henry left this description – gleaned from standing on top of his roof – of the freemen's families leaving for a hunt in October 1803. Not much would have changed by the time the Lagimodières arrived four years later.

Antoine Payet, Guide and 2d in command, leads off the van with a Cart drawn by two Horses and loaded with his own private Baggage, Cassettes (small trunks), Bags, Kettles, Mashquemotes &c. Madam Payêt follows the Cart with a child of one year old on her back, very merry. Charles Bottineou follows, with two horses and a Cart loaded with one and half Packs, his own Baggage and two young Children with Kettles and other trash hanging to his Cart.

Madam Bottineau follows with a young squalling Child on her back, and she scolding and tossing it about. Joseph Dubord goes on foot with his long Pipe stem and calumet in his hand. Madame Dubord follows her husband on foot, carrying his Tobacco Pouch with a broad bead Tail. Antoine Thelliere, with a Cart and two horses, loaded with one and a half packs of Goods and Dubord's baggage. Then comes Antoine La Pointe, with another Cart and two horses, loaded with two pieces of Goods and Baggage belonging to Brisebois, Jessmin, and Poulliotte, and a Kettle suspended on each side. Auguste Brisebois follows with only his Gun on his shoulder and pipe in his mouth fresh lighted. Mis. Jessmin goes next, same as Brisbois, with Gun and Pipe puffing out clouds of smoke. Nicholas Pouliotte, the greatest smoker in the North West, has nothing but pipe and pouch. Those three Fellows, having taking the farewell dram and lighted fresh pipes, send forth clouds of smoke and go on brisk and merry, playing numerous pranks &c.

Domin Livernois with a young mare, the property of M. Langlois, loaded with weeds for smoking, an old Indian Worsted bag (Madame's property) and some Squashes and Potatoes, and a small keg of Fresh water and two young whelps howelling &c. Next goes Liverhois' young horse drawing a Traville loaded with his own Baggage and a large worsted Mashquemcate, belonging to Madam M. Langlois. Next appear'd Madam Cameron's young mare, kicking and raving and Farting, hawling a Traville which was loaded with a bag of Flour, some Cabbages, Turnips, Onions and a small keg of water, and a large Kettle of Broth. M. Langlois, who is master of the band, now comes on leading a horse that draws a Traville that is nicely covered with a new painted Tent under which is laying his Daughter extended at full length and very sick. This covering or canopy has a pretty effect in the Carivan and appears at a great distance in the Plains.

Madam M. Langlois now brings up the rear of human beings following the Traville with a slow step and melancholy air attending to the wants of her daughter who notwithstanding her sickness can find no other terms of expressing her gratitude to her Parents than by calling them Dogs, Fools and Beasts &c.&c. Rear guard consisted of a long train of Dogs, twenty in number, some bred for Sleighs, others for Game, and some for Pets of no use whatever only to snarl and destroy meat. The total forms a string near a mile long, and appears like a large band of Assineboines.[21]

By mid-October the buffalo hunters returned to their home base at Pembina. The Lagimodières didn't stay long. In November an incident occurred that turned them into fugitives.

Not far from their wigwam lived a tall, attractive Cree woman with a baby girl and young son. That her husband was of European descent was obvious – both children were fair, and the little boy had reddish hair. She knew no French, so Marie-Anne couldn't speak with the woman, but Jean-Baptiste had a long, unhappy conversation with her. It must have been bad news, because the woman created a terrible commotion, screaming, wailing, and gesticulating wildly.

When Marie-Anne returned to her tent, she noticed her neighbour watching her. The woman suddenly spit out something in Cree so stridently, so furiously that Marie-Anne thought she must be demented. Later when she told Jean-Baptiste of the encounter, he nonchalantly shrugged his shoulders and quickly changed the subject.

Jean-Baptiste owned two dogs that had thick grey fur like wolves, and white eyes with a touch of blue. They showed no interest in either of the Lagimodières. Marie-Anne was a little afraid of them. One morning, Jean-Baptiste left the camp early. Marie-Anne was sitting outside her tent on a bench when, to her surprise and delight, her Cree neighbour arrived with some corn pudding for the family. She made Marie-Anne understand that this was a special dish, with plums and melon added, exactly the way her grandmother made it. Then she left. Marie-Anne was in the middle of sewing a seam when she ran out of thread. Placing the bowl on a nearby tree stump, she went inside her wigwam to look for some. In a few seconds she heard a loud crash. The dogs had knocked over the pudding and were busy eating it. By the time she got to them it was all gone. Suddenly they were vomiting. Within fifteen minutes they were dead.

After the commotion that followed, Jean-Baptiste finally confessed. The Cree woman was his "country wife." They had lived together for four years. Her children were his.

CHAPTER SIX

—

OF COURSE JEAN-BAPTISTE would have taken a country wife.* There
was no way he could have survived in the Canadian wilderness
without one. But why did he settle Marie-Anne at the exact location
where his Indian partner and children were awaiting his return? It
seems such an insensitive, cruel thing to do. Did he think the two
women would live together in peace? All the western tribes practised polygamy; it was an economic necessity. A widow's survival
depended on being taken in by her husband's brother. And having
several wives added to a man's prestige; as one journal writer put it,
the Indians believed that "all great men should have a plurality of
wives."[1] But the Lagimodières were devout Roman Catholics. How
did Jean-Baptiste think they could live in a *ménage à trois?* And what
of Marie-Anne's shock and sorrow? She may have realized that for
Jean-Baptiste having an Indian helpmeet and bed mate was

---

* At this point the Cree woman vanishes from the record, and neither
she nor her children are heard from again.

unavoidable, but what she found unforgivable was the nonchalance with which he had lied to her. How could she trust that he was telling her the truth ever again? Of course, she had no alternative but to continue in her marriage. Returning to her family in Quebec was not an option. Not only was there no way to get there, but Marie-Anne was expecting a baby in three months' time.

Not long after she'd left Maskinongé, she realized she was pregnant. Her conditions made the voyage even more perilous; morning sickness was a huge problem. And now she was on her way to a place where there was not only no midwife, but no women to help her during the delivery. After the autumn buffalo hunt, women and children returned to the relative comfort of the Pembina camp.

There was no question that the Lagimodières had to leave Fort Pembina immediately. There were plenty of guns in the community, and they were frightened of the violence that the insulted Cree woman and her extended family might inflict. Conveniently the fall buffalo hunt was underway. Alexander Henry reported on October 31, 1807: "We saw all the different gangs of Freemen along the hills. Buffalo are in abundance." Jean-Baptiste and Marie-Anne joined the trek to the Hair Hills sixty-five kilometres to the west. Their belongings were piled on a travois pulled by a horse. Marie-Anne rode in the chaise while Jean-Baptiste walked beside her, holding onto the reins. He would have tried hard to avoid ruts and holes so that she, in her pregnant state, wouldn't be shaken about too much.

Once their families returned to Pembina, the freemen gathered at what was known as the Grand Camp, near the head of the Pembina River, where in late fall the bison sheltered themselves against winter storms, in the dense bush. But it wasn't just big game the hunters were after. The streams were thick with fur animals – otter, marten, mink, fisher, raccoon, and of course, the almighty beaver. This was where the real money was to be found, and Jean-Baptiste was after a fortune.

The journey along the Pembina River was truly breathtaking. The trail curled up and down hills full of hardwoods, maples, oaks, elms, all suited out in a blaze of colour – purples, russets, yellows, oranges. Soon though, the hills became steeper, the path obscured by the falling leaves, the air chillier. The Lagimodières must have been relieved when they arrived at Grand Camp.

Accommodation at this place was much cruder than the cozy comfort of the wigwams the freemen enjoyed at Fort Pembina. It consisted of a wooden shack with a dirt floor, and since nothing else but the buffalo hunt mattered in this world, the tools used to skin and butcher buffalo were the only ornaments.

As Alexander Henry had noted, buffalo were plentiful that season. The calves bellowed all night long. Bushes, grasses, everything was trampled down. The willows were torn to bits, the bark of many smaller trees stripped away by the shaggy animals scratching themselves, the muddy banks of the river hammered into cement by the constant pounding of hooves. Dung, thick and hard, was piled everywhere. The camp stank terribly, full of hides waiting to be tanned and drying meat and bones, like ghosts seeking revenge.

As the wife of a hunter, Marie-Anne understood that she must learn something about the butchering process. Jean-Baptiste, covered with blood, called out the cuts as he sliced them from a cow – one small hump, one large hump, two tenderloin, two shoulders, two heavy *epoulets*, two *fittaits*, one belly, one heart, one rump, one brisket, two sides, one backbone, one neck, one liver, one tongue. There was a feast of smoked liver, salted tongue, sliced roasted hump.

As the days grew colder, Marie-Anne spent most of her time inside the hut, feeding wood and buffalo chips into the fire. The weather was so frigid that you could freeze to death on the way to the privy; snow fell constantly. She was alone much of the day, and sometimes the night, as Jean-Baptiste and the other men were away hunting.

Jean-Baptiste realized that, with no other woman present, he would have to deliver the baby himself, cut the cord, and comfort his wife. The prospect terrified him, and in early January he decided they had no choice: they had to return to Fort Pembina.

Bundled under a buffalo robe, Marie-Anne rode in a carriole, a one-person sleigh shaped liked a bathtub, pulled by four dogs. Jean-Baptiste walked on snowshoes beside the carriole, cracking a small whip to urge the animals on. The buffalo, with their triangular heads, were able to clear away snow to a depth of 1.5 metres to get at their feed, so patches of grass were evident everywhere – a strange sight at the height of a blustery winter.

One afternoon, clouds the colour of mother-of-pearl darkening to black jade scuttled across the sky. A north wind began to bluster, the snow whipped down. The travellers took shelter in an evergreen copse, but the storm soon wore itself out, and they started off again, only to discover that the trail had disappeared. Markings in the snow revealed that they were travelling in circles, and they realized they were lost. As they wandered about in the thick wood, Marie-Anne often had to get out and walk so that Jean-Baptiste could pull or carry the carriole through the tangled trees. She sank deep in the snow, often up to her thighs, or even covering her swollen belly. She was freezing, exhausted, nauseous. The possibility that her unborn baby might die here became a real fear.

Finally the couple reached a small iced-over stream full of huge boulders, called the Tongue River. Jean-Baptiste had been there before and knew exactly where the stream led. They followed it, climbing among the rocks and steep banks until they reached the open plains. From there, they headed northeast, and three hours later they reach Fort Pembina. Just in time. Two days later, on January 6, 1808, Marie-Anne went into labour.

The native midwives in camp quickly took over. All men including Jean-Baptiste were banished from the birthing wigwam. "A man has something inside of himself," Ojibwe women used to say, " . . . and if he came into the place of birth something would happen to that being in him; it might even die. The man wouldn't amount to anything after that."[2] The female elders gathered in what seemed to be a council of war. Marie-Anne was made to swallow a potion of roots, herbs, and bark – sunflowers, basswood and sweet grass, to name a few ingredients– to lessen the pain and to make the baby come quickly.[3] Until the cramps became too severe, she was encouraged to walk around the wigwam; if she had been an Indian, she would have been out chopping wood. One medicine woman is reported as saying, "If you make them walk around or work, the baby will be loosened and birth will be easy. We were told not to overdo, though."[4] Stoicism during childbirth was a point of honour. As an Ojibwe woman related some years later, "My mother-in-law was out trapping with her husband when one of her children was born. She cut the cord herself and continued to work."[5]

The birthing site was arranged just so, a bulrush mat placed on the floor, over it a thin layer of dry grass. Two poles, each ending in two branches, were fixed in the earthen floor a metre or so apart. A sapling was placed in the crotch of each pole.[6] When Marie-Anne's contractions came quickly and regularly, the chief midwife decided it was time for the mother-to-be to take the position for delivery. Marie-Anne knelt on the dry grass with her legs spread.

She grabbed hold of the sapling bar in front of her and pushed hard. When nothing happened, her elbows were placed on the outside of the pole. The more she supported herself with her arms, the less the pain. Meanwhile, the midwife massaged her belly with a cool, jelly-like substance, pushing downward as she rubbed. A strong push, a weak cry: the newborn fell between Marie-Anne's legs and was caught in the midwife's hands. The cord was cut by the oldest woman present.

The baby was a girl who had her mother's flaxen hair and bright blue eyes. Jean-Baptiste named her Reine. It's not clear why he chose such an unusual name. Georges Dugast claims it was in honour of the birthday of the ruling British monarch, King George III, but this seems unlikely as he was born on June 4. A more probable explanation is provided by a distant relative of the Lagimodières, Agnès Goulet, who wrote that the birth date, January 6, was the Feast of the Epiphany, a holy day celebrating the three kings who brought presents to the baby Jesus. In her biography of Marie-Anne, Goulet reported: "No bell memorialized the event, and nothing special was done at the request of the mother. Marie-Anne rocked the precious gift that life had given her. She was overcome by tears of joy."[7]

Reine Marie Lagimodière was not the first white baby born in Canada's west. Only nine days before, on December 29, 1807, at Fort Pembina, a British woman, Isabel Gunn,* had given birth to a son. Alexander Henry related the story in his usual vivid manner.

---

* In the journals of Alexander Henry edited by Elliott Coues, there is a footnote by the historian C. N. Bell, claiming that Isabel Gunn was in Pembina well before the Lagimodières. This adds weight to the theory that the Reine was born in 1808, not 1807 as some biographers have claimed.

At midnight he had been called to the fort's main hall, to attend to a young Hudson's Bay Company employee who was complaining of a terrible stomach ache:

> He stretched out his hand towards me, and in a pitiful tone of voice begged my assistance, and requested I take pity upon a poor help-less abandoned wretch, who was not of the sex I had every reason to suppose, but was an unfortunate Orkney Girl pregnant and actu-ally in Childbirth. In saying this she opened her jacket and display'd to me a pair of beautiful round white Breasts. She further informed me of the circumstances that had brought her into this sad dilemma. The man that debauched her in the Orkney two years ago, was now wintering above at the Grande Fourches. In about an hour after she was safely delivered of a fine boy, and that same day she was conveyed home to Heneys [Hudson's Bay Company post] in my Carriole, where she soon recovered.[8]

Since there was no priest available, the Lagimodières had to baptize the infant themselves. Two days after the birth, the half-breeds, the French Canadians, and their Indian wives crowded into the Lagimodières' wigwam. They stood in a circle around a birch-bark mākōk full of saltwater, which served as a baptismal font. Marie-Anne held the baby, while Jean-Baptiste poured a ladle of water on her head, made the sign of the cross three times, and intoned, "In the name of the Father, and of the Son, and of the Holy Ghost, I baptize thee Reine Marie."

As was the custom, the Lagimodières would have hosted a feast afterwards and those assembled would have brought gifts, such as a deerskin pouch, about the size of one's palm, beautifully embroi-dered with yellow porcupine quills and tiny red beads. It contained the newborn's umbilical cord, which had been dried in the sunshine.

Marie-Anne was advised to bury it under wood chips, so that Reine would grow up to be a skilled gatherer of kindling. Other presents probably included small white shells and bunches of birch cones – Indian mothers dipped these in a little maple syrup as a sweet taste for the baby – and buckskin twine on which the instep bone of a porcupine, the jaw of a squirrel, and caribou teeth had been strung; shells of turtles; and a skinned and dried duck's head. These were all intended as toys for the baby. They were hung on the cradle where "they catch everything evil as a spider's web catches and holds everything that comes in contact with it."[9] The lullabies sung by the Ojibwe women must have seemed a strange and poignant music to Marie-Anne. No words, just sounds – "Bō, Bā, Bā, Wē Wī, Wā."[10]

During the winter of 1808, Jean-Baptiste was away trapping furs and Marie-Anne had to rely on her Indian neighbours for help. When she arrived, she knew none of the native languages, and Michif, the mixture of Cree and French adopted by the Métis, was also incomprehensible to her. In a short time, though, she would become fluent in Cree and Ojibwe.

Tradition as well as availability dictated the materials employed in the care of an infant. Birchbark of the purest white was transformed into a waterproof bathtub as long as Marie-Anne's forearm, as wide as two stretches of her hand. To the bath water were added catnip, crushed spruce needles, and twigs of a swamp plant – all of which were supposed to make Reine strong and healthy. Rabbit pelts sewn together served as soft blankets. Dried swamp moss, with the bugs and weeds shaken out, made perfect diaper material.[11]

But the essential baby item was the cradleboard. Made out of cedar wood, it was usually just short of a metre long, and outfitted with a bow structure to protect the head and a footrest. Infants were not placed directly on the cradleboard; they were swaddled in rabbit skin, with the necessary dried swamp moss underneath, and positioned in a birchbark container. This device was placed on the board and held in place by two pieces of buckskin decorated with porcupine quills and beads. These were tightly laced together over the birchbark, beginning at the footrest and ending at the baby's waist. The cradleboard was then strapped onto the mother's back and supported by a strap around her forehead. Once she got the hang of the cradleboard, Marie-Anne was mobile again, free to perform the chores of survival that the buffalo hunters' wives were responsible for, especially wood-gathering. Each day the women marched in single file along a narrow path into the bush. Their axes rang out – raucous music shattering the still forest – until they staggered back with huge bundles of wood on their backs.

There was another essential task Indian women performed that dictated the success or failure of their husbands' business. This was transforming the stiff, thick buffalo hides into butter-soft leather used to make gloves, moccasins, satchels, and blankets. Marie-Anne would have learned the tanning process from an expert Cree woman; one can imagine the lecture.

"The first rule is that a freshly killed buffalo must be used. We want these robes to be worth something so an old dried-up piece won't do. I've already washed the blood stains from this one and have soaked it in this bucket for three days. We thread a rope through the hole that was left when the head was sawed off. Then we tie it to this big branch here. In my right hand I grab the hide at the tail end. It has to be taut. With the other hand I scrape off the hair.

"So that it won't be damaged by rough bark, we place the rolled-up hide neatly in a blanket and wrap it like this around a tree trunk. This big stick is placed into the overlapped ends. Now we twist it tightly, first to the right and then to the left, until the last bit of moisture is rung out. You don't want mould growing or your hide won't be worth a skunk's ass. In this large bucket I've boiled deer and weasel brains. Our hide will soak here overnight."

At dawn the next morning the work would begin again. "With my left hand I wrap the hide around my right wrist and arm until, you see, it looks like a gigantic cocoon. Then I ring it out again, as hard as I can. Now it's ready to be placed on a wooden frame. First we thread this rope made of basswood fibre into holes cut into the hide. Then we tie the hide to the four poles of the wooden frame until it is stretched as taut as a bow.

"Now the work really begins. We use this chisel-like device to scrape the hide on both sides in all directions. It's important you put your entire weight behind your scraping. How smooth and soft the hide will be depends on how much strength you can muster."

After five hours of hard labour the smudge was prepared. "We place these bits of birchbark on burning embers until they glow. Then we add the cones of the white pine and the Norway pine. Whatever you do, don't use Jack pine cones. They make a terrible colour.

"We sew the sides of the hide together with basswood twine until we've made an airtight pocket. Then we tie the head end of this hide packet to a tree; the tail end we place around the rim of the smudge bucket; the smoke wafts upward. Be careful! I've seen many a skin scorched by shooting sparks. Once we get the colour we want, we take the hide down from the branch. We remove the twine, turn it inside out, sew the edges together, and smudge the other side."[12] The process was complete.

By now Marie-Anne would have adopted Indian dress; she simply couldn't have performed her duties in European garb. She donned deerskin moccasins and leggings, her long skirts exchanged for a blue sackcloth petticoat falling to just below her knees, her European-style chemise replaced with calico-coloured blouses with full sleeves. Her hair was kept in a long braid down her back. And she might have sported a necklace of flattened silver coins, jewellery favoured by native women of the time. Never, though, would she have forsaken the gold crucifix she had worn on a chain around her neck from childhood. Indeed, what must have been most alien to Marie-Anne, the cultural idiom she had the most difficulty dealing with, was religion. That the *sauvages* were heathen and barbarians had been drummed into her since childhood. What else could she believe?

While some of the freemen had taught their native wives bits of Christianity, such as bedtime prayers, few had been baptized. Most were deeply involved in their own religion, practised for centuries. For the Ojibwe, the Midewiwin (Grand Medicine Society) was the most powerful spiritual force in their lives. There were two aspects to its rites: a life-giving ceremony conducted by a learned medicine man to cure those with serious illnesses – this involved the "killing" and "resurrection" of participants – and a passing along of tribal history and mores, an enunciation of the art of healthy, successful living. As one historian writes, "The key to long life was proper personal conduct and the appropriate use of herbal medicines and music. Men should neither lie nor steal. They should be moderate in speech and manner, and should respect women." To become a Midew (shaman or medicine man) bestowed enormous prestige. A fur trader explained that with the Red River Ojibwe, "almost every great man or chief among the Indians is likewise a Juggler or doctor of physic [medicine man]."[13] Women were also ordained into the priesthood.

In his journal, Alexander Henry gives a sense of the importance of the Midewiwin among the Pembina Ojibwe:

[We] found the Indians were busy employed in making the Grand Medicine a ceremony generally performed every spring, when they all meet and when there is always some novice to be admitted into the mysteries of this grand and solemn affair. On this occasion two young men were received, a woman and M. Langlois's Girl. There are many curious circumstances reported concerning the admittance of women into this Great mystery of mysteries. The most ancient and famous for the art among the men, it is said, have every privilege allowed them with a novice and are granted every favour they wish to enjoy.[14]

The sacred drums, deep-voiced and strident, did not let up for four days and four nights. Marie-Anne heard them throbbing, heard the rattles hiss like so many snakes, the high-pitched chanting, the moans of ecstasy. Never before had she felt so completely isolated, so completely alone, and not for a moment did she doubt that her Roman Catholic faith would one day prevail among the *sauvages*. It would take a long time and many awkward experiences before she came to appreciate the power of Indian spirituality.

By spring of 1808, the war between the Ojibwe and Dakota Sioux had heated up once again. Fort Pembina was living in fear. The Ojibwe were forest-dwelling people who lived on moose, deer, fish, maple sugar, wild rice, and berries. When white adventurers arrived in the west, the Ojibwe developed a taste for European goods, including alcohol; fur trapping quickly became an essential part of the economy. Those Ojibwe who camped at Fort Pembina had originated in the forests of the Sault Ste. Marie area and, as the beaver stock there became depleted, they followed the fur traders westward to areas north and south of Lake Superior. This territory had traditionally been occupied by the Dakota Sioux, a buffalo-hunting people who were great warriors and not interested in yielding a single hectare of their land to the Ojibwe interlopers. Chief Little Crow II explained to U.S. Government agent Thomas Forsyth in 1819 why the Dakota Sioux refused to consider a peace treaty with the Ojibwe:

[Little Crow] observed that a peace could easily be made, but said it is better to carry on the war in the way we do, than to make peace, because, he added, we lose a man or two in the course of a year, and we kill as many of the enemy during the same time; and if we were to make peace, the Chippewas [Ojibwe] would over-run all the country lying between the Mississippi and Lake Superior . . . why then should we give up such an extensive country to another nation to save the lives of a man or two annually.[15]

Naturally, animosity developed between the two Indian nations, and over the years it grew more and more fierce. The Dakota Sioux had several advantages in this struggle, most importantly, their skill with horses and guns. As an Ojibwe warrior explained: "While they keep to the Plains with their Horses we are not a match for them; for we being foot men, they could get to windward of us, and set fire to the grass; When we marched for the Woods, they could be there before us, dismount, and under cover fire on us. Until we have Horses like them, we must keep to the Woods and leave the plains to them."[16]

In 1780 a smallpox epidemic wiped out huge numbers of Cree and Assiniboine who had been living in the Red River Valley. The survivors welcomed their allies the Ojibwe to the beaver-laden territory. By this time, all three tribes owned horses and were finally able to take on the Dakota Sioux. Alexander Henry reported in September 1804, for example, that Ojibwe and Assiniboine had formed a war party of three hundred men, 150 on horseback, and were off to hunt down Dakota. The Red River came to be known as the "War Road."

When the fur traders moved into the Red River Valley, they brought guns and ammunition and walled forts, which provided the Ojibwe and other First Nations with protection against their enemy, and encouraged them to continue doing what they were so skilled at – trapping fur-bearing animals. Nevertheless, they lived in constant terror of a Dakota Sioux ambush.

These passages from the journals of Alexander Henry vividly describe the insecurity that plagued everyone in the neighbourhood near Fort Pembina:

August 26, 1800: We stopped for the night, the Indians told me they had seen a wounded Bull near this spot, which they suppose must have been shot by Scioux. This was enough to give an alarm. We pitched upon an advantageous spot, at the entrance of the meadow, to defend, ourselves, in case of attack.

September 8, 1800: About dark the canoes arrived. The men fatigued and in bad humour. They had again seen a wounded Buffaloe on the east side of the river, and a bunch of leaves laid upon the shore where some persons had drank. This had given them a very serious alarm and had I not told them this morning that I should stop here, I really believe they would have returned down the river.

August 23, 1801: My people have been in one state of alarm the whole Summer, our Indians telling them almost every day that they saw the enemy.

December 1, 1801: No Indians will remain there [at Grandes Fourches], all gone below. Our people there are continually in a state of alarm, and keep watch day and night.

May 12, 1802: An Indian and his family arrived in a small Canoe from Red Lake who bring news of the Scieux having killed seven Saulteaux [Ojibwe] in that quarter, all nearly related to those who are camped at this place and all intoxicated. The man was scarcely landed before the Camp and Fort were in an uproar. Crying, bawling, howling and lamenting the death of their relations. *November 26, 1803:* An Indian arrived from above, one of the Scieux having killed three Saulteaux that were working the Beaver on the Fallevoine River.

April 28, 1804: On my return to my Fort, I found all the men in a state of alarm, and all the woman and children had fled to the Woods. They had been informed by the old Indian Woman that the Indians [Sioux] were preparing to attack the Fort.

An ugly incident occurred on July 3, 1805 when a war party of fifty Dakota Sioux attacked a group of Ojibwe buffalo hunters camping on the Tongue River. The first to die was Alexander Henry's father-in-law, the chief called Old Buffalo. Henry records:

He had climb'd up a Tree to look out if the Buffalo were near hand, about eight Oclock in the morning, as they were tented there to make dried provisions. He had no sooner reached the top tree, when two Sieux discoverers who lay near the foot fired their two Guns at the same moment and the Balls passed through his body. He had only time to call out to his family who were in the Tent about 100 paces from him, saying "save yourselves the Sieux are killing us," and fell dead to the ground, breaking several large branches of the tree with his body as he fell.[17]

The women and children started running across the open plain to the heavily treed Wood Peninsula, on the Tongue River. The men followed on foot, those with guns took up the rear. They had gone a four hundred metres when they saw the Dakota war party bearing down on them, full speed. The Ojibwe kept firing at the warriors, and through crafty manoeuvres and expert marksmanship prevented them from rushing upon the women and children, who continued to fly toward the forest. They were within two hundred paces of the woods, and freedom when the enemy finally caught up. At that point, the Ojibwe split in three directions; two groups escaped into the bush, but a young chief, Auguemance, and his people were caught in the Dakota Sioux's path.

Auguemance waited deliberately, with his gun loaded, until the enemy came near. Then he aimed at the one horseman galloping at full speed, who appeared to be the chief. He knocked him to the ground and then blasted several others. Auguemance was finally shot dead, but, by taking on his attackers, he had provided enough time for most of the children to escape into the woods. Several of Auguemance's own offspring were not so lucky, although one daughter did survive to tell the story, which Henry recorded in his journal:

Our twins were so little they could hardly walk. Mama couldn't tote both on her back, so she asked my auntie to carry the boy and she took the girl. When my auntie heard the hideous war whoops, she became so frightened she tossed my brother on the ground and ran. Mama heard our baby screaming behind her. She kissed me and said, "Take courage, my daughter, try to reach the woods. Find your elder sister, she'll take care of you. She loves you. Take courage, take courage. Run fast my daughter." My mother picked up my brother and was running away when she got a blow on the head with a war club. She drew out a knife from her sheath and plunged it into the man's neck. But another man came along and hacked her with an axe. Then he did the same to our babies.[18]

Fourteen others were either killed or taken prisoner.

Auguemance's body was found the next day. His four limbs had been severed, his belly and breast excised, and the amputated parts thrown over his face. His penis and testicles were hacked off, and then stuck into his dead wife's mouth. His scalp had been lifted from his head, and the flesh cut away so that his skull could be removed. It was later used as a liquor goblet whenever the Sioux felt like bragging about their prowess as warriors.

The massacre seemed to appease the rage of the Sioux, at least for a while. There were no recorded assaults until the spring of the following year, 1806, when fifty Sioux warriors attacked Ojibwe hunters from Sandy Hill River, some eighty kilometres south of Pembina. An Ojibwe chief, his eldest son, and a Canadian engagé were killed. Thereafter, things remained quiet around the fort until December 1807, when Alexander Henry received a disturbing dispatch. A Dakota Sioux war party had assailed a large encampment of Ojibwe at Grosse Isle near the Folle Avoine (Wild Rice) River. The highly respected Chief Taybashaw, his eldest son, and an old woman were slaughtered. "The Saulteux [Ojibwe] had fought like heroes," wrote Henry, "against superior numbers and obliged them [Dakota Sioux] to retreat, by which means the Camp was saved."[19] Soon after the Ojibwe retaliated, attacking a camp of Dakota Sioux, destroying twenty-eight of their thirty tents, and killing many dozens. Seven Ojibwe died.

An all-out war was declared, but paralysis set in among the terrified Ojibwe. As Alexander Henry reported: "Indians now all Camped at the Fort drinking and very troublesome. They are now in such a state of consternation from the Scieux having fell in with them, that they have given over all Idea of hunting this season, and are now collecting around the Houses and are going Northward so as to be out of all danger. This affair caused a serious loss upon my department."[20]

Jean-Baptiste was probably still in the Fort Pembina region in August 1805, so he would have known first-hand the details of the grisly attack that year. Whether he told Marie-Anne about the tragedy isn't known. Certainly, she would have heard about the battles that took place in the fall and winter of 1807. By spring 1808 there was terror in the air, a tension as taunt as a bow that played on the already raddled nerves of the people of Pembina. The events of July 22 proved to be the last straw, not only for the Lagimodières but for everybody else.

The Ojibwes' tents – housing twenty-two men, fifty women, and a large number of children – were pitched in a range between the Pembina River and the fort. Alexander Henry relates what happened:

The night was dark and still. When about midnight a discharge of fire arms were suddenly heard, on the south side of the Panbian [Pembina] River accompanied by a most tremendous hooping and yelling in the same quarter. The Indians were first alarmed by some Balls passing through their Tents. They instantly started up, and called out to a party of two families, that were camped on East side of the River if it was them who had fired. They answered no, when at the same moment another discharge was made on the South side of the little River again, which instantly convinced the Indians who they had to deal with. Not one gun was then in their Tents. I had taken them all from them previous to their drinking to prevent their doing mischief among themselves. They now instantly rushed up the hill to the Fort. The gates being shut they climbed over the

Stockades, and in a moment and rushing into the house informing us of our danger, and caught hold of their guns run to the Gates, which were by this time opened, and thronged by women and Children, pushing in with their Baggage &c. They now exchanged Two or Three discharges with their enemy when the firing ceased on both sides."[21]

Henry dragged out his cohorn (a small cannon) "loaded with one pound of powder and 30 balls" and fired it at the Dakota Sioux. The Ojibwe were sure that scores of their enemies lay dead outside the stockade. But they were disappointed. Henry's famous mortar was all sound and fury. It managed to do in only one Sioux warrior, who was decapitated. Everybody joined in the search, but his head was never found.

Not all the freemen were at their Fort Pembina camp that night. As Henry wrote:

I went upon the top of my house being the most elevated situation on the Fort. I immediately perceived a large body of people on horse back moving towards us on the Cart road . . . I soon recognized them to be a party of Freemen coming with loads of Grease. They soon arrived and were much astonished to learn, the narrow escape they had with the Scieux, who I am confident would have shown them no mercy.[22]

Rather than riding along the Red River Road as freemen parties usually did, they followed a path along the foot of the Hair Hills and Tongue River, which was dense with willow and other trees. These provided camouflage from the retreating Dakota Sioux warriors who were riding only a mile and a half away. If Indians had encountered them, the freemen and families would surely all have been slaughtered – indeed two freemen who had wandered off alone were killed.

It's not known if the Lagimodières were amongst this group or had fled to the fort for safety. Whatever the case, they decided that it was time to leave this too dangerous place.

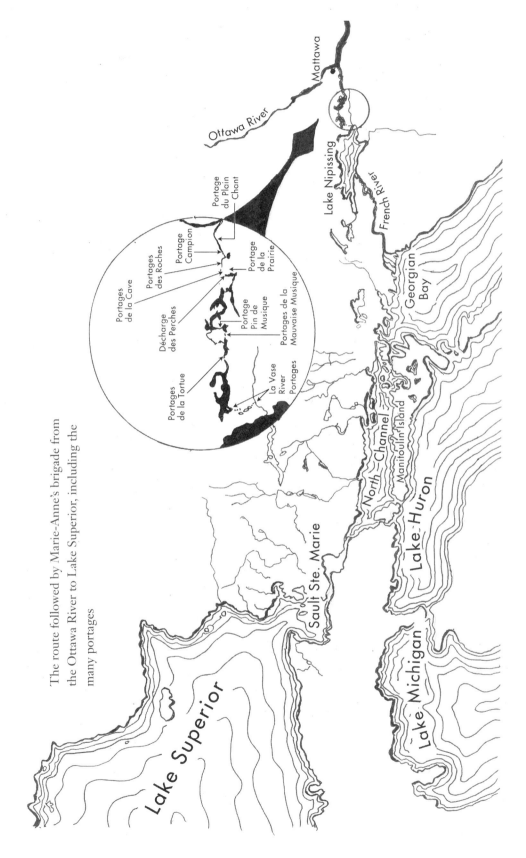

The route followed by Marie-Anne's brigade from the Ottawa River to Lake Superior, including the many portages

Ottawa River

Mattawa

Portage du Plain Chant

Portage Campion

Portages des Roches

Portages de la Cave

Portage de la Prairie

Décharge des Perches

Portage Pin de Musique

Portages de la Mauvaise Musique

Portages de la Tortue

La Vase River Portages

Lake Nipissing

French River

Georgian Bay

North Channel

Manitoulin Island

Sault Ste. Marie

Lake Superior

Lake Huron

Lake Michigan

—

PART TWO

FORTS DES PRAIRIES

CHAPTER SEVEN

—

INDIAN WARFARE WAS NOT the only reason the Lagimodières decided to leave Fort Pembina. Probably more important were financial considerations. By 1808 the fur trade had dried up; the animals had all but been trapped out.

In January 1805, Alexander Henry wrote of "the country being almost destitute of beaver and other furs." The numbers of peltries traded told the story dramatically. In 1804, 144 packs, each weighing forty kilograms, had been shipped out of Fort Pembina. Four years later the annual haul consisted of only sixty packs. This was exactly the number Henry had collected in his first year at Pembina, just as he was setting up, but now there were two to three times the number of hunters doing business at his post.[1] At the end of July, Henry announced that he was being transferred from Fort Pembina to Fort Vermilion, one of the North West Company's *forts des prairies* strung along the North Saskatchewan River that serviced the north country. Beaver here was not only plentiful, but their fur was especially thick and glossy.

The Lagimodières prepared to leave for the same neighbourhood. Jean-Baptiste had formed a partnership with three other
freemen, and with them and their Cree wives, they would travel
the nearly fifteen hundred kilometres to Edmonton House
(where the present-day city is located). Marie-Anne's biographers
write that all that is known about the partners are their last names –
Chalifoux, Paquin, and Bellegarde. There's scant mention of them
in the historical records, but there is a Michel Chalifoux listed as
a voyageur serving with the North West Company in the Red
River district in 1804, the same time that Jean-Baptiste was working
at Pembina, so he is likely the same person. And in a journal entry
of July 13, 1810 Alexander Henry mentions a "Challifoux"
freeman arriving at Edmonton House, which also places him in the
right time and place. In his journal of May 21, 1810 Henry refers
to a freeman "Pacquin" from whom two horses had been stolen
from behind Fort Vermilion, and on June 19 of the same year he
writes, "H. B. men off in two canoes for the Columbia, with nine
men, including the two Pacquins." These men were probably
brothers. Finally, Charles Bellegarde is listed as a "voyageur,
steerer" in Henry's 1800 Red River brigade, returning from Grand
Portage. Jean-Baptiste probably made Bellegarde's acquaintance in
1801 or 1802, when he too was working for Henry. Bellegarde is
also included in a list of freemen living in the Red River Settlement
in 1814 (where the Lagimodières were settled at the time.)[2] All
three partners must have hunted and trapped in the North West
before, because each was married to a Cree woman whose family
lived not far from the Hudson's Bay Company's Edmonton House.
(Like almost all native women, their names are lost in history.)

It's unclear whether the Lagimodière party was part of Alexander
Henry's brigade. It was customary to travel in groups for safety
reasons and Henry mentions that freemen were travelling with him,

but as usual, he doesn't name specific individuals.[3] Whatever the case, they all made the journey by canoe, first along the Red River, then north up Lake Winnipeg to Grand Rapids and the ends of the Saskatchewan River. This shallow, fast-flowing body of water carried them fifteen hundred kilometres westward to the foothills of the Rocky Mountains.

The two canoes lay low, heavy with supplies. In one travelled the Paquins and the Chalifoux, in the other the Bellegardes and the Lagimodières. It had rained heavily during July and the river was swollen, the current strong and wayward. The steersmen, Lagimodière in one canoe and Chalifoux in the other, had trouble keeping on course. On their second day out, a wind suddenly sprang up. Jean-Baptiste's canoe jerked into a semicircle and ran aground. Jean-Baptiste jumped out onto the beach, which had turned into a mushy bog; thick black mud stuck to his feet like mortar. He managed to push the bow out into the current but then jumped into the canoe so strenuously that it almost tipped over. Marie-Anne held tightly to Reine, praying that her husband didn't drown them all.

In some places along the winding Red, the forest was dense with poplar and maple, in others, the meadows reached to the horizon. Along the narrow stretches, the willows formed an arch over the water like a cavalry guard saluting a bride and groom. This was a very different trip from the one Marie-Anne made from Lachine. She was a veteran traveller now, but propped beside her in her cradleboard was her precious baby. She would insist that they be very cautious.

After a day's travel the party camped at The Forks, where the Red meets the Assiniboine, the location of present-day Winnipeg. Here were the ruins of an old French establishment – a portion of a chimney sticking up, a cellar overgrown with weeds. This was

Fort Rouge, an advance depot built by La Vérendrye seventy years earlier. It had also been the summer gathering spot of the Ojibwe – hundreds of families met to gossip, play games, get married, plan the winter trapping, and harvest wild rice. In 1783 the first wave of smallpox had hit, and thousands upon thousands died at this spot. For years snakes overran the place; the Indians believed they lived in the graves of their ancestors.

In the spring of 1808 the water was high, which fortunately for the Lagimodières meant the route from the mouth of the Red to the mouth of the Winnipeg River required no portaging and the going was relatively easy. The same could not be said for 450-kilometre-long Lake Winnipeg. It was totally unpredictable.

Voyageurs considered it the "damnedest" body of water in the entire *pays d'en haut*, worse even than Lake Superior. Squalls descended like devils. Only when it was changing direction did the wind let up. The waves didn't swell, they chopped. And because of the steep cliffs and swamps, there was hardly a place to land.

As usual, Alexander Henry is vivid in his description of a storm he, and perhaps the Lagimodières if they were with him, encountered on Lake Winnipeg on August 14, 1808:

The wind sprang up again ahead West, and the swell increased amazingly. Our position was rather unpleasant. The sea dashing with great violence against the rocks, and the extreme darkness of the night, and every appearance of the wind increasing made me anxious to find a convenient place to land. We crept on as near the shore as the surge would admit of, when having shipped a great quantity of water we discovered a small cave with a beach of round white stones . . . Here we unloaded and remained for the night, very happy to find ourselves in so comfortable a berth. The wind continued all night.[4]

Henry's party never stopped battling storms the entire time they were travelling on Lake Winnipeg. On August 19, just as they were reaching Horse Islands and the mouth of the Saskatchewan River, a near-fatal incident took place:

> Wind sprang up fair. We hoisted our sails and scud on very fast. The wind increased. We took in a double reef. Still we had too much sail and were in great danger of perishing. We furled our sail, now almost instantly leaving only about a foot of canvas, which even then required the assistance of two men to support the mast and yard from being carried away. The shore would not admit of our landing, and on passing along I observed a nine-gallon keg laying upon the beach which I supposed at first to be empty but in a short time after, I observed another of the same kind. I now began to suspect they might be part of a cargo that might have perished along this coast in the late severe gales of wind."[5]

One can imagine Marie-Anne clinging to her baby as her canoe was buffeted about like a leaf on a pond.

North West Company voyageurs always followed the quick route, crossing the lake at Grassy Narrows, and then travelling up the west side, where there were ten major traverses across bays. Hudson's Bay Company employees, on the other hand, stuck to the east side, where there were almost no risky traverses and shelter was easier to come by. With an infant on board, the Lagimodière party likely took the safer way, although it meant an extra couple of days of travelling.

They awoke each day at the break of dawn, and were on their way in half an hour. And every afternoon at about two, a squall was sure to froth up, forcing them to shore. They spent hours around the campfire, the men talking about business and their exploits as buffalo hunters, the women about their childhoods and their families. In later years, Marie-Anne spoke of the strong bonds of friendship she formed with the Cree women; by this time she was living Indian-style and had much in common with them. She said she had loved them like sisters.

Finally, after a week and a half, the two canoes arrived at the Hudson's Bay Company's Cumberland House. It was a place of enormous significance. Built in 1774, it marked, as one voyageur rudely put it, the occasion "when the HBC finally got off its arse."

For a century and a half, from the time of Cartier's original bartering session in 1534, the French operating out of Quebec City and Montreal had the fur trade to themselves. But in 1665, two *coureurs de bois*, fed up with rules and regulations imposed by authorities in New France, had defected to the British. Pierre-Esprit Radisson and Médard Chouart Des Groseilliers (later known as Mr. Radishes and Mr. Gooseberries to generations of schoolchildren) convinced a clique of wealthy London investors to sponsor a trading expedition to Hudson and James bays. When the *Nonsuch* returned with her hold full of valuable furs, certain British businessmen, including the king's eccentric cousin, Prince Rupert, realized they had struck gold. On May 2, 1670, King Charles II granted the prince and nineteen fellow "adventurers" a Royal Charter, giving them exclusive trading rights to Hudson Bay and its drainage basin, an incredibly huge area, 7.7 million square kilometres, covering one-third of present-day Canada. which became known as Rupert's Land. The Hudson's Bay Company was born, and within a decade it established three trading posts on the east side of the bay, with York Factory, situated at the mouth of the Hayes River, serving as the hub. Then, for the next seventy years, the company sat like a fat sultan –"sleeping by ye baye," as one HBC servant put it – waiting for the Indians to come to it.

The French Canadians laughed as they aggressively moved into the company's territory and captured its business.

Even though the HBC was in effect the landlord of Rupert's Land, the French never stopped thumbing their nose at the company. York Factory was captured in 1697 and operated as a French post until the 1713 Treaty of Utrecht (which ended the War of the Spanish Succession) gave monopoly trading back to the British. That didn't stop the Canadian fur traders over the next decades from setting up posts along the multitude of waterways lacing Rupert's Land to intercept the natives and their furs on their way to York Factory and the other smaller posts on Hudson Bay. It was simply easier for an Indian trapper to trade his furs in his own territory than endure weeks of travel eastward.

With the conquest of New France by the British in 1759, the HBC expected that their monopoly would finally pay off and profits would soar. And for a few years, Indians did make the long trek to the bay. But in Montreal and Quebec City a group of enterprising Scottish and American entrepreneurs, using the system developed by the French, barged back into business, and once again began intercepting the Indians and their peltries on their way to Hudson Bay. The HBC's returns fell precipitously. As one servant wrote in 1772, "What few furs I have received are mostly damaged and what the Pedlars [the Canadians] inland would not take."[6] The HBC answer was to send men into the interior to gather intelligence and try to convince the Indians to trade at York Factory, but this strategy didn't accomplish much. Finally, the Hudson's Bay Company's governors saw the light and realized that if they didn't set up posts convenient to their customers, the Indians, they would be out of business. They built Cumberland House, thereby laying the foundation for profitable inland trade.

The gutsy Samuel Hearne, the explorer of Canada's far north, was chosen to inaugurate this expansion. Unlike the North West Company, the HBC did not own canoes of its own, nor could it rely on brigades of tough voyageurs. And HBC employees were a puny lot, not at all at home in the bush. As Hearne wrote, his men were "entirely unacquainted with . . . every other duty that is not Emediatly Preform'd at the [York] Factory, none of them ever having ben farther from the Forts than a Wooding or hunting Tent."[7] Of the eleven men assigned to Hearne's expedition, only six reached their destination without mishap. One was abandoned en route by his Indian scouts, who stole all his supplies. Four others were also deserted by their guides, and endured the winter in the wilderness.

The trip, via the Grass, Goose, and Sturgeon Weir rivers, was long and arduous. Twelve weeks into the voyage, the travellers were close to starvation, but fortunately they managed to shoot some swans flying overhead. They finally reached Saskatchewan River country in early August. Hearne then spent three weeks searching for the perfect spot for a trading post.

The place he finally selected was on Pine Island, and at first it seemed ideal. It was located near three bands of Indians who regularly brought moose meat, fish, geese, and furs to trade for European goods. Most importantly, it was at the hub of a network of rivers and streams that provided access to the rich fur country west along the Saskatchewan River and into the north country. The only problem was that the aggressive Montreal "peddlers" once again moved in. "The men at Cumberland House," writes one historian, "were operating under extreme handicaps. Not only were they a handful of men, but they were encircled by rival traders who allowed few Indians to reach the post."[8] In 1789 Peter Fidler described the place as a squalid group of buildings: "Life was routine, monotonous. The occasional Indian came in to trade, but the men spent much of their time fishing, mending nets, hunting, making repairs to the buildings and tending the gardens."[9]

In 1790 the HBC built a new, larger Cumberland House, and at once the North West Company constructed its own post right next door. The place became "the Grand Central Station" of the fur trade.[10] The HBC had left the vast Churchill River–Lake Athabaska region to the North West Company, but it came to dominate the fur trade along the Saskatchewan River. Cumberland House became its interior administrative centre; the North West Company's post, a supply depot. Alexander Henry the Younger, who was at Cumberland House at about the same time as the Lagimodières, described the North West operation in his journal entry of August 25, 1808:

> This post is not kept up by us [North West Company] so much for the propose of trade as for the convenience of a depôt for provision to supply our northern Brigades. In the Spring of the Year we bring down the Saskatchewan to this place from three to five hundred Bags of Pemmican and upwards of 200 Kegs of Grease. . . . The H.B. Co. have a more permanent Establishment here than us and be said to have the whole of the Trade in their own hands, which I believe is the sole instance of the kind in the NW.

As an independent freeman, Jean-Baptiste Lagimodière could have done business with either the North West Company or the Hudson's Bay Company. Sometime during this 1808 journey, he decided to throw his lot in with the English. There were several reasons for this; perhaps all of them informed his decision. There was a conservative streak in Jean-Baptiste's makeup – he was anything but the revolutionary his grandson Louis Riel would become – and the HBC, in his mind, represented authority, the establishment, the monarchy. And he was likely fed up with Alexander Henry the Younger, who went out of his way to disparage the freemen; such rudeness undoubtedly put Jean-Baptiste off the Canadians. Or he might simply have been smart enough to realize that, in the end, the London company, with its shorter supply routes and its access to vast capital resources, would eventually obliterate the Montreal group – which is exactly what happened in the amalgamation of 1821. Whatever the case, Jean-Baptiste's loyalty to the Brits became unshakeable and would have important consequences for his family in the future.

Jean-Baptiste and his partners wanted to stock up at Cumberland House – it was the first opportunity since Fort Edmonton – which gave Marie-Anne and the other women a chance to rest for a few days. They would have encountered many Cree milling about; during the ferocious smallpox epidemic of 1781–82, the post had become a refuge for the ill, the elderly and the incapacitated and it had remained as such. It was also a rendezvous point: the Woods Cree and Ojibwe left their families here when they were away trapping beaver, collecting bark for canoes, or travelling to York Factory.[11]

By this time Reine was seven months old, with fat, pink cheeks, a mass of blonde curls, and the blue eyes of her mother. According to biographer Georges Dugast, everyone at Cumberland House was bowled over by mother and daughter. He claims that Bellegarde had gone ahead of the rest and lied to the natives gathered at Cumberland House, claiming "the French woman was good but that she was very learned in medicines and that if any one offended her she had the power to cause their death by merely looking at them." Naturally, when the Lagimodières arrived, everyone "tried to shew themselves at the best before her. 'Have pity on us,' they said, 'we only wish to look at you,' and they took an unspeakable pleasure in gazing at her."[12] Father Dugast was racist and wrong-headed about native people, and the story is probably apocryphal. Still, it gives an inkling of the stir that Marie-Anne and Reine caused.

By the end of August, the Lagimodière party was ready to travel again, with the addition of an extra hand on board. History records the man only as Bouvier, but he was a freeman like the others, probably born of a French-Canadian father and Indian mother. Another person to help paddle and carry cargo was welcome.

Pine Island, where Cumberland House was situated, is shaped like a hand, the spaces between each splayed finger a canal cutting through the heavy green foliage. In 1808 it hardly ever stopped raining, so these channels were overflowing with brown, syrupy water. The muskrat reeds and goose grass were almost completely submerged. The trees had broken from their moorings, leaving the banks muddy and ragged. On this broad Saskatchewan River – *kisisk ciwani* is Cree for "swiftly flowing water" – the Lagimodières' team had to paddle upstream for over nearly one thousand kilometres to reach their goal.

John Arnot Fleming was a surveyor who travelled the river fifty years after the Lagimodières. He gives an idea of what they were up against:

The Saskatchewan or "the river that runs swift" is truly well named, for even upon the smoothest and deepest part of the river, long lines of bubbles and foam, ever speeding swiftly but noiselessly by, serve to indicate the velocity with which this mighty artery courses unceasingly onward, swelling as it goes, with the gathering of its many wide-spread tributaries to mingle its restless and muddy waters in the Arctic seas.[13]

The first day there was a fine breeze and sails were hoisted on both canoes. They skimmed past ash, poplars, pine, and tamarack. Now and then a sandy beach was spotted, poking through the dense forest. One canoe was slightly damaged, and to gum the gash the party stopped at a place called Barren Hill. At the top was a lovely plateau of flowers and grasses. To the north lay a great green forest splashed with yellow and red, but to the south stretched a wretched panorama. A forest fire had devastated the area and mangled black trees lay across one another like Christian martyrs burned at the stake. Marie-Anne must have come to realize that her new home was a place of frightening extremes.

At this point the men put aside their paddles – the current was too strong for them. The bottom of the shallow Saskatchewan consists of sand and gravel; poles easily found a foothold, and so were used for the remainder of the voyage.

The most difficult part occurred where the riverbed dropped steeply. The flow here was so strong it had terrorized generations of voyageurs. Paddling was no longer possible; the canoes had to be pulled by ropes, "taking the line" as the voyageurs called it. Two men remained in the canoe to keep it steady; from the shore, two others pulled it along inch by inch. If the trail along the river's edge was clear-cut, the women walked, each taking turns carrying Reine on their backs; often they sank to their knees in the muddy bog. If the pathway was too overgrown or too dangerous, they rode in the canoe, adding more weight for the groaning men to pull. Alexander Henry described an incident along the way that almost resulted in tragedy:

> One of our [men] in the course of the day had a narrow escape of
> being drowned while in the act of disengaging the line from one

of those embarras [obstacles] which so frequently occur along those steep banks; the Line getting clear unexpectedly gave him a sudden jerk that tossed him into the River head long, and [he] was caught by a freeman in one of the Canoes, after having been carried down the stream some distance and swallowed a great quantity of water.[14]

It's tempting to think that the freeman who saved the Nor'Wester's life might have been Jean-Baptiste Lagimodière.

Once the open meadow was reached, it was relatively smooth going. Mile after mile, the tan-coloured river wound its way though the Great Plains, the only relief from the flat landscape the weeds and flowers which grew on the banks, and the odd sighting of a buffalo herd or the tracks of a moose or grizzly bear. Now and then a flotilla of voyageurs or a band of Indians passed by. Greetings were loudly exchanged.

As September nudged out August, the leaves began to turn. The majestic yellows, oranges, russets, and dark browns not only paraded along the shore but were reflected brilliantly in the water. Chokecherries were everywhere. It seemed, in many ways, like Valhalla. But one night in mid-September, a horror descended that haunted Marie-Anne for the rest of her life.

A perfect camping place was found located in a cove with willow trees to which the canoes were tied, a sandy beach, loose rocks for a fireplace, and kindling for a fire. The women made a delicious rabbit stew with bannock; the men allowed themselves an extra grog of rum. Everyone was relaxed, happy, hopeful.

Bouvier left to relieve himself in the bush. The others continued to chat until suddenly a terrifying scream rang out. All jumped up and ran into the bush. They found Bouvier pinned against a tree. Standing upright on her hind legs was a huge grizzly, batting the man's head back and forth like a boxer punching a bag.[*] Two cubs were standing nearby. Jean-Baptiste immediately ran for his gun, but before he returned, the bear took Bouvier's two cheeks in her paws and ate his face. The bones, assaulted by the animal's razor-sharp teeth, splintered. Jean-Baptiste was frightened that he might wound or even kill Bouvier if he attempted a shot, so he tried to ram the animal with the butt end of his rifle. This did nothing but enrage her, and she gnawed with even more gusto on Bouvier's scalp. Bouvier shouted out, "Shoot, shoot. I'd rather be shot than eaten alive." Jean-Baptiste got as close to the grizzly as he could, took aim, and hit her in the chest. She crumpled to the ground. Then he killed her cubs.[15]

The men carried the unconscious Bouvier back to the campsite and wrapped him in blankets. Marie-Anne placed the bark of red willow on the mauled flesh and then applied a tourniquet made from her handkerchief to staunch the flow of blood. One of the other wives added water to a concoction of herbs and grasses she carried with her, beat it to a pulp, then plastered it on the wounds.

---

* Probably the Lagimodière group was not travelling with Alexander Henry at this point since they would not have wanted to wait around as he stocked up on buffalo meat and other provisions for his fort. However, his journal does verify the existence of grizzlies in the neighbourhood. On September 7, 1808, he wrote, "We perceived the vestiges of a Grizzly bear where he had devoured a Calf Buffalo in the course of the day. We fresh primed out Guns and continued on through a long thicket of Willows, every moment in fear of meeting this voracious animal. On coming to an open spot we perceived him ahead of us running away at full speed along the river among the Hummocks of wood. We chased him and fired, but he got into a thicket, and now being nearly dark we did not think it prudent to molest him any more for the present."

These were ghastly. One eye had been ripped out of its socket; the flesh around it, either eaten or torn away, revealed crushed bones; and the nose had disappeared altogether, leaving only two bloody holes. Marie-Anne had with her a liniment that supposedly eased pain. She smeared it on the shattered face, but realized that the instant Bouvier came to it would be of little help. His terrible groans, mounting to a roar of anguish, were torture to listen to.

They laid the injured man on a stretcher made of birch branches, over which blankets had been tied and this device was placed in the canoe. Fortunately, a Hudson's Bay Company flotilla came by, headed in the same direction, and one of the men volunteered to take Bouvier's place paddling the canoe. Marie-Anne always considered the two-week voyage to Edmonton House to be one of the worse experiences of her life. Bouvier needed twenty-four-hour attention. The drink of water he cried out for in the night might make the difference between life and death. A strange noise emanated constantly from his swollen lips, a high-pitched cry that at times sounded bizarrely like a hyena's laugh. It kept them all awake night and day. Reine was frightened and never stopped whimpering.

Everyone was overwhelmed with relief when they finally arrived at the fort and Bouvier was carted off to the infirmary. Although he eventually recovered, he was left blind, his face horribly disfigured. He would spend the rest of his life relying on the compassion of others.[*]

---

[*] Georges Dugast writes that Bouvier lived at Edmonton House for many years, but once the first missionaries reached Red River in 1818, he pleaded to be sent to St. Boniface. He lived at the rectory there and whittled crosses and crucifixes, which he sold to the public.

CHAPTER EIGHT

—

ONCE THEY PASSED EAGLE HILLS, the group split up. The three Cree women set off to join their families at a camp in the Strong Woods, 120 kilometres east of the trading post – they could hardly wait to get there as they had missed their children terribly. Their husbands headed for the foothills of the Rockies to trap the thickest, glossiest furs found on continent. Hopefully, family fortunes were to be made. Jean-Baptiste would follow once Marie-Anne and Reine were settled. They would spend the winter at the Hudson's Bay Company's Edmonton House.

Jean-Baptiste felt comfortable with this arrangement because he much admired the chief factor in whose care he was leaving his wife and daughter. Before he returned to Lower Canada, he had spent a winter at the fort and had gotten to know James Bird.

Thirty-four years old in 1808, Bird was a Londoner who had signed on with the Hudson's Bay Company at the age of fifteen and served his four-year apprenticeship at York Factory. He was recognized for his quick thinking, his ability to take charge, and his no-nonsense attitude. (That he was also hidebound, vindictive, jealous, and egotistical hindered his career only in later years.) He served as chief at a number of HBC establishments, and in 1803 he was placed in charge of all inland posts in the Saskatchewan country, from Cumberland House to the Rocky Mountains. His hospitality toward Marie-Anne indicated how much he admired Jean-Baptiste's abilities as a buffalo hunter and fur trapper, and how much he wanted to retain his services. Unlike Alexander Henry the Younger, Bird appreciated the freemen he dealt with. "They bring in more furs than all the native tribes combined, excepting the Iroquois," he wrote to his superiors.[1]

Without waiting for official approval, he offered Jean-Baptiste and his associates hard cash for at least a portion of their pelts – eleven Canadian pounds per pound weight of heavily furred winter beaver, the same amount per five and a half pounds (2.5 kilos) of the thinner summer beaver. This was a breakthrough concession. European goods – tobacco, knives, kettles, cloth – had traditionally been the only currency the HBC had dealt in and was still the only exchange available to Indian trappers. In October 1808, Bird had told a delegation of freemen, including Jean-Baptiste, that he was taking a real chance. Until he got permission from the London Committee, he was paying out of his own pocket.[2]

Edmonton House was one of the many trading posts strewn along the North Saskatchewan River like pearls on a necklace. Early on, the French built forts at the traditional Indian summer rendezvous spots, and the Nor'Westers were smart enough to copy them. By 1780 over three hundred Canadian fur traders were doing business along the Saskatchewan River.[3] The establishments there were perfectly situated: from the north, Woodland Indians, mostly Cree and Assiniboine, came to trade their precious beaver furs and other pelts; from the south the Indians on horseback brought supplies, pemmican and dried buffalo meat, as well as buffalo hides and wolf skins. Quickly, however, the beaver and other fur-bearing animals disappeared in areas immediately around the posts; as one author wrote, the motto was "Trap an area clean – if you don't, your competitor will – and then move on."[4] By the early 1800s fur traders had pressed northward to the subarctic forests, where the best furs were to be found. The *forts des prairies* became primarily supply depots; as William McGillivray explained, they existed, "to procure provisions to enable them to carry on trade to the northern parts of the country."[5] And what a vast territory it was, stretching westward from the junction of the North and South Saskatchewan rivers to the Rockies, and from the Athabasca River south to the upper reaches of the Missouri.

At the end of summer in 1795 the North West Company had constructed the first post at the junction of the Saskatchewan and Sturgeon rivers, called Fort Augustus (named in honour of the future King George IV). Beaver and otter were said to be so abundant there "that the Women and Children kill them with sticks and hatchets."[6] Word of this cornucopia travelled, and in November of that year the Hudson's Bay Company set up shop right next door at what they called Edmonton House. From that point, on both places would serve as the administrative centres for their respective companies.

Seven years after the posts were built, the forests around them had been stripped bare; the huge amount of firewood – eight hundred cords per year – had to be hauled longer and longer distances.[7] Both establishments decided to move thirty-two kilometres further upriver. But there was more to this decision than lack of kindling. Only a short time after they were vacated, both forts were burned to the ground by Siksika (Blackfoot). As one writer put it, "This was neither an accident nor an act of God –

rather it appears to have been in response to an insult, a deal gone bad [a defective gun, perhaps], or the increasingly poisonous atmosphere between the traders and the Indians."[8] Indeed, antagonism and the contempt felt by the First Nations people for Europeans and Euro-Canadians would colour the Lagimodières' entire stay in the North West.

Fort Augustus II and Edmonton House II were erected on the north bank of the Saskatchewan, on the flats of a jutting bluff where the city of Edmonton sits today. The river was narrow at that point and the current very strong. Although the HBC traders and the Nor'Westers were bitter rivals, the two trading posts were built side by side with only an interior wall separating them. There were good reasons for this – small independent traders from Lower Canada would be shut out and, more important, the palisades served as protection against Indian attack. A common stockade of massive vertical logs, 4.5 metres high, surrounded both compounds. Competition for Indian clients bearing furs was fierce, and yet there was much coming and going between the populations of each fort.

Alexander Henry best described what life was like at a fur trading post in the early nineteenth century. On September 13, 1808, at about the same time as the Lagimodières had reached their destination, Henry arrived at his North West Company post, 320 kilometres to the east of Edmonton House: "At sunset we sighted Fort Vermillion, in a long, flat bottom of meadow, directly opposite the entrance of the Vermillion river, which falls in on the S.[askatchewan]. A large camp of Slaves [Plains Indians] began to whoop and halloo as we came down the hills, and appeared rejoiced to see us."[9] A year later he wrote of the people: "We are much crowded: there being present [at a dance] 72 Men, 37 Women and 65 Children."[10]

By the early 1800s, the North West Company was supporting between 1,200 and 1,500 women and children, the families of their employees. By 1808 the company was fed up with this encumbrance. As historian Sylvia Van Kirk writes, "Given the enormous quantities of food consumed by traders and their families, the company could not afford to add this heavy burden when faced with the expense of having to fight its competitors."[11]

The Hudson's Bay Company had never sanctioned marriage between their "servants" and native women. It didn't much matter; nobody paid attention to the rules. While eventually it was frowned upon for the ordinary stiff to dwell within the post with his native family, the HBC officers continued to take live-in wives, whose chief objective was, according to one report, to "dispense the property of the Company on the most undeserving of objects for the most selfish reasons." James Bird himself had married "in the custom of the country" several times; sometimes he lived with more than one spouse at a time. He produced many children – so many the exact number remains unknown. Bird stayed with the last of his Indian wives (which certainly wasn't the case in many country marriages) and eventually moved his family to Red River when he retired.

The story of one of the apprentice clerks at Edmonton House was typical of a practice that would become more and more prevalent. The clerk's British-born father worked for the Hudson's Bay Company for twenty-one years, rising in the ranks to senior clerk. He met Bridgette Star Keeper, an Assiniboine from the Milk River region and married her *à la façon du pays*. They had three children and seemed to be a happy family; the mother was a jolly woman devoted to her husband. Yet the moment he retired, he left his family with hardly a word. He returned to Plymouth and married an Englishwoman in a church ceremony. His country family never heard from him again.[12] When Marie-Anne heard this story, she probably couldn't help thinking of Jean-Baptiste's two other children now abandoned by *their* father.

While there might not have been as many people living at Edmonton House as there were at Fort Vermilion, the place was still jam-packed. In fact, life at any fur trade post was primitive, constricted, and uncomfortable. At Fort Vermilion, four or five families – sometimes as many as twenty people – as well as a number of bachelors shared the same large dormitory.[13] Fortunately, at Edmonton House, living quarters were partitioned off. Marie-Anne and Reine had at least some small amount of privacy. And, of course, they didn't have to winter in a wigwam on the open plain. She and Reine would be fed and they needn't worry about freezing to death in the middle of the night.

Their accommodation was typical of that offered an HBC working-class family. It consisted of one fairly large room with a crude wooden table in the middle on which was stored an assortment of iron kettles and pots, wooden bowls, ladles, plates, and spoons. Two wooden benches on either side provided seating. As well, there were two bunk beds with thin mattresses of straw and Hudson's Bay blankets thrown over top, a chest decorated with carved bouquets of flowers, and two armchairs made from willow branches. There was a wooden cradle for Reine attached to a frame that allowed it to swing back and forth. There was actually a window and, although it was covered with rawhide, it allowed creamy yellow light to penetrate the room. A good-sized stone fireplace dominated one wall. And there may even have been a few luxuries: a thick buffalo robe as a blanket for Marie-Anne, several rabbit skins sewn together as a comforter for Reine, bearskins to make the willow chairs comfier, and even a small wooden desk with a tree stump as a seat.[14]

Marie-Anne was given the choice of either eating with the workers and their families or dining in her own quarters. While Jean-Baptiste was still at Edmonton House, she likely preferred to cook for him, but once he left, she would have joined the others.

The mess was a large room with row upon row of long wooden tables and straight-backed chairs. Two immense fieldstone fireplaces were located at each end of the room. These provided warmth only; the back room was a well-equipped kitchen with a huge fire to cook the food and with all the herbs and spices necessary to create tasty dishes. An oven was located outside, where bread was baked. There was plenty of oatmeal porridge for breakfast, and fresh and dried vegetables from Mr Bird's well-tended garden were served – turnips galore, carrots, cabbages, onions, cucumber, spinach, cauliflower, radishes, beets, and potatoes. There were fresh and salt geese, salt pork, ducks, partridges, plovers, whatever was shot that day, as well as deer, moose, rabbit, beaver and, of course, buffalo – pemmican, beat meat (buffalo that had been pounded with tallow to make it tender, or at least edible) and, in season, fresh roasts. Fish was served, but the HBC employees, almost all Brits, didn't like it much.

Forty people ate three meals a day there. It was bedlam, with kids of all ages running around and screaming, women trying to serve the food, and men calling out wisecracks and jokes.

Marie-Anne may have found the etiquette of the place stifling. Bird had a reputation for being pretentious, demanding that those under his command follow the rules – clerks weren't supposed to socialize with labourers, white men were not supposed to have anything to do with native women who weren't their wives. Everyone had to dress and act as though they were living in London. Everything from the plates on the table to people's shoes signalled their station in life.

Although they were all Aboriginals, the women who lived in the compound considered themselves a cut above because they were married, country-style, to white men. They prided themselves on dressing "English." Marie-Anne would have found it necessary to once again don ankle-length skirts, petticoats, aprons, bonnets, and leather shoes. She may even have used the pressing iron she brought from Maskinongé, for the first time since her arrival in the west. Her hair was no longer braided in a pigtail but well brushed and pinned up into a bun. Her manners and speech took on a distinctly ladylike cast.

As the days darkened and the snow never ceased falling – Bird would write in his journal about its "extraordinary depth" – the cold seeped into every corner of the fort. The women busied themselves stretching buffalo hides to make pemmican bags and pack cords. Marie-Anne may have helped in this chore, although the Lagimodières hadn't had much time to collect the remnants of bison on their journey westward. She might have worked in the kitchen, but more probably all there was for her to do was stack wood on the fire, sweep their room, and keep an eye on her energetic one-year-old.

There wasn't much contact between the fort's residents and Indian customers. The actual trading of furs was carried out in a separate building; natives were not welcomed near the living quarters. Still, every now and then Marie-Anne would have encountered the Blackfoot going about their business at the fort. They probably stared at her pale skin, and blue eyes. Was she a wicked shaman or a medicine woman? She in turn must have found them fascinating.

The men were unusually tall and well built, with large but symmetrical features and heavy eyebrows. The young wore their hair loose and flowing except for one lock, which was cut square and suspended from the forehead between the eyes to the top of the nose.

The elders twisted their plaits into gigantic knobs at the crown of their heads. The women sported the usual two thick and glossy pigtails. Both men and women smeared their bodies and clothes with a red compound of berry juice and minerals and painted their faces with a glossy grey substance. These people were very different from Marie-Anne's close friends, the Cree wives of Jean-Baptiste's partners.

Marie-Anne probably found them frightening looking and they did have a reputation for fierceness. The old men liked to brag that they had killed at least twenty people with their bare hands.[15] They, like the Cree, habitually stole horses, as many as three hundred from enemies' camps in one year.

The folk at Edmonton House obsessed over the politics and intrigues of the various Indian tribes, if only because war and turmoil were in the air, and this could prove dangerous to anyone living in the North West. Since the arrival of fur traders, there had been a symbiosis among First Nations that had proved beneficial to everyone. But in the last few years this had spun out of control like a top gone mad. Ferocious wars were the result.

In 1809 the northwest plains were dominated by the Blackfoot (also known as Niitsitapi) Alliance, a loose coalition consisting of three main tribes: the Blackfoot (Siksika), the Blood (Kainai) and the Peigan (Piikani, or Muddy River). The three groups shared a common language, customs and traditions – the sun dance, for example – and intermarried. This is not to imply that they weren't separate peoples with separate leaders and decision-making bodies. As one scholar writes, "While war probably never occurred between these kindred nations and was probably barred by mutual consent, there cannot be said to have been any formal alliance."[16]

The Blackfoot speak an Algonkian language, as do the Cree, Ojibwe and Mi'kmaq but the northwest version is quite different from the central and eastern versions. This suggests to scholars that the Blackfoot must have been separated from other Algonkian speakers for many centuries, and therefore have "ancient roots" on the northwest plains.[17] And archaeologists have shown that there were hunting communities in the territory since shortly after the end of the last ice age.[18] For centuries, therefore, the Blackfoot enjoyed a relatively secure existence, hunting the vast herds of bison, first with the *atlatl* (a device for throwing a spear or dart) and subsequently with bow and arrow. Then "the horse and gun revolution" burst upon the scene, profoundly altering the culture.

At the end of the sixteenth century, Spanish conquerors introduced horses in Mexico, and over the next 150 years this amazing means of transportation made its way northward. By the early 1700s the Shoshoni, located south on the Great Plains, had acquired the horse. They immediately put this advantage to devastating effect by waging war on their northern enemies and, in the process, usurping their territory. Young Man, a Peigan chief, described his people's first encounter with horse-mounted attackers:

> The Snake Indians [Shoshonis] and their allies had Misstutim (Big Dogs, that is Horses) on which they rode, swift as the Deer on which they dashed at the Peeagans, and with their stone Pukamoggan knocked them on the head, and they had thus lost several of their best men. This news we did not well comprehend and it alarmed us, for we had no idea of Horses and could not make out what they were.[19]

The Blackfoot bands and their allies were forced to flee from the South Saskatchewan River northward to the Battle River, which allowed the Shoshonis to prevail on the plains.

But the tide turned very quickly for the Shoshonis. They couldn't prevent the Blackfoot coalition from obtaining horses; soon the Blackfoot, Blood, and Peigan developed into expert equestrians, tending and breeding large herds. As well, the Blackfoot had turned for help to those who possessed a white man's invention even more deadly in warfare than horses – guns.

The allies who had access to the white man's weapons were the Cree and Assiniboine, who dwelt in the woodlands north of the Great Plains. They had been among the first to travel to the HBC's posts on Hudson Bay – Cree became the language of the fur trade – carrying away in their birchbark canoes iron pots, iron knives, ammunition, and guns to trade with the buffalo-hunting tribes further west and north. Historian Arthur J. Ray states that "using the arms they obtained at the Bay, the Cree quickly assumed the role of middlemen in the evolving trade network and expanded their trading areas with force."[20]

Cree ancestors had moved into the valley of the North Saskatchewan and South Saskatchewan rivers below The Forks long before the white traders arrived, at least by the fifteenth century, and probably much earlier than that, over the years expanding westward into the parkland and forest north of the Great Plains. But, according to Theodore Binnema, "there is no reason to question the long-held belief (based on documentary evidence and [native] oral traditions) that Cree bands became permanent residents only during the late pedestrian or early equestrian era."[21] Once, that is, they found out how lucrative it was to deal with the Blackfoot. And, of course, the Cree and Assiniboine, now becoming more plains than woods people, soon wanted horses, which they could get from the Blackfoot.

It was a mutually beneficial relationship that went on for decades, until fur traders began establishing posts along the

Saskatchewan. At that point the Blackfoot began to deal directly with the white man, and the Cree role of middleman eroded. The various alliances crumbled as one acrimonious skirmish followed another, usually to do with stealing horses, for which the Blackfoot and Cree were notorious. In January 1807, seven months before the Lagimodières arrived at Edmonton House, James Bird wrote a note to J. P. Pruden, the chief factor at Acton House, illustrating how dicey the situation was:

> Point out to them [the Blackfoot bands] as forcibly as possible the necessity there is of their being on a friendly footing with the Southward [Cree] Indians for to have a safe & easy Intercourse with us and above all that if they value our Friendship & assistance it will always be necessary for them whatever Quarrels may arise among the Indians, to consider us a party unconcerned, Friends to all, sorry for their dissentions and at all time willing to do every-thing in our power to compose them.[22]

Fur traders were desperate to maintain peace among the various Indian tribes for good reasons: a war would not only interfere with the fur trade but also disrupt the post's supply of food and, in minus-thirty-five-degree weather with snowdrifts two metres high, this was no little thing. James Bird's journal during the first winter Marie-Anne spent at Edmonton House indicates how much the white population depended on the Indians to ward off hunger:

> *January 20th*: Sent two men with Horses and Sledges with the Sussees [Sarcee] . . . to try if a little meat can be got from their [buffalo] Pound, as we have no prospect of getting even a small stash from any other quarter, owing in some measure to the extraor-dinary depth of snow.

February 7th: Three Blood Indians young Men arrived, sent by the Sussee to inform us that they have the meat of 20 cows on a scaffold for us.

February 16th: Sent fifteen Men with Horses & Dogs to the Sussees Tents for meat, our Hunters being unable to furnish us with half the Quantity requisite.

The Indians who were most helpful in supplying Edmonton House were the Sarcee (James Bird calls them Sussee, others call them Sussez, Sussekoon, and Sussi). He wrote of them, "This tribe of Indians are the best disposed, the Cree only excepted, towards the white people of any belonging to this settlement."[23] They were a strange, solitary tribe, and also the most unconventional, as their teepees revealed. These were decorated with beautifully executed triangles, circles, and stripes, finely drawn wolves and otters, and huge buffalo painted in black and red, almost life-size.

The Sarcee were a people with a most peculiar history. Athapaskan-speaking Dene, they had, in a remarkably short period of time, transformed themselves from trappers of beaver in the northern woodlands to hunters of buffalo on the plains.

Anthropologists believe that all of the First Nations belonging to the Athapaskan linguistic group (including the Navajo in Arizona) originated from a region around the Bay of Alaska. About eight hundred years ago, a tremendous volcano in the Saint Elias Mountains erupted, forcing the Indian nations to flee the area. One band, the Beaver, eventually settled in the Lesser Slave Lake region. Sometime around 1730, and for reasons unknown, the Sarcee split off from this group and headed for the plains. They were befriended by the Blackfoot nations, so much so that many fur traders thought they were part of the alliance. As well, for decades they consorted with the Woodland Cree as trading partners, but by the 1880s there had been a serious falling-out between the two. Horse theft was the probable cause.

The Sarcee developed a reputation as fierce warriors. The explorer David Thompson called them "brave and manly";[24] an English traveller described them as "a small but very brave and mischievous band."[25] They would play a distressing role in Marie-Anne's future.

There was one other band of Plains Indians who often visited the *forts des prairies* – the Gros Ventre (also called Atsina). Although of Algonkian stock, their language was very different from that of the Blackfoot, to whom they were closely allied. The nation likely originated in the sixteenth century in the interlake region of Manitoba. Some time around 1550, it split in two: one group, called the Arapaho, migrated southwest and affiliated with the Cheyenne; the other moved to the forks of the Upper and Lower Saskatchewan rivers. There's a particularly strong current there so the Cree named them the Waterfall People. James Bird described them as "Falls Indians"; other Europeans called them "Rapids Indians." But the name they were best known by was Gros Ventre – Big Bellies.

Despite the help of the Gros Ventre and other First Nations, as spring approached in 1809, a serious food shortage plagued Edmonton House. Bird sounded the alarm in his journal. On March 12, he wrote: "it will be impossible for us to procure a sufficiency of fresh meat, and there is no prospect of our being able to procure any considerable quantity of dry Provisions, the great depth of snow having prevented the Slave [Plains] Indians from pounding or running any great number of Bulls."[26] Six days later he added: "Nine Men arrived with the last of the Bull Meat killed by our Hunters; should they meet with no more success, I must be under the Necessity of sending the greater part of our Men to

Paint Creek to live till our Embarkation."[27] This meant they would have to fend for themselves for the duration. Finally, on March 22, sixteen bison bulls were hunted down and butchered. Bird continued: "Bad as the meat of these animals is & as far as it must be fetched, under the present circumstances we are happy to be able to get it."[28] Everyone, including Marie-Anne, must have breathed a sigh of relief.

On March 25 the chief factor wrote that two freemen had arrived at the fort. While he doesn't name them, undoubtedly one was Jean-Baptiste Lagimodière. Of all the buffalo hunters, he had the closest links to Bird and Edmonton House.

He must have been delighted with Reine. She hadn't been walking when he left and now here she was trying to scramble up his leg. And he had good news for Marie-Anne. The trapping had gone exceptionally well; they would be able to pay off their debt to the Hudson's Bay Company and have money left over.

Marie-Anne didn't have much chance to fatten up her now-skinny husband. In four days he left for the spring beaver hunt at Fighting River (Battle River), which marked the boundary between the Cree and Blackfoot. Before he left, she told him her important news – she was expecting their second child.

On April 13, the ice broke on the Saskatchewan River. Swans were heard honking their eerie cry overhead, and the snow began its long melt. More and more First Nations people arrived to trade their winter haul of furs. On April 21 a huge band of Muddy River Indians (Peigan) wound their way to their campsite near the trading posts. First, though, they had to cross the Saskatchewan River, the young men, without a stitch of clothing on, swimming their horses through the strong current.

Marie-Anne must have been impressed at the panorama – over two hundred white teepees, strikingly painted with otters, butterflies or moths, stars of the Big Dipper, circles, reindeers, all representing specific Spirit Beings. The women wore elaborate tooth and cowrie shell jewellery. The chiefs, fifty in all, were decked out splendidly in their buckskin suits, intricately decorated with porcupine quills, and their ceremonial eagle feather headdresses, also beautifully quilled, all as a show of respect to the chief factor. But Bird had bad news for them. What the Indians wanted to trade for the skins of "700 wolves, five Bears, 50 Beavers, besides Red Foxes & provisions" were tobacco and ammunition, but both Edmonton House and Fort Augustus had run out of the items. The only thing on offer was liquor, and the Indians had no choice but to accept this. The fort population was expecting a drunken brawl, but James Bird condescendingly wrote that, "they still behaved extremely well."[29]

Jean-Baptiste finally arrived home and Marie-Anne must have been overjoyed to see him. For one thing Edmonton House had degenerated into cramped, foul-smelling quarters. She could hardly wait to camp out on the open plains, but if she was to join her husband, Chalifoux, Bellegarde, Paquin, and their wives for the buffalo hunt, she had to be mobile.

That spring, Marie-Anne turned herself into an expert equestrian. Her first mount was a slow, fat mare. At first they plodded along the prairie trails, Jean-Baptiste walking beside her holding the reins. Then as Marie-Anne felt comfortable and got the knack of squeezing with her knees and gently kicking with her heels, she and the horse trotted alone. Soon she was galloping across the plains. Jean-Baptiste purchased a four-year-old, an experienced buffalo hunter. He was a beautiful animal, greyish with stark white mane and muzzle, and forelegs that were black as tar. Marie-Anne called him Argent (Silver). Like all the native women, she was outfitted with an Indian-style saddle. The frame was made of cottonwood covered with rawhide and stuffed with buffalo hair.

Two horns, a pommel protruding in the front and the cantle at the back, both made of wood, were attached to the sideboard.

In early June the Lagimodières set out to meet their three partners and their wives at South Branch House, on the South Saskatchewan River. Strapped to Marie-Anne's saddle on one side of Argent was a cradleboard carrying Reine, and on the other side a bag of supplies, for balance. Jean-Baptiste rode his own horse and held the reins of another that pulled a cart full of their goods. They didn't worry about a successful hunt. The topography, vegetation, climate on the northwestern plains all combined to support vast herds of buffalo. And it wasn't just bison that thrived in the area. Elk, deer, antelope, bighorn sheep, grizzly and black bears were abundant, as well as the predators – large packs of wolves, crows, ravens, coyotes, and foxes.

New grasses begin to shoot up on the prairies as early as late March. This nutritional food combined with the swarms of biting insects lured the bison onto the open plains. Most of the calves were born between early March and late June, and yet this wasn't the best hunting time. While the buffalo population increased at this point, the herds were widespread and highly mobile, since water was readily available and grass rather thin.[30] Not until the rut in early to midsummer when the mature bulls mingled with the cow population did the herds swell and hunting was most fruitful.[31] Alexander Henry the Younger gives a sense of how these huge beasts dominated the environment at that time:

> The ravages of the Buffalos at this place is certainly astonishing. . . .
> The willows are intirely trampled and torn to atoms, even the bark
> of the smaller trees are in many places totally rub'd off by the Buffalo
> rubbing or scratching themselves against them. The Grass upon the
> first bank of the river is entirely worn away. The numerous paths

(some of which are a foot deep in the hard turf) which comes out of the Plains to the bank of the River, and the vast quantity of dung which lays in every direction, gives this place the appearance of a civilized Country where Cattle have been kept for many years.[32]

Marie-Anne always remembered that summer of 1809 as one of the most pleasant of her life. The weather remained hot and sunny for much of the time. Sunsets of unbelievable colours spread out so magnificently they hurt the eyes. Their small entourage moved often, following the woolly bison. They halted sometimes for a night, sometimes for a week. A spot was chosen beside a river or in a clearing near a clump of trees where a camp of four tents was set up around a stone-edged fireplace, with a variety of pole structures used for curing hides and drying meat. The men went off each day hunting buffalo, skinning and butchering them on the spot. Once the flesh and hides were brought back to camp, the women took over, producing the pemmican to sell to the fur traders at the forts. By this time Marie-Anne would have been skilled at this job, slicing the buffalo meat into very thin strips, then hanging them up to dry. Once the meat was completely free of even a drop of moisture, it was beaten with hammers until it was flaky, almost powder-like. Meanwhile, buffalo bones were placed in a huge pot and boiled until the marrow fat could be skimmed off the top. Berries were dried in the sun and these, along with the fat and some grease, were added to the flaky meat. Then the mixture was packed into leather bags called *parflèches*.

One morning after they had packed up camp and prepared to move on, Marie-Anne mounted Argent. Young Reine, nestled in her cradleboard, dangled along the horse's side. Suddenly, the pounding of buffalo hooves was heard. There was an explosion of dust on the horizon as thousands upon thousands of the shaggy beasts stampeded towards them. Marie-Anne's horse stopped dead in his tracks, but only for an instant. Then he bolted, galloping as fast as he could toward the river where the herd was crossing. Marie-Anne could do nothing to stop him. In his wild flight, Argent's movements grew increasingly erratic. Criss-crossing the plain, he pounded the earth so hard that stones and mud were propelled upward. Marie-Anne shielded Reine with her one hand while, with the other, she clutched the reins. Above all, she knew she mustn't panic, mustn't let go. Then she heard the thud of a horse's hooves behind her. Jean-Baptiste's horse did a kind of dance, cutting and wheeling across Argent's path. Finally the runaway came to a halt and Jean-Baptiste grabbed its reins.

An hour later, Marie-Anne knelt in the silver grasses and, with the help of her Indian companions, gave birth to a baby boy. Although he was a month premature, and therefore rather small and sickly, he was alive. The baby was baptized Jean-Baptiste Junior, but nobody ever called him that. He was known as LaPrairie, a nickname so appropriate that it stuck for his entire life.

CHAPTER NINE

—

THE JOURNEY NORTHWARD to Fort Edmonton was painfully slow. The carts and horses were loaded down with the season's catch: *parflèches* of pemmican, bladders of grease, tanned buffalo hides, smoked tongues, dried fruits, as well as all their personal effects. LaPrairie needed feeding several times a day, and, while Marie-Anne didn't need to dismount to nurse, she could hardly travel at a rapid speed. Everyone was as nervous as hunted deer. There were three Cree women in the group. A chance encounter with warriors of the Blackfoot, Gros Ventre, and Sarcee would almost certainly bring a deadly attack.

For over fifty years the northern alliance (the Cree/Assiniboine) and the southern coalition (the Blackfoot and their allies) enjoyed friendly relations based on a mutually beneficial business arrangement – the Cree wanted horses, which the Blackfoot had, and the Blackfoot wanted European goods, particularly guns, which the Cree middlemen obtained from the fur traders. When the HBC and Nor'Westers built posts along the Saskatchewan,

inviting the Blackfoot to trade directly with them, the inter-
dependency between the two blocs broke down. In the 1780s,
several violent incidents flared up – Peigans killing Cree, Cree
massacring Blood and Sarcee. In a particularly gory episode in the
spring of 1788, a small band of Gros Ventre was attacked by a war
party of Cree, who, it was reported, "fell upon them and killed the
leading man, after which they cut off his arms, head, Private Parts
and took out his bowels and then took what furrs they had
untraded from them."[1] Somehow, though, cooler heads prevailed.
Time and again, skilled diplomats, such as the Siksikas Chief Old
Swan and the white fur traders managed to broker peace. Then in
July 1806, only two years before the Lagimodières arrived at
Edmonton House, any good cheer that had existed between the
two tribes evaporated altogether.

It started innocently enough. A large war party of about four
hundred Blackfoot (Siksikas and Kainai) and an equal number of
Cree decided to combine their strengths and wage war on a
common enemy, a horse-thieving band of Gros Ventre. But along
the way an argument broke out about which horses belonged to
whom. A battle flared. Twenty-eight Blackfoot and three Cree
warriors were killed. James Bird wrote that suddenly the Cree were
"flying in all Quarters to conceal themselves in the Woods, and
that the Blackfeet threaten indiscriminate Vengeance." They didn't
have to wait long. Later that summer, as Bird reported, "four Tents
of south [Cree] Indians who were returning from the Muddy River
[Blackfoot] country quite ignorant of the late quarrel were on a
sudden attacked about 100 miles from this [Edmonton House], by
two or three hundred Blackfeet, two men made their escape, but
the rest, men, women & Children were either butchered or taken
Slaves."[2] For the next sixty years, periodical but constant bloody
warfare between the two factions was the norm.

The Cree women travelling with Jean-Baptiste and Marie-Anne weren't the only ones anxiously looking over their shoulders as they trotted along. The freemen knew that the usual friendly relations between white man and Indian – they had only to look at their wives to realize how cordial these were – had been soured by tragic incidents in the last few years.

In October, 1793, bands of Siksika and Gros Ventre attacked back-to-back trading posts on the North Saskatchewan River – the North West Company's Pine Island Fort and the Hudson's Bay Company's Manchester House. A gun battle ensued. The country wives of two fur traders were kidnapped, some of the staff badly beaten, and the forts pillaged. Anything that couldn't be carried off was destroyed. Scores of horses were stolen. The white traders killed several warriors during the melee. The Blackfoot and Gros Ventre swore revenge.

In January 1794, a band of Siksika arrived, supposedly to trade at Buckingham House and Fort George. The fur traders knew the Indians were determined to avenge the death of their kinsmen and they armed themselves to the teeth. Finding the forts too well guarded, the Blackfoot stole sixty horses, "threatening at the same time to *Scalp* the people & plunder the goods, as a Sacrifice to *appease the Spirits* of their deceased relations."[3] Not long after they left the forts, the warriors ran into three North West Company men who were returning home from another camp. The warriors relieved them of their gear and furs, then "stripd [them] to their shirts and had it not been near the House they must have perished."[4]

In June, 1794, an angry war party of 250 Siksika and Gros Ventre attacked the Hudson's Bay Company's South Branch House on the South Saskatchewan River. Since it was summer, almost everyone had left for York Factory. The warriors set the palisades on fire, then invaded the fort, destroying everything in their wake.

Three men, a woman, and two children were killed. Jacques Raphael, a North West Company interpreter, was an eyewitness to the devastation:

> The Ind[ian]s traced William Flea (by his blood) into the Cellar and Shot him dead. . . . finding no more Men about the House they plun-der'd it of everything, set fire to it and reduced it to Ashes . . . they stabbed Mags Annels Wife, kill'd two of his Children, which they put onto the mothers Belly . . . three young women belong[in]g to the Men they took prisoner with them . . . after plundering and destroy-ing our house, they went to the Canadians about 300 Yards distance intending to serve them in the same horrid manner.[5]

Fortunately the North West Company's post was better fortified and the traders were well armed. They were able to defend them-selves so that nobody at the fort was injured. Five warriors were killed and nine others were wounded.

In March 1802, a party of two hundred Gros Ventre attacked and killed ten Iroquois (close allies of the fur traders who had brought them west to trap furs) and two French Canadians from Chesterfield House. They hacked up the bodies, placed the scalps on the ends of poles, then paraded them past the trading posts. The Indians were furious that the Nor'Westers were intending to trap in Cypress Hills, which the Gros Ventre considered to be their domain.

In March 1805, a war party of fifty Hidatsas (Plains Indians whose homeland on the Missouri River was situated south of that of the Gros Ventre) travelled north with the intent of confronting a band of Blackfoot who had supposedly stolen their horses. They either couldn't find the Blackfoot or their enemy was too well armed. Frustrated and angry, they turned back. In the Moose Woods they encountered North West Company traders who were bargaining with some Cree. Then, as the trader and explorer François-Antoine Larocque described, the Hidatsas "attacked at day break, a volley was fired in Bouchés tent where three men were in bed asleep and all of them were killed."[6] According to other reports, two more Nor'Westers were slain in the onslaught.[7]

Bitter resentment lay at the heart of these attacks. The Blackfoot, Gros Ventre, Sarcee, and other allies were indignant at what they conceived to be unfair treatment by white people. They had a point. The Cree and Assiniboine were certainly favoured at the fur posts because these trappers brought in what the traders wanted most – beaver pelts. William McGillivray described the situation succinctly. Native customers were separated into two distinct categories: "those who have furs and those who have none: or, the Indians of the mountainous and Woody regions, and those of the Plains. The former furnish the rich and valuable furs."[8] McGillivray's brother Duncan wrote: "The *Gens du large* (Plains tribes) consisting of Blackfeet, Gros Ventres, Blood Indians, Piedgans, &c., are treated with less liberality, their commodities being cheifly Horses, Wolves, Fat & Pounded meat which are not sought after with such eagerness as the Beaver."[9] The one fur item which the Plains Nations did trap and counted on to procure European goods was wolf skins, but in the 1780s a glut on the market resulted in prices being severely slashed. By 1809 the North West Company wouldn't trade in wolf at all. For the Blackfoot and their allies, this was a serious blow for it meant that the Cree and Assiniboine would now be able to secure more guns and ammunitions – and, very quickly, obtain military superiority. Bitter rancour against white people was a natural outcome.

Alexander Henry gives an indication of how tense the situation was in the fall of 1809, while the Lagimodières were on their way back to Edmonton House. "The affair of last summer wherein the

Piegans were murdered has exasperated the Slave Indian Tribes [Blackfoot and allies] to the utmost degree, & they all appear bent on having revenge, either upon the Crees or us, although they are fully convinced that we are perfectly innocent in that affair." Two weeks later he wrote:

> Indians troublesome at the waterside in crossing and wishing to steal away our Boats. Some of them appear fully inclined to quarrel with us, while others seem to give themselves much trouble to prevent any disturbance between us. However to prevent surprise I was always careful to have my Swivel kept in good order, well loaded and frequently primed in their presence and always pointed directly at the center of the Camp on the opposite side of the River, giving them to understand that if any of them [were] to misbehave or hurt any [of our] people down at the water side I would that instant fire the Big Gun and sweep their tents away from off the Bank on which they stood.[10]

As well as the fear of Indian attack, the Lagimodières' journey northward was made miserable by a never-ending rain that was unusual for September. Water seeped into the tents at night until the travellers were damp to their very core. No matter how they had tried to cover up, the children's clothes were always soggy. The various rivers and streams were so swollen and swift that it sometimes took days to cross them, often precariously in a rough-hewn, fragile-looking raft. Some days hail as large and hard as musket balls rattled down on them. When they finally arrived at Edmonton House, heavy black muck lay everywhere. It was almost impossible to scrub things clean. Still, Marie-Anne must have been glad for the sake of Reine and LaPrairie that they were sheltered.

She quickly caught up on all the news. One of the dogs bit the clerk's little girl and was shot for his trespass. Somebody ran off with turnips from Mr. Bird's garden. The hen actually laid an egg, the first in six months. Mr. McKenzie, of Fort Augustus next door, was finally retiring after thirty-one years as a fur trader. The gossipers said he was worth eighteen hundred pounds. White and grey geese were seen flying together, an omen, insisted Chief Cow Buffalo, that the winter would be long. And, maybe most important, Mr. Bird, who was still at York Factory, sent word that he was finally laying down the law. There were to be no more country marriages between his "servants" and natives, no matter how beautiful or obliging the women were. The gentlemen in the service of the Hudson's Bay Company were to pay strict attention to this regulation, as they must serve as role models to the other employees. "At this moment I have 85 mouths to feed. I don't want one more sucking at our teat," he was reported to have said.

Many at Edmonton House thought this was rather hypocritical of Bird since he had married, *à la façon du pays*, at least five Indian women – sometimes at the same time – and had fathered a brood of children.

When the chief factor finally arrived back at Edmonton House from York Factory at the beginning of November, he had more to worry about than his employees' marital problems. Once again, native people were threatening violence against whites – this time it was the Cree who were on the warpath.

During the afternoon of October 9, two young Cree men arrived at Fort Vermilion, presided over by Alexander Henry, next door to Paint Creek House. One of them snuck into the Hudson's Bay Company post and took several loops of rope. With this he intended to steal as many horses as he could. Henry wrote: "He was no sooner gone, when his companion turned King's evidence, and declared him to be a Horse Thief, &c. Instant search was made for our horses and fortunately all [were] collected though [it was] dark and Rainy."[11] That night the young man was apprehended by one of the Nor'Westers and brought back to the fort. After a so-called trial, he was taken to the edge of the river and positioned before fifteen riflemen and executed. Henry rather self-righteously protested; it was, he wrote, "much against my own inclination I must confess. I had various reasons for not wishing he should be punished with death. Corporal punishment was all I desired, but my neighbours [the HBC] insisted upon killing him.[12] There was a good reason that Henry didn't want the man killed – to raise the wrath of his kinsmen was dangerous indeed. And certainly the Indians were enraged.

On November 7, an elderly native woman brought news that the Assiniboine and Cree had declared war on all white people and that an attack was imminent. "They were coming up both sides [of the river], determined to go to Fort Augustus, sweep the river clear of whites and steal every horse."[13] Henry immediately sent a courier with a warning letter to Fort Augustus/Edmonton House.

Heavily armed guards were posted at the guardhouses and gates. Marie-Anne and the other fort residents watched through cracks in the palisades as the long, long line of warriors, colourful in war headdresses and painted faces, trotted toward the posts. Jean-Baptiste had left for the winter trapping grounds by this time, and Marie-Anne, with an infant and small child to care for, was particularly vulnerable. But then, everybody was terrified. Suddenly the warriors let out a frightening whoop, waved their rifles above their heads, made a ninety-degree turn, and rode away.

It turned out that this particular party were on their way to make war against a group of Gros Ventre who were accused of raping Cree women. Indeed, in the days to come the most difficult problem facing the chief factor was preventing all-out warfare among the various Indian nations.

Bird must have been a good chess player, so adept was he at juggling which Indians he should be doing business with and when. One afternoon a small band of the Flatheads arrived. Bird gave the order to get rid of them as quickly as possible and a clerk rapidly noted down the pelts they brought in and the supplies they took away. He shoved the items into their arms, including a half-rope of tobacco as a gift to their chief, and shooed them out the door. In half an hour a band of over one hundred Blackfoot, the Flatheads' deadly enemies for centuries, arrived. More than 230 dogs and thirty horses pulling travois were parked just outside the fort. Everyone realized that a massacre had probably been averted. And who knows how the Flathead allies would have retaliated. Perhaps they would have destroyed both adjoining forts.[14]

That year the two trading posts decided to celebrate the festive season jointly with a Christmas Eve dinner given by the Hudson's Bay Company and a New Year's Day dance sponsored by the North West Company. Evergreen bows and pine cones tied together with red ribbon were pinned up everywhere. Mr. Bird gave his permission for the linen and fine china to be used for the night. The cook spent days preparing the banquet. There was a thick stew of fresh buffalo meat mixed with potatoes, turnips, parsnips. and carrots, all retrieved from the root cellar. The tongues were boiled then rolled, cooled in the snow, sliced very thin, and served with mustard and bannock. And there was a delicious whitefish pulled up from under the ice the day before. Rum punch flowed freely and there were sweets for the children. Chairs of all shapes and sizes were rounded up and brought into the mess. As the population of Edmonton House had doubled, it was very crowded, but nobody minded at all. Before the meal was served,

Mr. Bird conducted a service, reading from the Book of Psalms and the Book of Common Prayer of the Church of England. Carols were belted out, and the chief factor gave a sermon pointing out how neighbours must be kind and respectful to each other.[15]

Jean-Baptiste had promised to return home for the festivities, but Marie-Anne was disappointed when by New Year's Day he still hadn't arrived. Nevertheless, she put on her one good dress over her buckskin leggings and moccasins and walked the short distance to Fort Augustus through the towering snowbanks.

The dining hall there had been emptied of furniture, and three fiddlers were whirling out a jig. But the news arrived that evening made everyone uneasy. There had been yet another massacre among the Indian nations.

The slaughter occurred 150 kilometres north of Edmonton House. A party of Sarcee came across a band of Cree camping on the Pembina River. There were only women and children and a few elders in the camp – apparently all the able-bodied men were away trapping. A few months earlier, several Sarcee had been shot by Cree warriors in a vendetta involving horse theft. The Cree on the Pembina River had nothing to do with the shooting, but that didn't matter. The Sarcee murdered everyone in the camp, all 151 people, including many of the wives and children of Jean-Baptiste's partners.[16] Only the Bellegarde family survived intact, either because they weren't there or because they ran away. Marie-Anne must have been devastated. These women had been like sisters to her and she had grown to love them.

Three days after Marie-Anne was told about the tragedy, Jean-Baptiste finally arrived at Edmonton House. He found his wife lying on her bed, covered with blankets and skins. She had a high temperature and seemed unable to hear anyone. After a few days, when they had all but given up on her, Marie-Anne opened her eyes and asked for a glass of water. Over the next week she gradually gained back her strength, until by the fifth day she was sitting up. Many at Edmonton House were sick that winter. Epidemics of influenza, scarlet fever, typhus, dysentery, and scurvy were common at all the fur trade posts.[17]

Once his wife was well enough, Jean-Baptiste prepared to leave. His traps had all been baited and he had to recover the catch.

There was much excitement at the fort that spring. The employees of Edmonton House and Fort Augustus had never involved themselves much in the rivalry that had poisoned the Hudson's Bay and the North West companies and that had featured cheating, stealing, brawls, and murder. Isolation had forced them to be cordial. But not long after Mr. Bird's sermon on love and friendship, hostilities broke out. It began when the Bay's Hugh Isbbistor arrived at a camp of Flatheads at the same time as the Nor'Wester Louis Gervois.

Hugh Isbbistor explained what happened to an assembly gathered in the square of Edmonton House. He had had more success trading than Gervois, and he could see that his rival was piqued by this. While Isbbistor continued his business with the Indians, Gervois rushed back to Fort Augustus and informed his boss of what had happened. Five hours later five men waylaid Isbbistor a few metres from the gate of Edmonton House. They grabbed his gun and threw it into the snow. As Isbbistor reported, "By superiority of numbers and strength they deprived me of the fifteen beaver skins I had carried on my back all the way from the Indian camp."

After hearing his man out, a furious chief factor marched next door and insisted on confronting Hugh McDonald, Fort Augustus's new head man. McDonald disdainfully dismissed Bird's demand to return the pelts, insisting that they were the property of the North West Company. The Flatheads had always traded with the

Nor'Westers. The furs were stolen from under Gervois' nose, he insisted. Bird replied that this was utter nonsense. The Indians were simply better disposed toward Isbbistor than Gervois. Those furs were obtained peaceably and fairly and must be returned.[18]

But the chief factor knew that nothing could be done. The Nor'Westers outnumbered the HBC men three to one. That very day he wrote to London, "Your Honourable Servants readily bear the depravation of what they experience in winter and other trials of this place; but to endure, without hope of redress, the continual insults of the depraved Canadians is too mortifying a condition for any man to put up with."[19] Since it took months for a letter to travel to London, Bird knew it wouldn't relieve the situation one iota, but it probably soothed his wrath a little.

The residents of both establishments were now on tenterhooks, expecting more violence to erupt. It didn't take long.

A clerk set out on his weekly excursion to the HBC's horse camp accompanied by Cardinal, a Cree buffalo hunter who also worked for the company. After the young man had inspected the animals to his satisfaction, he said goodbye to the horse keeper and he and Cardinal made their way back along the trail. Cardinal excused himself for a moment and disappeared into the bush. The clerk continued on at a slow pace. Suddenly before him stood six Nor'Westers, all drunk, all barely able to walk. They all laughed uproariously as they pulled the young man from his horse. He stumbled and fell, smashing his forehead into a tree branch.

At that moment Cardinal reappeared. He raised his rifle and pointed it at the nearest Nor'Wester's head, telling them all to run as fast as they could. After they took off, he grabbed their horses' reins, and led them back to Edmonton House.[20]

Both bosses were outraged and it was a long time before friendly feelings prevailed again. In the end, the HBC clerk was allowed to keep one horse as compensation. Given his paltry salary, his humiliation might have been worthwhile.

The spring of 1810 was slow in coming. There were storms and more storms. By mid-April, the snow off the trails was still up to one's waist. There was not a smidgen of grass to be seen anywhere. Jean-Baptiste finally arrived home from the spring beaver trapping but he couldn't have been very happy. The fur harvest had not been as good as the year before, and two of his horses had died. The HBC horse keeper told him that the mare had probably lain down for a rest. The deep snow under her melted from her body heat and made a hollow in which her back got wedged and, with her legs sticking straight up, she couldn't stand. She probably perished of thirst and hunger.

Spring finally arrived and preparations were made for the trip to the plains. LaPrairie, like his sister before him, would ride in a cradleboard hanging from the horn of his mother's saddle. But what to do with roly-poly Reine, who no longer fit into a papoose? The Lagimodières may have followed the example of the Blackfoot, devising a box made from buffalo hide in which pillows stuffed with goose feathers were placed. The adults rode their own mounts, of course, another horse pulled the travois with Reine's box lashed to it, and a fourth, a wooden cart with huge wheels that carried their supplies.

In May, just before they left, another terrifying incident occurred. The children had fallen asleep in the afternoon and Marie-Anne decided to fetch some water. She had to scramble down the steep bank, which took about ten minutes. On her return she met Chief Factor Bird, who said he had seen a Blackfoot woman carrying a white child. Marie-Anne ran until she spied the Indian ahead of her walking quickly toward her camp. Georges Dugast relates what happened next:

She [the Blackfoot] had almost reached her people when Madame Lajimoniere seized her by the shoulder. "Give me my child," said she, stopping her, "Give me my child that you have stolen." The squaw did not understand the words, but she knew what the gesture meant though she made believe not to understand and pretended to be very much astonished, as thieves do when accused. However Madame Lajimoniere opened the hood that the woman had carefully closed and there was her little child smiling quite happily. When the squaw saw that she was discovered she pretended that she was only carrying him away to play with him and made no resistance to restoring him. She could hardly claim him for hers, his complexion would at once betray him, so she let Madame Lajimoniere take the child and for the present renounced her design of bringing up a little Canadian and making him into a Blackfoot.[21]

The Lagimodières left Edmonton at the end of May. The prairie was a carpet of low-growing blue flowers as velvety to the touch as a queen's gown. The wild rose bushes were covered with buds. The frogs croaked their hearts out. The rivers and creeks swarmed with strange brown insects, two long legs protruding from their underside, which nobody could remember seeing before. White and grey geese flew overhead. Many varieties of songbirds trilled their faithfulness.

This was the first time the Lagimodières had gone on the buffalo hunt by themselves. So recently after the death of their wives, the partners were in no mood to join in. They might also have been paralyzed with fright. Dugast records that Bellegarde and Chalifoux, as well as two other men named Caplette and Letendre, had been trading with Cree trappers when a band of Sarcees attacked. "The men only escaped death by prompt flight to the fort."[22]

Naturally, Jean-Baptiste didn't want Marie-Anne and the children left alone at night, so he planned to travel shorter distances than was his custom while searching for buffalo. Fortunately, the day after the family left South Branch House, a herd so huge it blackened the plains for miles was spotted.

The next day Marie-Anne, with LaPrairie in his cradleboard and Reine seated in front of her, rode to the top of the hill to watch the head of the household in action below. They spotted the bull lying on its belly in the grass. Jean-Baptiste flattened himself to the ground. He took aim and shot the huge animal in the heart. The legs, neck, and tail stiffened all at once, blood gushed from the mouth and nostrils, then the shaggy head fell back.

By this time, both Marie-Anne and the children must have been glowing with health, recovering from a winter of shrivelled cabbage, pemmican, and bannock. Fresh food was always available. If Jean-Baptiste didn't find buffalo, he shot smaller game, rabbits, geese, ducks. If they were camped close to a stream or lake, they fished for their dinner. And berries of all kinds were plentiful. Most days followed the same pattern. Jean-Baptiste left at daybreak, after a quick breakfast of tea, bannock, and fruit, and returned as the purple-pink sunset spread across the horizon. Marie-Anne spent her time looking after Reine and LaPrairie and dealing with the buffalo catch.

One morning, the Lagimodières awoke to find their horses missing. They surmised that they had either been stolen or that they had wandered away looking for a more lush pasture. Jean-Baptiste decided that he had to go after them, following their tracks. Marie-Anne was left alone with the children. During that day she tried not to alarm her offspring by showing her own fear but, in fact, she was terribly worried. What if Jean-Baptiste couldn't find the horses? There was no help for hundreds of kilometres.

When the sun went down and he still hadn't returned, Marie-Anne realized she must spend the night alone. She would have been scared of many things – wild animals, the thunderstorms which had been violating the evening calm for days and, of course, warring Indians.

The next morning Marie-Anne awoke to the distant sound of horses' hooves. She was so relieved that Jean-Baptiste had returned that she started making him breakfast, but when she stepped out of the tent, she saw a dozen Indians galloping toward her. As they approached, their vermilion and black war paint and their head-dresses – the snow-white feathers tipped with red – glistened in the sun. She knew exactly what to do.

With LaPrairie in his cradleboard on her back and Reine at her side, she stood waiting. When the warriors arrived, they must have been amazed at the bizarre whiter-than-white people with light hair and sky-blue eyes. By sign and gesture, they asked Marie-Anne where her husband was. She signalled back that Jean-Baptiste was not at home, but away rounding up their horses. She knew that the language spoken was neither Blackfoot nor Cree, and that fact, as well as their flat features, convinced her that these were Sarcee, perhaps the very ones responsible for the massacre of the wives of Jean-Baptiste's partners and Marie-Anne's beloved friends. Still, she realized the safety of her children and herself depended on her appearing unconcerned and hospitable. She fetched a slab of buffalo meat from the cache and made a stew with potatoes and wild herbs which the Sarcee ate with relish.

In the early afternoon, Jean-Baptiste finally showed up with the horses; he had found them wandering some fifty kilometres away and had no idea how they had gotten there. He was nonplussed at the sight of the teepees in a circle around his own tent, and at several of the younger men playing with his children. He surmised that they were friendly, but Marie-Anne told him of her suspicions. There was good reason for their distrust. Immediately the Indians told them that until those Sarcee who were at that moment doing business at Battle River House returned safely they would not be allowed to leave. A lot of blood had been shed, and they were afraid of reprisals from the white traders.

During the night, while everyone slept, the Lagimodières decided to make a dash for it. LaPrairie, in his cradleboard, bumped along at the side of Marie-Anne's horse. Jean-Baptiste placed Reine on the saddle behind him, wrapped a blanket around her, and tied it to his shoulder strap. They galloped as fast and as hard as they could, stopping only for a few hours during the night for a bite of bannock, a drink of water, and a short rest. Marie-Anne never slept – there wasn't a moment she didn't hear pounding hooves, ferocious war cries.

On the fifth day they let up the pace a little until Reine shouted out. The child had glanced behind her and seen a dust cloud rising from a dozen galloping horses. They drove on in a frenzy until at last they spotted the sentry posts of Edmonton House and Fort Augustus in the distance. By sheer luck the transport ferry had just arrived on the south bank of the Saskatchewan. The Lagimodière family clambered aboard. When they were halfway across the river, the warriors raced up to the shore and gave out a loud and terrifying cry.[23]

CHAPTER TEN

—

THE TRADING POST in which the Lagimodières sought refuge was not the one they had left in spring. During the summer, Edmonton House and its neighbour, Fort Augustus, had moved lock, stock, and barrel to White Earth Creek, one hundred or so kilometres to the north (at present day Smoky Lake). It had been Alexander Henry's idea, a product of his fear of Indian attack. On February 13, 1810, he wrote,

> Mr. Hughes and myself determined to abandon Fort Vermillion and Fort Augustus, and to build at Terre Blanche. The latter, being a more central place, will answer the same purpose as the two present establishments and save the expense of one of them; it will also draw all the Slaves [Plains Indians] at one place, where we can better defend ourselves from their insults . . . By this means, we hope to divide the Slaves from the Crees; if it succeeds, it may save us a great deal of trouble and anxiety.[1]

Chief Factor James Bird felt that the Hudson's Bay Company posts – Paint River House (next door to Fort Vermilion) and Edmonton House – had no choice but to follow suit. In only two months, June and July, a stockade enclosing both Edmonton House III and Fort Augustus III, the main houses for the bosses, dormitory wings for the staff, kitchens, storehouses, and the shops and stores had been constructed. At that point there were 135 men, women, and children living at the North West Company fort, and eighty-five people – in a few months the population would swell to 106 – at the HBC post.[2]

It quickly became clear that the relocation was a mistake. The Blackfoot seldom showed up, the Cree were as "troublesome" as ever, there was little firewood, and a nearby swamp incubated "very large and troublesome" mosquitoes, as well as gigantic horseflies. Alexander Henry fled Terre Blanche in September of 1810, moving on to take charge of Rocky Mountain House. Four years later, he would drown in a boating mishap at Fort George in Oregon. In 1812, James Bird moved back permanently to Edmonton House II, which never seemed to have closed down altogether.

In their flight from the Sarcee, the Lagimodières had left behind everything. Four months' worth of provisions, all their personal belongings – Marie-Anne's mother-of-pearl combs, LaPrairie's turtle-shell rattle, Jean-Baptiste's rosary – the buffalo hides so far collected, and the bison meat waiting to be made into pemmican. Jean-Baptiste realized that he would have to return to their camp quickly, before everything was either taken by humans or eaten by animals.

It was a stifling summer. Alexander Henry reported that on July 29 the temperature reached ninety-one degrees Fahrenheit (thirty-two degrees Celsius). Cooped up in such close quarters, Marie-Anne and the few others who had remained at the trading post must have thought that they had descended into hell. It was so hot that buffalo meat rotted in a day and had to be cut up, dried, and made into pemmican as quickly as possible. The fort's women were all busy at these tasks.

Everyone's nerves were stretched taut. The Indians could attack at any time, or at least that's how the white population felt. One afternoon, four naked half-breed boys ran into the fort, blurting out that they had found some feathers tied to a piece of red cloth on the riverbank. Even more frightening, they had also spotted a human arm tied to a log. It floated right past them, they said, but they couldn't catch it. In a panic, the man in charge – James Bird had gone to York Factory for the summer – sent two men in a canoe down the Saskatchewan, but the current was too fast and they found nothing.

Among the First Nations, the killing battles continued. Assiniboine and Cree warriors had proclaimed war on the Crow Mountain people; ten were massacred in one battle. Flatheads slaughtered sixteen Peigans. Kinsmen were even fighting among themselves: the Little Girl and Saskatchewan bands, both Assiniboine, decimated each other.

In his journal entry of October 31, 1810, James Bird described the atmosphere that was poisoning the plains. The previous August a battle had raged between a party of Gros Ventre and Muddy River Indians (Blackfoot). The Gros Ventre were defeated – fourteen of their warriors were killed. But as far as Bird was concerned, the worst of it was that a North West Company clerk named Macdonald had been travelling with the Gros Ventre and now the infuriated Muddy River Indians were determined to ambush any white man who was conveying goods back to the forts. This had been confirmed by "the Muddy River Indians themselves who stopped French canoes, which were bound for the Columbia, a Little above old Acton House and this band of Indians . . . declared that another is laying on the banks of the river."[3]

And the humans weren't the only ones on edge. The animals were acting strangely. A pack of dogs killed two colts tethered nearby. In retaliation, the cooper shot the miscreants, four from Edmonton House and three from Fort Augustus. He had to bury them immediately – their bodies had already begun to stink. James Bird's brown hen sat on eleven fertilized eggs, but by the third day of the heat wave something was obviously amiss. When the bird was shooed away, two eggs were found to be missing, one was rotten, and there were eight dead chicks. Huge flocks of pigeons arrived and plucked up the newly grown barley by the roots. The beet leaves withered.

On August 18 everyone rejoiced – the heat wave had broken at last. Only three days later, when the fort's residents emptied their chamber pots outside, they saw ice sparkling in the morning sun. Overnight, a pan of water had frozen.

Jean-Baptiste finally showed up, and the family headed for the plains. At that point the Lagimodières teamed up with Chalifoux, who now had a new country wife and children in tow. They spent the remainder of the summer and early fall hunting and butchering buffalo and making pemmican, and in the early fall they turned to trapping beaver. Alexander Henry ran into them on his way to Rocky Mountain House. "At Vermillion river we met two freemen, La Gimonidère and Challifoux, with their families, beaver hunting."*

---

* As far as I can determine, this is the only time Alexander Henry mentions Jean-Baptiste Lagimodière by name, and even then he spells it wrong.

The prairies were not as beautiful that autumn as they usually were. Fires had ravished the luxuriant grasses, huge patches had been transformed into black-as-tar expanses. The inferno had started in the spring, and it continued through summer, driven on by a hot, dry wind.

Wildfires on the Great Plains were usually beneficial, at least as far the bison were concerned. The blazes burned down trees that invaded the prairie, promoting the growth of rich nutritional grasses on which animals fed and grew fat. Prickly pear cactus that was easily digested once it was singed was a particular favourite. Indians knew that setting fires not only meant more and better food for bison, it also created ideal conditions for berries and prairie turnips. First Nations people also used prairie fires to control the movement of buffalo herds. Historian Theodore Binnema writes:

> They could burn areas of the northern mixed prairie in the autumn (or even the winter) to direct the bison towards their wintering grounds and to encourage grasses in those areas to sprout earlier in the spring. They could burn fescue grasslands in the spring to drive the bison onto the plains and to encourage the fescue grasses to grow . . . Traders frequently mentioned that Indians burned the prairie near trading posts to keep the bison out of their reach during the winter. This practice forced the traders to buy the provisions from Indian bands during the winter, rather than hunting for themselves.[4]

During 1810–11 there were an unusually large number of fires. Whether they were set by native people or by an act of nature, they would have dire consequences for everyone.

Jean-Baptiste wanted to make up for last year's poor catch of beaver skins, so he and Chalifoux intended to travel farther this season – right into the Rockies and perhaps beyond. "These Freemen think beaver grows like grass on the other side of the mountains," remarked James Bird, who also had returned from his summer away. But Marie-Anne could understand why Jean-Baptiste was tempted. All the talk in both trading posts was about the extraordinary adventures of the North West Company's David Thompson. Three years earlier, the geographer-explorer had crossed the Rocky Mountains by the Howse Pass, and found the source of the Columbia. This season he planned to travel the entire river from its source to its mouth. Everyone was envious of the lush furs he had collected from the Indians along the way.

Not long after his papa left, LaPrairie came down with a cold. He developed a fever, and soon his cough was so bad his little chest hardly stopped heaving. He wouldn't eat and would hardly take a drink of water. Marie-Anne dosed him with tonics, applied mustard plasters, kept the fire at a roar. Nothing seemed to work, and by the fourth day she was at her wits' end. Finally one of the fort women told her to wrap LaPrairie in a bearskin and follow her to the nearby Indian encampment.

Both the baby and Marie-Anne were stripped of their clothing and enfolded in a blanket, for modesty's sake. Then they were led into the lodge, a wigwam made from willow branches and covered with buffalo hides with an opening so small Marie-Anne had to get down on her hands and knees to crawl inside. Seven women of varying ages sat in a circle around a pit; they signalled to the white woman to join them. Everyone was naked. As the long braid of sweet grass burned, they wafted the smoke toward themselves and toward Marie-Anne and LaPrairie. A pipe was passed around as the singing and mournful prayers, led by eldest person present, a medicine woman, continued. Several young girls brought in bricks so hot they glowed red and placed them in the firepit. At a signal from an elder, the opening flap was shut tight, plunging the lodge into blackness.

The elder then threw cold water on the stones and sang, "Wake up, great Stone Spirit, wake up. Send our messages to Māmawiwiyohtā, the Creator of All Things." Around the circle each person gave her name – "So the Creator can recognize you," one elder whispered – where she was from and the name of her clan; most had Bear or Loon lineage. When it was Marie-Anne's turn, she said, "I am Madame Lagimodière, from Lower Canada, of the Muskellunge clan." The elders nodded their approval.

Meanwhile, the steam rose. It was so hot Marie-Anne almost panicked, especially when she noticed that LaPrairie had stopped coughing. Perhaps he was dead. But then he gave a pathetic but loud sob.

Finally, the opening flap was removed and cool air rushed in. The Indian women scrubbed Marie-Anne's moist body with buffalo sage leaves until she felt as though her skin was coming off, then splashed her with cold water.

After the ceremony, Marie-Anne was given a cloth bundle filled with herbs – rat root, shrill-voiced herb, raven's beak fungus and bear root among others – and told to mix in a small amount water. The potion was spooned into the little boy's mouth.

The next morning LaPrairie's condition had improved; two days later he was bouncing around as usual. His mother never discovered whether it was the session in the sweat lodge or the medicine that saved LaPrairie's life. In her later years, she was often asked by white people how her children had survived in such primitive surroundings. She would bring out a little pouch tied with string, explaining that it was by this medicine, which was sent by Māmawiwiyohtā, not caring at all that they looked at her aghast.

On November 8, the Saskatchewan River froze and one of the most crippling winters that Aboriginal peoples or fur traders had ever experienced descended. The temperature seldom rose above minus twenty Celsius, often lingered at minus twenty-nine, and fell as low as minus forty. The wind from the north blew longer and stronger than anyone could remember. But it was the never-ceasing snowfall, the "extravagant banks," as James Bird wrote, that astonished everyone. It wasn't something that people merely waited out in a certain amount of discomfort – they almost starved to death.

Each year Edmonton House stored away a supply of pemmican from the main depot, Cumberland House, but the community mostly relied on the Plains Indians, a few freemen, and their own employees to hunt for their basic food throughout the winter months. That autumn few Blackfoot, Gros Ventre, or Sarcee visited the twin forts. The bosses blamed the lack of customers on the new location. But on December 4 a sharp alarm bell sounded. James Bird wrote, "The young Blackfeet Men traded their wolves for Tobacco and returned to their tents. They slept four nights on their way to the House & say that there are no Buffalo near." A week later, another Blackfoot party arrived with a similar story. Bird's unease began to mount and his journals begin to tell a story of desperation: "This is a piece of very unpleasant News as we are 106 Mouths and our Hunters Can with difficulty provide us with a sufficiency of meat." On December 18, more Blackfoot showed up at the post. "They have slept nine nights on their way to the House and tell us that they saw scarcely a Buffalo in their whole journey & that there are few even at their tents, which is an unpleasant piece of intelligence as our provisions are becoming very thin." A day later: "The man that is tenting with our Hunters arrived for something to eat as the Extreme Cold weather and scarcity of Animals prevented their killing any these several days. This news Reduces me to the necessity of Borrowing Beat meat from our Neighbours."

It mustn't have been a festive Christmas at Edmonton House that year because the day after, Bird admitted, "Found myself under the Necessity of again borrowing Beat meat from our Neighbours." On December 31, the fort's own hunters managed to kill five male bison, and on January 5, after seventeen days on the lookout, another hunting party returned "with the meat of two old Buffalo Bulls." It wasn't exactly delicious fare but it kept the wolf from the door, at least for awhile. Six days later, two HBC employees from Acton House arrived, begging for supplies. "They have the greatest difficulty in procuring provisions even of the poorest kind sufficient for their subsistence, and have not seen any Indians from the plains since the fall. The cause of their and our distress for Provisions is, the Burning of the plains between the red Deer & south Branch Rivers which has prevented Buffalo from coming this way as usual." Two days later the situation had deteriorated further. "We are now reduced to the necessity of serving out a few dried berries & a little old fat to the men for present subsistence, & for want of provisions to give them for their journey, I am unable to send off the men who arrived from Acton House. Thus we are an hundred Mouths without more than two days provisions of any kind in the House."

Fort residents, including Marie-Anne, didn't know which was worse – the cold or the hunger. The snow was so deep it wasn't easy for the men to travel any distance into the bush, so firewood was carefully rationed. The children sat huddled over the fireplace, trying to warm their hands on its few embers. At night, as the wind howled through the fort like a deranged animal and the temperature dropped to minus fifty, the adults cuddled their offspring close and covered themselves with blankets, coats, anything they could find. Oatmeal was still being served, as well as a few dried peas and berries and small pieces of meat so tough they could barely chew it – the children wouldn't even try. There was a great deal of sickness at the fort – influenza, colic, gout, rheumatism, lung inflammation, pneumonia – but the worst of all, especially at times of famine, was scurvy. Teeth fell out, gums bled, legs swelled, eyes sunk into the skull, spots blemished the skin, and death often followed. Marie-Anne would have learned what to do from her Cree friends. Despite Reine's and LaPrairie's protests, she force-fed them tart cranberries she had earlier dried and a bitter tea of spruce needles and dogwood bark. All anyone could do was pray that this horrible winter would end.

The people at Edmonton House did not starve to death. The hunters were able to provide enough meat – mainly the carcasses of old bulls they found frozen to death on the plains – to keep the populace alive, but it was a terrible struggle. Not until February 15 did the danger finally pass, and the hero of the moment was, in all likelihood, Jean-Baptiste Lagimodière.

James Bird first alluded to a "Free Canadian" in his journal entry of January 4, 1811. He had been "engaged to hunt" along with four HBC servants. Bird never referred directly to Lagimodière – he never named individuals in his journal except for a few HBC brass – but it seems unlikely it could have been anyone else. Jean-Baptiste's links to both the Hudson's Bay Company and Edmonton House were much stronger than any other freeman's. Marie-Anne was by now firmly entrenched; James Bird must have got to know her and the children well. Jean-Baptiste had developed the fierce loyalty toward the Hudson's Bay Company for which he would later become famous. Most important, he had a reputation for being a remarkable hunter. At first he didn't do much better than anyone else. On January 20, Bird reported: "It appeared from the accounts of some Canadians sent to discover Buffalo that there is not a Bull to be found to the South within 80 miles of the place & that our Freeman has killed no more than one bull." Finally, though, on February 15, Bird received this good news: "Two men arrived from our free Canadian hunter who informs us that he has killed 15 cow buffalo." The next day Bird sent off a party of twelve horses and sleds to bring back the meat. The famine was over.

That winter's discontent wasn't only about having enough to eat. The fur hunt was also a disaster. Beaver were as scarce as daffodils. That shortage, along with starvation, had forced the Cree from the bush. As James Bird reported on January 6, 1811: "Had the mortification to learn from a young Cree that their relations, and indeed most of the Indians belonging to this place, had made no hunt whatsoever. Men that were accustomed to killing 80 or 100 beaver have no more than 10 . . . the reasons assigned for this Diminution in this hunt are . . . the extreme severity of the winter and Extraordinary Depth of Snow." The valuable marten had also all but disappeared: "The Indians all suppose they must have been Destroyed by the fires which raged in the woods last spring." Even less valuable skins were scarce. The horrible cold and six-foot-high snow drifts had destroyed the Plains Indians' horses, which "prevented them from running wolves."

The season's trap had been a disappointment for Jean-Baptiste Lagimodière. He had planned to spend the winter near Rocky Mountain House, but the dreadful weather probably made him turn back, for he was at Edmonton House for the holiday season. In the second week in March, he bid Marie-Anne farewell and headed for the Battle River. He intended to meet up with some Blackfoot acquaintances of his, and together they would trap beaver on the river and the creeks that flowed from the south into it. James Bird wrote that the freeman "found the Blackfeet too apprehensive of Meeting with their Enemies who inhabit the Banks of the Missouri River to be prevailed on to Accompany him."[5] Reports arrived at the fort that the Blackfoot were "wretched" from trying to subsist on so little food. Jean-Baptiste was back at Edmonton House by April 17 with little to show for his hunt.

Finally the wind shifted to the southwest, and almost overnight the temperature climbed. On May 5 the ice on the Saskatchewan River broke. Soon the purple heads of wild crocuses had popped out of the slush. A flock of nine white swans flew by – a loud, clear *klooo, kwooo* honked out. Everyone in the fort thanked God that they had survived the terrible winter.

To make up for the poor haul of buffalo and furs, the Lagimodières decided that as soon as the weather permitted they would leave for the bison hunt. This year they would journey much further south in their quest.

It's not known whether the Lagimodières travelled with other freemen in the spring of 1811, but probably they were accompanied by the Chalifoux family as well as others. An incident occurred along the way once again involving LaPrairie, now two years old, that made them all nervous. It's related by Marie-Anne's biographer, Georges Dugast. One day several Assiniboine arrived at the freemen's tents. The chief dismounted and asked to speak to Mme Lagimodière. Jean-Baptiste, who had some proficiency in that language, agreed to act as a translator. It was obvious that the old man was enthralled with LaPrairie. Dugast described what happened next:

The chief represented that they desired to have the boy and taking the rope which held the finest horse he put it in her hand making signs that he would give it in exchange for the child. As one can well imagine Madame Lajimoniere refused his offer and made signs that she would never consent to such a trade. The Indians believing that she was not content with one horse drew up a second and put the cord of this one also in her hand . . . She said to her husband, "Tell him that I will not sell my child that he would have to tear my heart out before I would part with him."; "Very well!" said the Indian, "take the horses and one of my children." "No!" said she, "you can never make me consent to such a trade," then taking her child in her arms she began to cry. The Indian apparently was touched by her tears, for he ceased to insist on the [ex]change and went on his way with his people and horses.[6]

This was a most unsettling episode because the Lagimodières and the others were travelling to the Cypress Hills, which had traditionally been a hunting grounds for Aboriginal peoples; whites were not welcome there. Once again the Lagimodières were teasing fate.

It was an ideal place to track down buffalo. In the 1850s Captain John Palliser called Cypress Hills "a perfect oasis in the desert." Another visitor wrote, "No better summer pasture is to be found in all the wide North-west than exists on these hills, as the grass is always green, water of the best quality is always abundant, and shelter from the autumnal and winter storms always at hand."[7] Cypress Hills received more rain than the plains, and as well as supporting nutritional grasses which "cover the ground like a thick mat," it sustained forests of lodgepole pine, Jack pine, white spruce, and Douglas fir. But storms also descended with deadly speed; the Cree called the area Thunder Breeding Hills.

These hills are a strange phenomenon, huge mounds, almost mountainous in height, pushing up from the flat grasslands. Unusual animals – reptiles, insects, and birds – are abundant. According to Cree myth, the creatures have been left alone from the time God created the world. The native people were too frightened to hunt them down because they thought the woods were full of demons who made the winds howl and lightning flash.

After three weeks of travel, the party finally arrived at their intended destination – the southwestern part of the hills. The trail climbed upward, circling round and round until the plateau was reached. Here on the top of the prairie world, silver and yellow grasses stretched for miles. Marie-Anne kept her eye out for a spot she thought was suitable. She found it in a circular grove of mixed poplar and birch, with evergreens standing behind like tall soldiers. There they camped and the preparations began. A bed of moss was laid on the ground, branches of lodgepole pine cut. Two days later, Marie-Anne gave birth to her third child. Jean-Baptiste baptized the baby Marie-Josephte, after his mother. But like her brother before her, she was forever known by her nickname, LeCyprès.

Despite all their efforts to get there, not long after the birth, the Lagimodières give up on the buffalo hunt and headed north again. Exciting news had reached them. A colony of English-speaking immigrants was to be established at the forks of the Red and Assiniboine rivers, under the patronage of the Scottish philanthropist, Lord Selkirk. It was expected that eventually thousands upon thousands of farmers, poor crofters from Scotland and Ireland, would settle in a huge area that was now called Assiniboia. The Lagimodières decided at once to join them. It had been such a hard year – the near- starvation, the anxiety of conflict with the Indians, the poor fur catch – but that was not the primary reason they decided to give up on the North West. At Red River, they imagined fields of wheat tall as a man's belly button. Cattle grazing. Orchards full of apples. Pretty houses with gardens. And most important, a church with an imposing steeple and bells clanging them to mass every morning. The children could finally be baptized as God ordained.

The Lagimodières probably didn't realize it, but it would be many years of unremitting hardship before this paradise became reality.

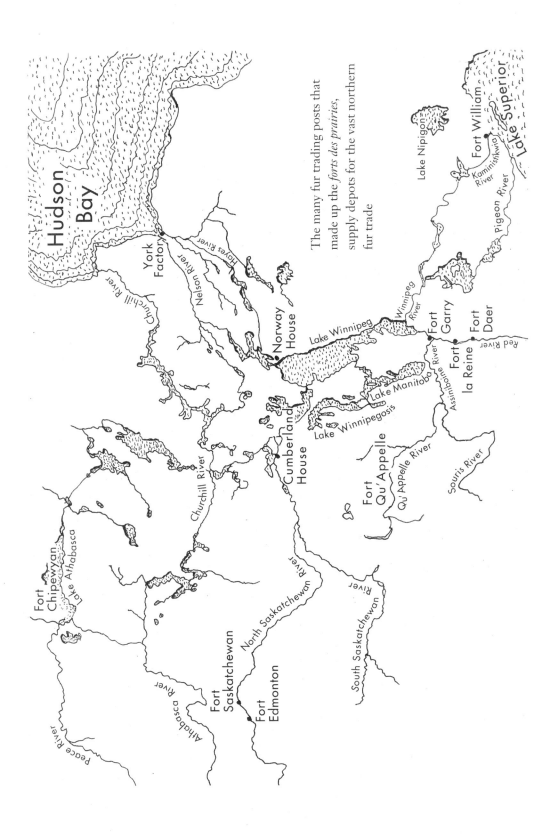

Hudson Bay

York Factory

Hayes River

Nelson River

Churchill River

Norway House

Lake Winnipeg

Winnipeg River

Fort Garry

Fort Daer

Red River

Fort la Reine

Assiniboine River

Lake Manitoba

Lake Winnipegosis

Cumberland House

Churchill River

Fort Qu'Appelle

Qu'Appelle River

Souris River

South Saskatchewan River

North Saskatchewan River

Fort Saskatchewan

Fort Edmonton

Athabasca River

Peace River

Lake Athabasca

Fort Chipewyan

Lake Nipigon

Fort William

Kaministikwia River

Pigeon River

Lake Superior

The many fur trading posts that made up the *forts des prairies*, supply depots for the vast northern fur trade

PART THREE

THE SETTLEMENT

CHAPTER ELEVEN

—

WHEN THEY REACHED EDMONTON HOUSE, the rumours were confirmed. European immigrants were on their way to the Red River Valley. The Lagimodières had to quickly wind up their affairs as the last brigade of the season headed for Red River was about to embark. This time they travelled in the relative comfort of a York boat, a large, open vessel, pointed at both ends like a gigantic pea pod and powered by oars. Several other families travelled with them, mostly HBC or North West Company servants who were retiring but who wished to settle permanently in the west with their country wives and half-breed children.

On the morning of the departure, Marie-Anne found herself once again saying goodbye to people of whom she had grown fond, including Chief Factor James Bird, who told her that he planned to settle himself at Red River with his current country wife when he retired. Marie-Anne herded her small children aboard, the two eldest waving farewell to the crowd gathered on the dock.

They went the same way they came, along the curving molasses-coloured Saskatchewan River, but this time they travelled with the current, not against it. It was not exactly a comfortable journey, but the weather held – even the pernickety Lake Winnipeg remained calm – and in three weeks they were on the Red River. They continued southward until a few days later they reached The Forks, the juncture of the Red and Assiniboine rivers where Winnipeg stands today.

Marie-Anne and Jean-Baptiste must have been amazed by what they saw. On the exact spot where three years ago only black snakes and the ruins of a fort had been visible, an imposing citadel had been constructed. Fort Gibraltar was situated on the west bank of the Red River just at the mouth of the Assiniboine. Five-metre palisades with a squat guardhouse at each corner enclosed a beehive of buildings – two residences for forty-odd workers, stables, carpentry and blacksmith shops, a meat house and kitchens, stores, and an ice house. The fur trader Colin Robertson wrote, "This is not only a strong place but very comfortable lodgings, such as I have not been accustomed to for some time past."[1]

Since Fort Gibraltar's construction in 1810, the North West Company had solidified its control of the pemmican trade in the Red River and Assiniboine valleys, much to the grief of the Hudson's Bay Company. The place wasn't used as a fur trading post, but as a huge warehouse to store and eventually distribute pemmican and other essentials to the fur traders and their families in the interior. Every North West Company canoe had to pass by The Forks either on the way to the North Country or to Montreal. The last thing the Nor'Westers wanted was a colony of farmers loyal to the Hudson's Bay Company who might interfere with this traffic. With a settlement would come a town with all the constraining apparatus of civilization: government, judiciary, military, police.

But the Lagimodières were more interested in what was happening across the river, on the east bank, five kilometres south of Fort Gibraltar. This was where the first group of Selkirk settlers, an advance party of thirty-five men, was supposed to be building cabins and clearing land. There was no sign of them, an indication that the nobleman's grand plan was already descending into what could be called a comedy of errors if it weren't so tragic.

Lord Selkirk looked like an aristocrat, imposing and self-confident. He was tall, fine-featured with wavy, coiffed red hair. He was a good conversationalist, sincere with both those of his class and with ordinary folk, and people liked him the moment they met him. He was imbued with genuine enthusiasm, energy, and optimism, especially when it came to his grandiose plans. He also suffered from amazing self-delusion, often having no idea what he was getting himself and others into. He played with the lives of people as though they were puppets whose strings he erratically pulled. His schemes were complex and often imaginative, but if one plank was faulty, the entire project came tumbling down like a house of cards. This could be partly attributed to his being a terrible judge of character; because he spent most of his time in Scotland, it was essential that he employ responsible middleman to oversee his projects overseas, but almost to a man these people proved to be disasters. Thomas Clark, an Upper Canada merchant, financier and one of the few capable agents engaged by Selkirk, was perceptive when he wrote, "I think from his plans [Lord Selkirk] will injure himself very much without doing his people or the folks in Canada much good."[2]

Thomas Douglas, Fifth Earl of Selkirk, was born in the family castle on St. Mary's Isle near Kirkcudbright, Scotland in 1771. The youngest of five sons (two brothers died before he was born), he was brought up to live a philanthropic and untroubled life.

However, in rapid succession, his four brothers died of one thing or another until, at age twenty-eight, Thomas inherited the family title, estate, and fortune.

The Selkirks were Scottish nationalists, unusually liberal – at least for the aristocracy – in their political views. For his primary education Thomas was sent to an unorthodox academy run by the Unitarians. He then enrolled at the University of Edinburgh, studying arts and some law, but left without a degree. He spent the next few years in France, where his brother was involved in revolutionary politics. This was where his philanthropic urges blossomed. But his benevolence was put into action in his homeland. "The French Revolution had an impact on him," writes one historian, "and he went to France to study it at first hand. But, while he supported liberal ideals and good causes, he had little sense of direction in his life. It would be his tour of the Highlands in 1792 that made a huge impression on him."[3]

At the time many tenants in Ireland and the Scottish Highlands were being turfed from their small subsistence farms by "modernizing" landowners. Selkirk developed a genuine concern for their plight. The answer, he decided, was to move these poor, homeless people holus-bolus to the wilds of North America.

His first scheme was to ship rebellious Irish to Rupert's Land to form a colony somewhere near Lake Winnipeg, where there was "a climate . . . not more severe than that of Germany and Poland." (Needless to say, he had never travelled anywhere near the region.) Hemp cultivation would be a good idea, he decided. But the Colonial Office turned him down; "colonizing at all en masse" was frowned on. His next proposal was more successful. In 1802 he managed to buy large tracts of Prince Edward Island and established eight hundred Highlanders there. Despite protests among the settlers that Selkirk had not provided what he originally promised – farm equipment, seeds, etc. – the colony took hold. The next undertaking, though, ended in disaster.

For this venture he chose a site on the shores of Lake St. Clair (near present-day Wallaceburg, Ontario), where he decided sheep farming would prove a booming business. But it was swampy territory; the 102 settlers arrived at the height of the malaria season. Most fell ill immediately; eighteen died. Nevertheless Selkirk continued to pour money into his dream and the settlement struggled along. Finally, during the War of 1812, American soldiers ravaged the farms, sounding the colony's death knell. Half the original one hundred immigrants had died by then, victims of malaria, malnutrition, flooding, and poor management.[4]

None of this deterred Selkirk. He became smitten with the travel accounts of the famous explorer Alexander Mackenzie, in which he described the Red River Valley thus: "There is not a finer country in the world for the residence of uncivilised man . . . It abounds in everything necessary to the wants and comforts of such a people. Fish, venison, and fowl, with wild rice, are in great plenty; while, at the same time, their subsistence requires that bodily exercise so necessary to health and vigour."[5] Whether the area would be a similar paradise for "civilized" man seems not to have concerned Selkirk. He rushed ahead with his plans to plant an agricultural colony populated by Irish and Highlanders. A utopian, he believed his own propaganda when he wrote of how his Red River colony would thrive:

A man starts with nothing, but having planted five bushels of potatoes, he harvests sixty. On this, supplemented by a little meal of his own, he, his wife and his children manage through the first winter.

In the second year, there is expectation of 200 bushels of potatoes from planting ten. There would be land cleared and some wheat grown, and a cow almost paid for, along with adequate shelter and firewood. In the third year, 20 bushels of potatoes planted in 400 bushels harvested, 30 acres if land sewed.[6]

And so on until nirvana was achieved.

The one difficulty facing Selkirk was that the 1670 Charter named the Hudson's Bay Company the "sole proprietor of all the territories granted," including the Red River Valley, and the London Committee had earlier made it clear that settlers weren't welcome; it was felt that they would interfere with the fur trade. Selkirk solved the problem by buying up a large number of HBC shares. He was able to do so because earlier he had married an heiress, Jean Wedderburn, and with his own fortune, her money, as well as her brother's and Alexander Mackenzie's, he captured control of the company. In 1810 he presented his Red River Settlement project and, not surprisingly, it was accepted by the London Committee. On June 12, 1811, Selkirk was granted 300,000 square kilometres of land for the express purpose of establishing a farming community. The asking price was ten shillings, but in reality the settlement would cost Selkirk a good chunk of his fortune.

Even before the documents were signed, agents were combing the Highlands, Scotland's Western Isles, and Ireland for colonists. They eventually rounded up 125 men. Under the leadership of a magistrate called William Hillier, seventy-five were hired by the Hudson's Bay Company and were to be posted to various forts in the Athabasca country as a show of force against the North West Company. The other thirty-five labourers were assigned to Red River to lay the groundwork for the families who were to follow.

They were to depart from Stornoway, a port in the Outer Hebrides, but because of many difficulties, including officious customs agents, they were stalled there for a month, long enough for many to change their minds. At one point, a Scottish customs inspector climbed aboard their vessel. "Listen up," he said, in a low and solemn voice. "I will call the name of each and every enlisted man aboard this ship, and he must say aye or nay to the question: Are you here of your own free will?" Several yelled out "nay!" and escaped. It didn't help that the newspapers were full of stories describing what a dreadful place the Red River Territory was. "Fit only for Eskimos in the winter and black men in the summer" was how one esteemed journal put it.[7] The HBC's claim that the Nor'Westers bribed the reporters into writing these accounts was nonsense. Nevertheless, the propaganda obviously put many off, because *engagés* ran away even before they reached the ship. Another bunch deserted when they got a taste of Governor Miles Macdonell's vile temper. Finally, the governor was so upset at the disappearing recruits that he ordered the captain to sail off, leaving a much-needed pile of equipment and supplies on the dock.

It was a terrible voyage with fierce westerly winds blowing all the time; it turned out to be a long journey, indeed some people say the longest in history. Governor Macdonell planned to use the time on board to whip his settlers into shape, training them how to use a musket and other useful skills. Unfortunately, one by one they were felled by horrible seasickness.

While the colonists' *Edward and Ann* was a creaky old vessel with rotten ropes inhabited by rats, the ships sailing with them, the Hudson's Bay Company's *Prince of Wales* and the *Eddystone* were trim, modern vessels. The crew and passengers aboard these ships were seasoned servants of the HBC and used to winter storms galloping down from the north. The captain of the *Edward and Ann* had never seen an iceberg before. Intent on disparaging the "ridiculous mud-diggers," the HBC people went out of their way to be miserable to the settlers.

When the colonists finally arrived at York Factory, it was so late in the season that ice had already formed on the rivers and lakes. There was no question that they would have to remain there for the winter.

In the meantime, the Lagimodières had joined a small but thriving community already situated in the Red River Valley.* Many French-Canadian and Métis freemen and their families had moved from Pembina and settled south of The Forks. Baptiste Roy, an old friend of the Lagimodières, had moved there in 1804. He later stated, "I have cultivated a piece of ground of my own . . . My house was about 40 paces distant from the opposite shore and the NW fort . . . I used to sell the produce to the gentlemen of the NWC or the HBC."[8]

Among their many employments, the freemen cultivated gardens and sold the surplus to the fur traders. They obtained seed for prairie vegetables – wild onions, turnips, tomatoes –from the Mandan Indians, and seeds for growing potatoes, cabbage, and carrots from trading post's gardens. Father Charles Bourke, a priest who had accompanied the Selkirk colonists to York Factory, met several Canadian freemen there, and quizzed them about the land's agricultural potential. In his journal entry of July 3, 1812, he paints a picture of The Forks as a virtual Garden of Eden:

---

* Historians have always insisted that the Selkirk settlers established the first agricultural settlement in the Red River Valley. This simply illustrates a long-standing bias against Canada's First Nations peoples. Buffalo hunters were simply not supposed to be able to use a hoe.

A robust strong man about 50 [had] remained there for 25 years.* I stuck close to this Canadian, as he satisfied my curiosity in every point of view – he was a simple, honest, well-behaved man, had all the appearance of steadiness – and a good sense about him . . . He said that land was incomparably fertile in the production of potatoes and all sorts of vegetables, without the exception of any, that the rice was growing wild there, and that when it is ripe there, those that know the good of it, gather their annual provisions, there is not in fact in this world any that could or will produce better grain . . . they make their own suggar there, the country tea, they gather in the season; they make their own soap, and provisions of all sorts abound there. Buffalo, deer; fish of every kind and the feathered creation, multiplied about to infinity. I ate some of the suggar he brought with him made by the Indians, as good as any west Indian suggar; the soap they brought was far preferable to the factory soap from Europe.[9]

Bourke also tasted Red River potatoes and declared they were as good as any he had eaten at home – quite a compliment from an Irishman.

Twenty kilometres south of Fort Gibraltar (at present-day St. Charles) Jean-Baptiste built the family's first home. A makeshift affair – a one-room shack without windows, measuring fifteen square metres, with a crude fireplace and chimney on one wall – it was smaller and dingier than the cell they occupied at Edmonton House. Marie-Anne kept it clean as best she could, sweeping the

---

* Bourke did not mention the name of this individual but he was probably one of three freemen who were at York Factory at the time. These were Bottineau, Peltier, and J.B. Roy, all men whom Jean-Baptiste Lagimodière would have known well from his previous times at Pembina.

floor with her straw broom until the packed dirt actually shone, but it must have been a frustrating job. There was one bright light. The Bellegardes, with whom they had travelled to Edmonton House, lived next door. They had two boys still at home, and nearby were their eldest son, his wife, and two daughters.[10] The two families relied heavily on each other.

Few of the freemen remained in The Forks district for the winter. Their main occupation was still supplying the trading posts with pemmican and other bison products. Since Pembina was located closest to the buffalo migration routes, everyone moved there.

The junction of the Pembina and Red rivers looks much as it had when the Lagimodières left almost four years earlier. The two trading posts were still there – the HBC's Fort Pembina (a third structure, Fort Daer, would soon be built to accommodate the settlers) was located on the east side of the river, and the North West Company's Fort Henry, named after Jean-Baptiste's old bugbear, Alexander Henry, was situated on the west side. A community of Métis and freeman buffalo hunters and their families was gathered around each post. The Lagimodières knew most of these people, and many hearty greetings were called out when they arrived. Yet something different was in the air. The intense individualism was still there, but in some mysterious way the community had solidified.

What was germinating was the notion of a nation of people rooted in the intermarriage of French fur traders and native women, distinct and vibrant, who called themselves "Bois-Brûlés" and the "New Nation." (They eventually became known as Métis.) Historian Fred J. Shore writes:

> The Métis in Rupert's Land were the product of a social system devised by themselves from the materials at hand [furs, buffalo, horses]. Their basic unit was the extended family with its wide circle

of social, economic and political resources. While some of the families chose to remain close to the Aboriginal way of life, others engaged in practices similar to those of Europeans. The glue that held them together was their culture . . . The Métis were also fierce individualists who saw personal honour and freedom as the ultimate expression of existence . . . In all aspects of Métis life the ability to adapt and redesign for their own purposes became a hallmark of the people.[11]

Lord Selkirk had nothing but contempt for these people. He described them as "Canadians, mixed with the bastard sons of others, who have thrown off the restraints of regular society, & cohabiting with Indian squaws have formed a combination of the vices of civilized & savage life."[12] He would pay no heed to their claim to the land on which they had roamed for decades. The result, predictably, was tragedy.

During the winter of 1811–12, Selkirk's project was practically the only topic of conversation around the home fires at night; every aspect was analyzed, dissected, debated. Many thought that the idea of a farming community was nonsense. The only intention of establishing the settlement, they believed, was to interfere with the Nor'Westers' food supplies and starve their people in the interior. That way the HBC would have the entire fur trade to itself. The whole scheme made sense, they pointed out, when you realized that Lord Selkirk owned most of the HBC's shares. They also resented that Selkirk had never picked up a pitchfork or a hoe, never dirtied his hands at farming work; he had once spent a month or so working land on his family's estate at Baldoon, but that, they felt, didn't count. Many were deeply cynical. Why would anyone want to bring all those lost souls to no man's land – and at his own expense, too? Why didn't he do something for them in

Scotland or Ireland? Pay the rent owning on the land their families had been tilling for hundreds of years, for example. And they had heard that many a poor Scot and Irishman wished that the Earl of Selkirk would mind his own business. Twenty and counting, that was the number of dead from the foolish dream he concocted on the St. Clair River in Upper Canada.

But others, including Jean-Baptiste Lagimodière, thought that Selkirk should be given more credit. He had spent thousands of pounds of his own money coming to the aid of poor crofters who been driven out of their homes in the Highlands, their lands given over to sheep farms and deer parks. Surely his altruism should be appreciated.

Mostly it was the older men among the freemen who supported Selkirk's settlement, but they were very much in the minority. In a short time it became all too obvious that the buffalo hunters and the settlers, particularly their leader, would never see eye to eye. An oft-repeated saying displays their cynicism:

> When the plowshare disturbs the soil
> The beaver and the mink desert the streams.
> The deer flee.
> The wolf and fox are exterminated.
> Even the hardy muskrat can barely survive
> When the plough bites into the earth.[13]

In late spring the Lagimodières returned to their cabin at Red River. Just in time. Marie-Anne gave birth to her fourth child. He was baptized Benjamin, and unlike his brother and sisters he received no exotic nickname, an indication perhaps that the Lagimodières are already settling into a more stable life.

On August 29, almost a year after they were expected, the first band of settlers arrived at Fort Daer. Everyone was on hand to greet them and everyone was shocked at how thin they were, like cadavers, and how poor. Their leader, Miles Macdonell, called out the men's names – "Colin Campbell, County Argyll; John McKay, County Ross; Nichol Harper, Orkney; Martin Jordan, County Ayrshire . . ." – until all seventeen were introduced. Hugh Heney, the HBC's chief factor at Pembina, pronounced a few words of welcome, although it was obvious that he wasn't overjoyed at having all these extra mouths to feed. Several of the settlers gave nice little speeches of thanks but their brogue was so heavy that the French speakers in the crowd understood not a word. Nevertheless, over the next week, piece by piece, their terrible story unfolded.

Once the colonists arrived at York Factory, the HBC employees made no secret of their contempt, calling them *va-nu-pieds*, ragged fellows. There was no room for them, so the gates of York Factory were slammed in their faces. They had to trek thirty-seven kilometres up the Nelson River until they reached Seal Island, where there was clean water and plenty of wood. A forty-metre bluff would provide protection from Artic winds. There they set to work making brushwood shacks for the winter. With all that fish to catch and Lord Selkirk's money to buy provisions with at York Factory, they thought that they'd dine, if not like kings, at least like the bourgeoisie. But the HBC contingent at York Factory refused to hand over the supplies, even for money, and once winter set in the only food the travellers had was dried venison. Everyone's mouth became sore: gums swelled and bled, teeth fell out. The worst thing about the scurvy was the crushing exhaustion. They could hardly lift their spoons, never mind an axe. Finally, a Dene trapper came by and showed the cook how to make a brew of distilled spruce gum and various leaves. Those who took it got better, those who refused it remained sick. One poor soul died.

But it wasn't the lack of food or the cold that made life hell. It was the constant quarrelling between the Highlanders and the Orkney settlers who snapped at each other like fox terriers after the same bone. According to the Glasgow men, the Orkneymen were slow and stupid. According to the Orkneymen, the Glasgow men were lazy shirkers. On and on – it never let up.

On New Year's Eve every man received the traditional pint of rum. Then it began – teasing, heckling, taunting until all hell broke loose. By the end of the dust-up, five Orkneymen were so badly beaten that they hung between life and death for weeks. One man lost his eye and three others their teeth. Macdonell tried to impose heavy discipline, but the crofters simply ignored him.

The ice didn't melt until the end of June; the colonists didn't leave for the south until July 7. At the beginning the journey was quite pleasant. The Hayes River meandered along; its banks were so low they could see the watery meadow stretching to the horizon. The flowers and birds were magnificent. Then suddenly the river tumbled into a channel hemmed in by stone cliffs rising to twelve metres. The awkward bateaux had to be pulled by line – the travellers spent most of two months thigh-deep in icy water. The muddy banks were so slippery that the men would fall a dozen times during one morning. The portages were terrible – narrow pathways wound along rocky cliffs. One poor fellow did take a tumble. The group couldn't stop long enough to fish up his body. Finally they reached The Forks, all looking as if they had suffered the wrath of God.

CHAPTER TWELVE

—

SEPTEMBER 1812: While the Union Jack and Red Ensign were slowly raised up a flagpole installed that very day, a flute whined a pageantry hymn. Then "God Save the King" was sung by the assembled motley crew – Métis, Indians, freemen, British and French fur traders, wives and children, including the Lagimodières' brood. The Hudson's Bay Company servants strutted out, wearing their fine lace and serge, swords stashed in their cummerbunds; one even wore a plumed hat. Finally, the most resplendently dressed man of all, Governor Miles MacDonell, strode forth, squared his shoulders, and glanced around his vast domain, like Napoleon surveying his victory at Rivoli. The clerk read the declaration, formally transferring the territory now known as Assiniboia, 300,000 square kilometres, from the governor and Company of Adventurers of England Trading into Hudson Bay to the Right Honourable Earl of Selkirk. HBC Factor Hugh Heney then roughly massaged the document into French, skipping more words than he translated. Everyone clapped, including three officers of the North West

Company who were on hand to pay respects. At last, seven swivel guns boomed into the afternoon. Loud hurrahs echoed and the Red River Settlement was officially christened.[1]

At a later reception , the men were served a glass of high wine, the women tea, and the children gooseberry juice with a good dollop of sugar. It might have been at this point that Miles MacDonell first spoke to Jean-Baptiste Lagimodière. He wanted to hire him and two other seasoned buffalo hunters at thirty pounds per annum to assist the colony families who were about to arrive.[2] Jean-Baptiste would have been glad of the offer. Not only was he a fan of the governor and everything he represented, but he needed the money. The attraction between these two men seems odd, because on the surface at least they were so unalike – Jean-Baptiste, gregarious and trusting, MacDonell, formal and domineering. The governor, with his wide, stern face and neatly trimmed moustache, was the epitome of the stiff-backed military man; Jean-Baptiste still smacked of the wild prairie. Yet Jean-Baptiste would remain loyal to MacDonell after everyone else had turned their backs on him.

If there is a perfect example of Lord Selkirk's notorious lack of judgment regarding the character of those he put in charge, Miles MacDonell, first governor of the Selkirk Settlement, was it. Nary an historian has found a kind word for him.

The MacDonell family emigrated from the Scottish Highlands to New York State a few years before the War of Independence flared. Monarchists to a man, they joined the Loyalists streaming into Upper Canada, finally settling in Stormont County. There they picked rocks until a farm of sorts emerged. Perhaps it was the hard work this entailed, but Miles decided he preferred the military life and eventually was named captain in the Royal Canadian Volunteers Regiment. When that outfit was disbanded in 1802, he returned to a farm he had earlier homesteaded near Cornwall, Ontario. Tenants had ground it into disrepair, but the captain soon had it shipshape.

During his visit to Canada in 1804, Lord Selkirk was taken to inspect this model enterprise and was so impressed that, when the job of first governor of Assiniboia came up, he hired MacDonell and gave him dictatorial powers: control of an area five times as large as Scotland with absolute authority over the inhabitants, from natives to the factors of the Hudson's Bay Company's various posts. Lord Selkirk described him as "a gentleman in manner and sentiments with just the right ambition and administrative ability," when he was considering him for the job.[3] That MacDonell was also arrogant, stubborn to the point of pigheadedness, elitist, and prejudiced against anyone without pure white skin did not trouble the earl one iota.

Those who defended the governor – Jean-Baptiste for one – understood what a terrible burden he had taken on. Just feeding the settlers through their first winter would be a daunting task.

MacDonell was eager to stake out the boundaries of the new colony, but nobody from the HBC had thought of providing him with transportation. Finally, Alexander Mcdonell, his brother-in-law, cousin, and a rising concern in the North West Company, then stationed at Fort Gibraltar, loaned him his own saddle horse and sent a freeman to guide him. (Whether this was Jean-Baptiste is not known.) For three days, MacDonell stumbled about in the bush until finally he discovered what he considered was the perfect spot on the west side of the Red, just where the river performs one of its agonizing loops, below the mouth of Assiniboia River and north of Fort Gibraltar. It was utter desolation – a fire had recently swept through, destroying everything in its wake, and only some weeds and brushwood had regrown. This was just what MacDonell had been looking for: it would not be so difficult for the settlers to clear the land.

The location was called Douglas Point, after the colony's bene-factor, and the fort to be constructed nearby would bear the same name. The neighbourhood was to be surveyed into narrow plots with three hundred metres of frontage on the Red River, and with the rear portion running perpendicular to the prairies.[4] The farms extended back three kilometres as freehold, and there was to be an additional three kilometres on the prairie to grow hay. Each family was to receive the deed to one of these forty-hectare farms, free of charge. The Lagimodières must have been reminded of their childhood in Maskinongé, where the farms were just as narrow. When the settlers arrived, many were disappointed at the way the plots had been laid out.

Once the location was decided, the advance core of colonists began working the land and planting some vegetables and winter wheat for the contingent that was soon to arrive. Unfortunately, it was too late in the season for a decent crop, and the potatoes either rotted or were eaten by animals. Nothing was being readied for the colonists and the local population wondered if the great aris-tocrat who had dreamed up this scheme had ever spent five minutes, never mind an entire night, in minus-thirty-five-degree temperatures with a blizzard blowing around his ears.

But Selkirk's supporters, Jean-Baptiste included, continued to mouth the prevailing logic: The earl could only do so much. The colonists shouldn't be pampered. They must take responsibility for their own survival and for their own health and happiness.

On October 27, the second contingent – 120 settlers, including women and children – arrived at Gibraltar Point. Their two-month voyage by sea was as miserable as that of the first lot, but for different reasons. Their ship, the *Robert Taylor*, was sound enough, and the weather held – there was hardly a storm during the crossing. But on board lurked a devil by the name of Owen Keveny. He was the leader of the expedition and, if the settlers' accounts are to be believed, a more cruel and mean-spirited man would be hard to imagine. For the least infraction of his rules, a man was made to "run the gauntlet"; that is, to stagger between two rows of fellow passengers armed with bats who would beat the unfortunate black and blue. One young fellow, Thomas Langdon, resented Keveny's dictatorship and wasn't afraid to say so. The passengers were being treated like so many criminals transported to a prison, he insisted. He had to run the gauntlet so many times that finally he and some others mutinied. They devised a plot to knock the governor unconscious, take over the ship, sail to an enemy port, sell everything aboard including Keveny's gold watch, and with the proceeds give the colonists a good time. But the plot was discovered. Langdon was clamped in irons and eventually forced to sail back to England when the *Robert Taylor* returned.[5]

Fortunately the colonists had arrived early enough so that they did not have to winter at York Factory. After a gruelling month-long journey by bateaux, they reached The Forks.

As etiquette demanded, Marie-Anne would have travelled the twenty kilometres from St. Charles to Douglas Point to greet them, Benjamin, snug in his papoose, tied to one side of her horse, and LeCyprès in her cradleboard to the other side. Reine sat on the saddle behind her mother, secured in a blanket tied around her waist. LaPrairie was parked in front of her. With her blonde hair braided down her back, her skin now weathered to a honey colour, her limbs sculpted into muscles, Marie-Anne must have seemed the epitome of healthy, vibrant womanhood, especially in contrast with the newly arrived colonists. They were pasty-faced, dirty, their hair matted, their clothes in tatters.

Nothing had been prepared for the new arrivals – no shelter, no equipment, no clothing, no warm bedding and, most seriously, no food. If it were not for the generosity of the North West Company, they might not have survived. As one of the traders at Fort Gibraltar wrote, "I pitied them [the settlers] much and, as they were suffering severely for want of provisions, I made application . . . to afford them such immediate assistance as our mean would allow. This was not withheld; Miles MacDonell was directed to send his people to our establishment, where they received an ample supply of such provisions as we had."[6] This included wheat, potatoes, live stock, even clothing. Interestingly, the Hudson's Bay Company, supposedly the settlers' ally, provided little.

If they were to survive the winter, the colonists had to move on to Fort Pembina, where hopefully the buffalo hunt would provide protein in the winter. The problem was that the bateaux they arrived in were too wide to navigate the Red River, and there was no other transportation. Carrying their goods and their babies on their backs, the settlers were forced to walk all the way – 112 kilometres through virgin prairie.

The Lagimodières also moved south for the winter– their little shack had been boarded up, their goods placed on a travois beside the buffalo-hide boxes where the two eldest children snuggled together. They met the main party just below the Sword River. Marie-Anne must have been shaken at the sight. The women and the children were exhausted, ill, many in tears.

The Saulteaux, who had been hired as guides by MacDonell, helped out as best they could, handing out food, water, warm clothing. The settlers' children were pulled up onto saddles, or found places on the travois, but the natives would not give up their horses and were deeply resented for this. The settlers couldn't understand why the "savages" rode like lords of the plain while "civilized" folk were forced to march along like ants. The Saulteaux insisted on receiving payment for their services, and the colonists had to hand over personal belongings – an antique gun that was used at the Battle of Culloden, a gold wedding ring, a family Bible.[7]

The days grew shorter and chillier as the ragtag army slowly marched southward. At night a huge fire was lit, and the travellers were able to warm themselves, but few wigwams or tents were available, so most slept in the open air. By the second week in October, snow covered the ground where they lay on thin blankets.

Finally, on October 27, the bedraggled settlers arrived at the Pembina River. Governor MacDonell had sent an advance guard to build yet another fort, this one called Daer, acknowledging Selkirk's minor title. A few buildings – a storehouse, a kitchen, MacDonell's quarters – were finished, but there was no shelter for the colonists. Some of the freemen suggested that wigwams made of buffalo hide would be just the thing, but the governor wouldn't hear of it. As far as he was concerned, they must build their own houses with their own hands, never mind that the only material was brushwood, which hardly made for a sturdy dwelling.[8]

The exhausted men attempted to construct shelter strong enough to withstand a prairie blizzard and minus-thirty-five-degree cold. As the pathetic little village of huts sprung up, Jean-Baptiste and the other freemen ran around with a hammer, square-headed nails, wood, and rawhide, patching up holes, preventing roofs from caving in, improvising fireplaces. There were no windows or doors, and stacks of hay were used to stuff the openings. One family almost suffocated to death from the smoke.

Marie-Anne was pregnant again and she would have liked to set up camp near the North West Company's Fort Henry where her friends from previous years had gathered, but Jean-Baptiste felt an obligation to Governor MacDonell. He insisted they remain with the colonists.

The winter of 1812–13 was unusually mild and calm, which should have been a blessing, but instead turned into a disaster. The warm weather encouraged the buffalo to remain in the north. As well, a forest fire had denuded the prairie and blocked their way. When herds were spotted, Jean-Baptiste and the other freemen rushed to kill as many as they could. The colonists' task was to haul the meat back to camp, a job that sometimes took three days. "The men lost, hungry cold, and miserable would burrow into the drifts for shelters. Occasionally to keep from starving, they would have to kill and eat their sledge dogs."[9] Alexander Mcdonell, the governor's cousin, reported:

> They were obliged to perform this duty destitute of all necessaries, much as snow-shoes, caps, mittens, leather or blanket coats, socks, kettles, fire-steel or flint; and it is a fact that cannot be denied, that some of these wretches, for want of the means of making a fire, have buried themselves in banks of snow to prevent their being frozen to death, and have often been forced to eat the raw meat off their sledges.[10]

Since they had no horses and few dogs, they carried the carcasses on their backs. They arrived in camp bloodied from head to foot, looking like ghouls sent by Lucifer. Still, they were not working fast enough. Wolves devoured the best parts of the bison before they would cart away the carcasses. Governor MacDonell called on the hated Owen Keveny to come up with the answer and he was happy to oblige.

His solution was to yoke the men to sleds and, instead of horses, and make them pull loads of meat. To each transport was assigned an overseer who drove the team on, freely using his whip on the backs of these human beasts of burden. "Owen Keveny's going to get his throat cut if he doesn't watch out," one colonist said.* "I don't know a man who's ever been as hated as much as he."[11]

By December conditions had become so desperate the settlers began to ignore both MacDonell and his prohibition against dealing with the North West Company. They streamed cross the frozen Red, returning with bundles of snowshoes, caps, mittens, blanket coats, socks, kettles, and flint to make fires, none of which Selkirk's agents had seen fit to supply.[12] And, of course, bags of pemmican. The North West Company gave them credit because they wanted to curry favour – part of a campaign to convince the colonists to move elsewhere.

The chief factor at the HBC post in Pembina had tried to help out and was furious at Governor MacDonell's total ineptitude in organizing the supplies. On January 12, 1813, he wrote, "I have strained my warehouse of every pound of meat, and made slaves of the hon. Compy's servants to draw provisions for him and his people, yet for all this, these two proceeding days the common people at Fort Daer have been fasting, owing to all Captain MacDonell's provisions being expended."[13]

On January 27 the immigrants' rations were cut by half, but somehow enough resources were found to hold a wake to which the Nor'Westers were invited. As Miles MacDonell wrote in his journal: "Today at 3 o'clock buried Mr. McLean's child, the Gentlemen of the three forts & all my people attend. Mrs. McLean is distressed."[14]

---

* Three years later Owen Keveny was murdered by Charles de Reinhard, who was an employee of the North West Company, and by a Métis called Mainville.

By February not a bison was seen anywhere. The entire populace was living on the small game they could snare and whitefish
that were pulled through the ice. The pemmican MacDonell had
bought from the freemen had all been used up.

The food shortage became so desperate that several families
were ordered to move out onto the plains and fend for themselves.
It will prove how self-sufficient you can be, the governor told
them, never mind that the women and children had never seen
snowshoes before, that equipment traditionally used to capture
their prey – bivouacs and pounds for example – were totally
unknown, or that, as a Nor'Wester said, "not a man among them
has shot a buffalo before."

On a cold and blustery day, the Campbell and McKewen families left the protection of Fort Daer with their belongings on their
backs and struggled along a prairie path that seemed to lead to
nowhere. Many of the freemen who watched them leave thought
the governor was insane. Didn't the stupid man understand they
would freeze to death in a couple of hours? Alexander Mcdonell
explained what happened next:

> As might be forseen, these miserable people had not proceeded far,
> before the women and children were overcome by the cold, and
> with difficulty reached a bluff of wood, not far distant, where,
> having been furnished with the means of making a fire by the
> Canadians, they encamped for the remaining part of the day and
> following night. Next morning they continued their journey,
> sinking up to their knees in snow, and as I was informed, cursing
> Lord Selkirk at every step.[15]

Macdonell did not make much of the help given by the freemen,
but apparently it saved the colonists' lives. They lit fires, melted

snow for drinking water, and hunted small game so the settlers didn't starve to death. Jean-Baptiste was in the vicinity at the time, and he could well have been one of the rescuers. The group finally reached the Pembina Mountains "half famished and nipped by the frost, where they remained till the latter end of the winter, and suffered many privations."[16]

During all this time Miles MacDonell was hardly sharing in the misery. His cousin Alexander went out of his way to invite the governor to share in the comforts of Fort Henry. He spent many days sitting in front of a roaring fire, drinking brandy, smoking a pipe, nibbling on sliced buffalo heart, and telling boring stories about his days in the Royal Canadian Volunteers. The colonists, his own employees, and the freemen all came to despise him – just what the Nor'Westers at Fort Henry were trying to accomplish.

Throughout the long winter, the freemen were not the only allies who helped the settlers to survive. The Saulteaux were "the only friends the colony ever had," according to one HBC boss.[17] Their attitude toward Europeans would remain diametrically opposite to that held by most of the Métis.

In the late 1700s, the Ojibwe had moved from the Great Lakes to the Red River region, following the westward expansion of the fur trade, in the process filling a vacuum that had been left by the near-extinction of the Cree and Assiniboine population, a result of the 1780–82 smallpox epidemic. The devastated Cree welcomed them, inviting them "to eat out of the same dish, to warm themselves at the same fire, and make common cause with them against their enemies the Sioux." "Your presence," they said, "will remove the cloud of sorrow that is in our minds."[18]

For the next two decades, the Western Ojibwe camped at The Forks during the summer, and set out for their hunting and trapping grounds in the forest in the winter. By 1800, however, several bands, known by this time as Saulteaux, were spending most of the year at Netley Creek, near the mouth of the Red River, between Portage la Prairie and Lake Manitoba, about fifty kilometres north of The Forks. It was an area rich in resources: one historian described it as having "large game in the river valley and plains; good stocks of beaver; productive fisheries in the river and lakes; and the considerable wetland resources – waterfowl, beaver, muskrat and plant foods [wild rice] – of the marshes at the mouth of the river."[19]

Even though they thrived in this environment, the Saulteaux lived in constant fear of Sioux attacks. This was one reason that right from the beginning they welcomed the Selkirk Settlement. Surely the Europeans would prove to be military allies and secure The Forks against their enemies. Also, there was a certain cachet, a sense of self-importance, in being considered vital to the interests of the British traders.

As well, the Saulteaux saw the colony as an opportunity to do business, a pleasant alternative to the fur companies, especially the traders at Fort Gibraltar. The Nor'Westers, aggressive and prone to chisel their customers, were loathed by many Indians. There had been many arguments, one reason why the Saulteaux were eager to align themselves with the HBC and the colonists.

Throughout the first years of the settlement, the Saulteaux provided the settlers with desperately needed provisions – wild rice, maple syrup, Indian corn, and, of course, meat. The settlers also hunted for buffalo, even though they weren't very experienced at it, had few horses, and mostly did the job by foot – fur trapping and gardening were their areas of expertise.

The wretched winter finally came to an end. Overnight, it seemed, the vast prairie was covered with a blanket of purple and pink flowers. The relieved colonists were eager to move back to

Point Douglas, where they could start breaking their fields, ploughing, and seeding as soon as possible. But until the harvest, the settlers remained in dire circumstances. As Alexander Ross, a long-time Red River resident wrote:

> Fish, as sometimes happens, was very scarce that season, as were roots and berries: so that their only dependence was on a harsh and tasteless wild parsnip, which grows spontaneously in the plains, and a kind of herbage or plant, equally wild and tasteless, called by our people *fat-hen*, a species of nettle; these, sometimes raw, sometimes boiled, they devoured without salt [as they had none.][20]

Marie-Anne wasn't able to travel back with the others. This pregnancy, her fifth in six years, was the most difficult she would endure. It was probably a breech birth, which often killed women during the nineteenth century. That there was no Catholic priest to deliver the last rites, should she succumb, must have upset her terribly, but fortunately she pulled through. The baby was a girl who was baptized Pauline. The near-calamity may have frightened the Lagimodières, for it would be six years before another baby arrived.

It wasn't until mid-June that Marie-Anne was strong enough to make the trip to the family's cabin at St. Charles. She had hoped that Jean-Baptiste would enlarge their one-room hut, or at least install a wood floor, but he was too busy helping the colonists. The work, after all, meant money in their pockets.

The settlers were supposed to be expert farmers, but as it turned out many were fishermen in their home countries and didn't know a spade from a plough. This didn't matter much; few farm implements had been provided anyway. They were expected to break the heavy prairie soil with only a hoe. The fields were finally cleared by burning the undergrowth, but the planting was too shallow and the ash damaged the growth. The main crop was supposed to be wheat, but half of the seeds brought from Scotland had been eaten by rats, and the other half were old and infertile. The livestock didn't fare much better; animals dropped dead, seemingly for no reason at all. On July 10, five merino sheep were killed by half-wild Indian dogs. This was the last of the herd, the two ewes and the ram having died the previous winter. The merinos had been an expensive luxury. Alexander Maclean, the one settler who was considered to be not of the peasant class, had insisted that Lord Selkirk purchase them. A pile of ploughs was left behind on the dock because there wasn't room for both them and the animals. The settlers deeply resented this foolishness, because not only did Lord Selkirk substitute sheep for ploughs, but he granted Maclean over four thousand hectares, a grand house, and a yearly allowance, all because the earl considered him more of a gentleman than the others.

The troubles continued. On July 12, the prize bull was executed; it had been unmanageable, goring anybody who got near it. Peter Fidler, an HBC surveyor, had paid the hefty sum of one hundred pounds for the beast. The herd had now shrunk to two cows and a heifer. On July 20, a flock of blackbirds arrived so thick that the settlers thought at first that it was an enormous black cloud. The birds were ravenous and ate everything in sight until the humans ran into the fields to shoo them away. On July 25, a huge swarm of grasshoppers descended. The peas, barley, corn, and wheat were stripped naked. All that was left were a few turnips and potatoes.[21]

By mid-August many of the settlers were sick, racked by fever and harsh chest coughs; forty-year-old John McIntyre and Jimmy Heron, age twelve, both succumbed to the illness.

It was not only drought, sickness, and hunger that plagued the colony. The antagonism between the North West Company and Selkirk's settlement was heating up in a most dangerous fashion. Colony Gardens, as the settlement's farm was ironically called, was situated directly on the supply highway of the North West Company. It was over this route that pemmican and other commodities moved inland from Fort William each fall. If they didn't get their supplies through they could starve to death. On the other hand, there were the colonists to think about. They had to eat, too.

In fact, both fur trading companies had valid arguments backing their claims to ownership of The Forks territory. If Selkirk could claim possession of Assiniboia by virtue of the Hudson's Bay Company's 1670 charter, the Nor'Westers could claim rights of access as successors to the early French fur traders and a fort that was built in the area in 1734.

At first Governor MacDonell went out of his way to mollify his critics, spending every opportunity talking and joking with the trappers and traders who crowded around Fort Henry when he was there enjoying the comforts of home. But this policy came to an end when he discovered that certain half-breeds refused to deliver buffalo meat even though it had already been paid for. (The hunters denied this.) Meanwhile, there was trouble brewing among the buffalo hunters. They resented the way Miles MacDonell flaunted his authority and were tired of arbitrary regulations being imposed on them.

In October, news arrived that another contingent of settlers had disembarked at York Factory. It was too late in the season to set out for Red River, but they would arrive next spring. Miles MacDonell was beside himself. The colony was threatened with hunger – how was he to feed another ninety souls?

On January 3, 1814, like Luther's ninety-five theses, the "Pemmican Proclamation" was nailed to the gates of Fort Gibraltar and other posts along the Saskatchewan. All provisions – meat, grain, vegetables – were embargoed for the year; the exporting of pemmican from Assiniboia by either the Hudson's Bay Company or the North West Company was prohibited without the permission of the governor. He might release some goods, but they had to be paid for at the customary HBC rates. If the Canadians, Métis, and Indians starved during the winter, that was their business.

The Nor'Westers and the Métis considered the proclamation to be an open declaration of hostilities. For one thing, they believed that MacDonell didn't have the authority to impose such outlandish laws. Interestingly, some years later William Coltman, who investigated the fur trade conflict for the British government, agreed with them. He pointed out that the appointment of Miles MacDonell had not been submitted to the Crown as was required by Parliament. Moreover, he had never taken an oath of office.[22] None of this swayed the governor, who continued to insist that it was his "indisputable duty to endeavour to secure to the British Empire this part of the Country."[23]

Thus began the Pemmican War, and the Lagimodières, all of them, would play a large part in this absurd drama.

CHAPTER THIRTEEN

—

THE RED RIVER SETTLEMENT was supposed to be the heart of a new society where not only immigrants from the British Isles would prosper, but where those who had retired from the fur trade, their native wives, and half-breed offspring would feel at home. Marie-Anne must have had doubts. Some of the settlers felt themselves superior to the Indians, the mixed bloods, and even French Canadians like herself. Yet they were utterly clueless about surviving in their new homeland; they would have lasted five minutes if left alone in the wilderness. And Governor Miles MacDonell echoed this arrogant attitude. The half-breed buffalo hunters he treated with haughty disdain. They later complained about MacDonell and his colonists that "no one would ask us in to take a Glass of Rum, or even to warm ourselves."[1] The governor had made it clear that he didn't give a fig about those who had lived in the territory for a century and a half. All that mattered were his settlers.

Still, Jean-Baptiste remained as enthusiastic as ever. So much so that he had quarrelled with the buffalo hunters under his supervision, and many were threatening to quit his team.[2] They couldn't see what seemed so simple to Jean-Baptiste, that the fur trade and the colony could not only co-exist but be of mutual benefit, the traders and buffalo hunters enjoying the vegetables grown at Red River, and the farmers appreciating the money they received for them.

At first Governor MacDonell's regulation prohibiting the exporting of foodstuffs from the Red River Settlement didn't mean much. It was winter and the water highways were iced over, so there would be little movement of supplies until the brigades set out in early summer. Meanwhile the colony had again moved to Fort Daer on the Pembina River, and the Lagimodières had gone with them. The move was a little easier this time around. While the buffalo were not exactly plentiful, the hunters were well organized to track bison herds within a couple of days' travel. And some of the settlers themselves had gained skill at killing the huge beasts.

And there were signs that the colony was starting to gel as a community. On December 18, the first wedding had taken place. John Cooper and Mary McKinnon were married at Fort Daer in a solemn ceremony. Everybody was there. "Two Salteau danced a reel after laying aside their Blankets &c and dressing themselves in clothes borrowed from our people."[3] For Christmas everyone was treated to potatoes, oatmeal, and a pint of liquor.

On New Year's Day, 1814, the Nor'Westers held a party at Fort Henry in honour of the colonists. It was a gay affair, with plenty of fiddles, grogs of wine, rabbit stew. Perhaps in response to his opponents' enticement, a day later MacDonell assembled the colonists at Fort Daer. They were made to stand while the entire Hudson's Bay Charter, the grant to the Earl of Selkirk, and MacDonell's commission as governor of the Territory, were tediously read out.[4]

Four days later the declaration prohibiting the movement of food-stuffs out of the colony was tacked to the fort's doors.

The battle for the settlers' allegiance continued. On February 15, a tea party lured them to the NWC fort. There was a roaring fire in the trading hall. Fancy dishes of cold tongue and beef and little bowls of mustard were laid out, Earl Grey tea was served in pretty cups. This was a far cry from the bleak environment at Fort Daer.[5]

Some of the freemen who supported the colonists could see through this hospitality. The Nor'Westers weren't just being friendly; they wanted to persuade the settlers to vacate the colony come spring.

In mid-March the tension was ratcheted up several notches. MacDonell's proclamation explicitly stated that all pemmican stored in the various forts throughout Assiniboia must be hauled to Fort Douglas and turned over to colonial authorities there. Most of the Hudson's Bay Company traders complied. The Nor'Westers paid no attention whatsoever. Colonist Alexander Maclean approached Governor MacDonell and offered his and other settlers' assistance in the event there was trouble, but MacDonell waved him aside. Don't worry, he said, the Nor'Westers' impertinence is "the last struggle of an expiring party and when once foiled in it they would never trouble us more."[6]

In May, as the ice melted, the pemmican that had been obtained from the Indians and Métis in places such as the North West Company's Fort Qu'Appelle and Fort La Souris and stored away began to move down the Assiniboine River, eventually swinging toward the Red. The foodstuffs were urgently needed because Nor'Westers, both traders and voyageurs, travelling south from the Athabasca region were always short of rations, and sometimes near starvation by the time they reached The Forks.

With the Nor'Westers continuing to thumb their noses at his regulations, Governor MacDonell was beside himself with frustration. When, on May 25, an informer disclosed that ninety-six *parflèches* of pemmican were stored at the North West Company's depot at White Horse Plains on the Assiniboine River, he decided that firm action was necessary. He designated his secretary, a taciturn, blunt Englishman named John Spencer, as sheriff, and four of the burliest colonists as police. Jean-Baptiste Lagimodière and several other freemen were assigned to help transport the meat back to Fort Douglas.[7] This was accomplished without incident, but soon it was revealed that a much larger stash of pemmican was stored at Fort La Souris near Turtle River, south of Pembina, and was about to be shipped eastward.

MacDonell's posse arrived at mid-morning on June 10. La Souris was a small fort but a sturdy one, surrounded by the usual palisade. The main gates were bolted shut. Sheriff Spencer yelled out. "We are here under the authority of Miles MacDonell, governor of Assiniboia. We demand you open up immediately." No answer. The men waited for several minutes. Not a stir. Finally, with the axes and picks they'd brought along, they loosened three of the posts in the palisade and entered the fort. They then pried loose the warehouse door and inside found 479 bags of pemmican, nearly four hundred kilograms of dried meat, and ninety-three kegs of fat. All of this was loaded in canoes by Jean-Baptiste and other freemen, and transported to the HBC's Brandon House, not far away. It was now clearer than ever to the Nor'Westers that the colony was simply an extension of the Hudson's Bay Company. The governor would act entirely with the British company's interests at heart.

What mystified the HBC intruders was that they knew the North West men were in Fort La Souris, hiding all the time. Why had they remained quiet? Why hadn't there been a blast of guns? To some, this silence indicated that the Nor'Westers were acquiescing and that MacDonell's rule was being accepted. Others were not so sure. The Nor'Westers and the half-breeds would surely think the escapade nothing but theft, and would be fighting mad. The latter supposition would prove all too correct.

Governor MacDonell felt more self-confident after this coup, but the euphoria didn't last long. A week later a contingent of Nor'Westers occupied Brandon House, where the pemmican captured at Fort La Souris had been stored, and arrested Joseph Howse, the Hudson's Bay Company chief factor in charge there. He was sent to Montreal to be tried for stealing their supplies.

In retaliation Governor MacDonell mounted a shiny brass cannon on the battlements of Fort Douglas. This was a show of force – any brigade carrying forbidden cargo could be blasted out of the river. But just three kilometres away, at the North West Company's Fort Gibraltar, the voyageurs, the Métis, and the Canadian traders were arriving on their annual trek from the west and the north. They vastly outnumbered any contingent, whether HBC servants or colonists, that MacDonell could muster.

Nonetheless, the Nor'Westers were in an awkward situation. Their supply route had been crippled by the Americans' disruption of shipments on the Great Lakes during the War of 1812. The British government had granted permission to the North West Company to send trade goods through Hudson Bay. The only way this would work, however, was with the agreement of the HBC. Realizing they were boxed in a corner, the Nor'Westers at Fort Gibraltar finally told Governor MacDonell that it was "necessary for the existence of your infant Colony that a perfect understanding & an intercourse of mutual good offices should exist between us & you."[8]

With a number of freemen and several Indians, their faces in war paint, standing by, ready to undertake "an attack well arranged,"[9] negotiations began. After a few days of parleying, a truce was signed on June 17.

MacDonell handed over 176 bags of the pemmican that had been taken from the North West Company's Fort La Souris. In return, the Nor'Westers agreed that in autumn they would send canoes to York Factory to bring back oatmeal for the settlers, and that they would provide 175 *parflèches* of pemmican to the colony the following winter. The agreement saved face for all concerned, and a collective sigh or relief was heard throughout the Red River Valley. When the pemmican from the Fort La Souris theft was returned, the *parflèches* were immediately loaded onto the backs of voyageurs, who scrambled down the hill from Fort Douglas to the canoes anxiously waiting to take off up the Red River.[10]

In late June the third contingent of Selkirk settlers finally arrived, forty newcomers mostly from the Scottish parishes of Clyne and Kildonan in Sutherlandshire. Predictably, the voyage had been a nightmare. Only a few days after they left Stromness, "ship's fever" broke out. Almost everyone got sick with the horrible headache, high fever, and dysentery that typhus brings. One woman said she could find no words to describe the misery. All she remembered was the moaning that went on day and night, and searching her own body for signs of the red rash. Five settlers and two crew members died. The ship's physician, who was also the leader of the expedition, perished.[11]

The captain could hardly wait to get rid of his sick passengers, so once the *Prince of Wales* reached Hudson Bay, instead of heading for York Factory, it sailed straight across and landed at Prince of Wales Fort, at the mouth of the Churchill River. There was no one there to greet the passengers. All the supplies – and Governor

MacDonell – were waiting for them two hundred kilometres away at York Factory. No amount of pleading could change the captain's mind, and the poor people spent a horrible winter in little shacks at a place called Sloop Cove, twenty-five kilometres from the trading post. Their rations consisted of a little bit of oatmeal, dried partridge, and peas that were infested with worms.[12]

In early April, forty of the younger and stronger men and women set out on foot for York Factory. It was very cold, the only food was the odd partridge or hare the men shot. Not one had ever seen snowshoes before, never mind used them; cramps crippled their legs for the entire trip of over 150 kilometres. One woman gave birth en route – a cave of sorts was carved out of a snowbank, and there the baby arrived. In only two days the mother was up again carrying her newborn through the knee-high snow. Somehow they made it to York Factory, and from there they travelled by bateaux to Red River. That anyone lived to tell the tale was a miracle

When Marie-Anne met the travellers, she was shocked by their appearance: skeleton-like, with pinched, pasty faces, their clothes in ruins, like victims of a horrible war.

The settlers who remained behind at Sloop Cove arrived at Red River in midsummer. They had had an easier time – a ship had carried them from Fort Prince of Wales to York Factory, and their trip by boat to Fort Douglas had not been too strenuous. Eventually one of their party carved a wooden plaque with the names of those who had perished since leaving the old country: John Sutherland, 50 years; Christine Gunn, 50; Katherine Gunn, 20; Donald Stewart (age unknown); Donald Bannerman, 50; George McDonald, 48; William Sutherland, 19; Hugh McDonald, age unknown; Samuel Lamont, age unknown; Dr. P. Laserre, 36.

Toughened by their ordeal, they recovered quickly and got down to the task of farming. Each family received forty hectares on the west side of the Red, as well as guns, some tools, and a horse. They immediately planted a crop of potatoes.

Jean-Baptiste was still being paid to help the colonists settle in, so he had no time for the family home, although he had taken the time to clear a patch of land behind his cabin and turn the earth over. The vegetables, grain. and flowers that sprung up were amazingly abundant. And Marie-Anne was mobile again. A wagon, a modified Red River cart, had been rigged; it carried Reine, LaPrairie, and LeCyprès and was pulled by one of the horses the Lagimodières had bought off the Saulteaux. Marie-Anne rode Argent with two-year-old Benjamin behind her; Pauline was still young enough for a cradleboard, which was either mounted on her mother's back or dangled from the side of the horse. As she travelled, Marie-Anne must have marvelled at the thriving fields of turnips, wheat, barley, corn, and potatoes. The settlers' shacks were turning into homes; some even had flower boxes at the windows. It seemed Selkirk's prediction that farms could flourish in the Red River Valley was becoming a reality. She probably didn't realize that real trouble was brewing in paradise, that by next year the earl's dream would lie in ruins.

There were several fronts to the storm threatening the peace that summer. The first rumble occurred far away at Fort William, at the North West Company's annual rendezvous. The company was in trouble financially, mostly because its supply routes were so over-extended that the expense of running the operation had become unsustainable. The bosses were in a sour mood, and the Pemmican Truce at Red River was considered a particularly nasty insult, "the compromise of our honour."[13] Those who had played a role were severely castigated for being too soft in negotiations with the HBC. John Pritchard, who had allowed Sheriff Spencer to steal his pemmican without a fight at Fort La Souris, was publicly branded as a traitor. The Nor'Westers' collective pride had been so injured that a consensus was reached: nothing short of a complete downfall of the colony, by fair means or foul, would satisfy. The Nor'Westers must defend their rights to the interior at all costs.[14] The man they chose to lead the charge was a veteran of the fur trade wars, Duncan Cameron.

Cameron's background was similar to that of his opponent, Miles MacDonell. Born in Scotland, he had immigrated to New York State with his parents when he was nine years old. Seven years later, during the American Revolution, he joined the loyalist King's Royal Regiment of New York. But he was too much of an individualist to enjoy the military life. In 1785, he began his career in the Montreal fur trade, first for a small independent outfit, then for the North West Company, eventually becoming a partner. He had worked in posts throughout the west, quickly gaining a reputation for outsmarting HBC servants in the battle for pelts. Something of an explorer, he possessed exceptional knowledge of the fur trade routes.

The moment Cameron was put in charge of the Red River Department, he assembled all the *engagés* in Fort William's Great Hall. In the presence of the wintering partners, he made them swear an oath to obey every order he issued as their commander, even if it meant going to war.[15] Then Cameron left Fort William with two warrants signed by the magistrate for the arrest of Sheriff Spencer and Governor MacDonell.

Another provocation to violence came that summer in the form of two proclamations by the governor of Assiniboia back at Red River. The first was an announcement that all the North West Company forts in Selkirk's territory must be vacated at once. It was simply a legality. Lord Selkirk had to officially announce that these places were his property or the Nor'Westers might claim squatter's rights. He didn't mean to act on the order, at least not right away, but again he enraged the other side.

The second declaration, issued on July 21 and once again tacked on the gates of various trading posts, prohibited the running down of buffalo on horseback. It was intended to give the colonists who hunted on foot a fair chance at the bison against the swift and skilled Métis, who naturally reacted with outrage. Historian J. M. Bumsted describes the situation bluntly: "To further display a disdain for the friendship of the Métis was beyond folly."[16] Even those freemen, like Jean-Baptiste, who supported the governor were put off by his heavy-handedness. To them, it was like forbidding a carpenter from using his saw, or a butcher his knife.

Four days later, on July 25, Governor MacDonell left for his annual visit to York Factory. On the way he suffered a nervous breakdown. He suddenly seemed to realize that he was a failure. He told the magistrate William Hillier, "I am a villain – the colony will be ruined all by my fault."[17] Not only had he antagonized the Nor'Westers and their entourage, but he was fighting with the Hudson's Bay Company people at Fort Pembina, and his attempt to keep the financial accounts for the settlement was a disaster. He was in such a state that his guns were taken away in case he attempted suicide. It would take three months of rest at York Factory before he recuperated.[18]

Meanwhile, on August 30, the Nor'Wester superstar Duncan Cameron, arrived at Fort Gibraltar to take up his command. He appeared before the astonished crowd wearing a full-dress military uniform – a scarlet tunic with epaulettes, a plumed hat, and a sword swaying at his side. Alexander McDougall presented him as the Captain of the Voyageurs Corps, Commanding Officer of Red River.

That evening Captain Cameron pounced. Seven Nor'Westers, armed to the teeth, circled Sheriff Spencer's little farmhouse. When he came out to see what was going on, he was arrested, his hands were tied behind his back, and he was led away to be incarcerated at Fort Gibraltar. The next day, the Red River populace, probably including the Lagimodières, watched as the canoe holding the prisoner swept past them on the way to Fort William, where he would be tried for stealing pemmican at Fort La Souris.[19]

Unlike Miles MacDonell, Duncan Cameron knew the value of the mixed bloods; four half-breeds working as North West Company clerks were named as "captains of the Métis," a title indicating their persuasive influence on their companions. Among them was the well-educated, well-connected Cuthbert Grant.

Grant's father was a long-time employee and wintering partner with the North West Company, and his mother was a Métisse. Cuthbert was sent to Montreal for his schooling, and in 1810, when he was seventeen, he was employed as an apprentice clerk with the NWC. Two years later he was put in charge of a small trading post on the Qu'Appelle River, and in August of 1814 he was assigned to Fort Gibraltar. Some months later he would be given the title of captain-general of all the half-breeds, in which capacity he would participate in a truly great tragedy.

Grant spent a great deal of time with the buffalo hunters and their families, trying to convince them that the North West Company had more of a legal right to the Red River territory than Lord Selkirk or the HBC. His cause was greatly helped by MacDonell's regulation forbidding them to hunt buffalo on their horses. They were still seething over this threat to their livelihood.

Jean-Baptiste, while he may have sometimes disapproved of the governor's leadership, never swayed in his loyalty to Lord Selkirk and the Hudson's Bay Company. But by this time he must have become a little nervous. There was a new pride, a new spirit, a sense of cohesiveness in the air, which the Lagimodières must have realized could be a powerful force in opposition to the colony.

The term *Métis*, derived from the Spanish word *mestizo*, meaning "mixed blood," was being used more and more often by the half-breeds to describe themselves. Recently, under the tutelage of Nor'Westers, they had begun to understand what Lord Selkirk had in mind for the colony. He had already written that mixed-bloods and whites should live separately, and they understood perfectly who would get the inferior land in that arrangement. None of the colony's leaders seem to have even considered that the Métis, who had lived in the North West for many decades, could lay claim to the right of first occupancy, or that they thought of themselves as a distinct nation, or that they would forcibly defend their native land.

At York Factory, Miles MacDonell had managed to pull himself together and tear up the letter he had written requesting "your Lordship be not prevented by any delicacy to send a suitable person to take my place, as I find myself unequal to the task of reconciling so many different interests."[20] On October 19, he arrived back at Fort Douglas loaded down with provisions for the colonists. With these supplies on hand, the vegetables and grain harvested in the settlement, and the meat the buffalo hunters promised to supply, it was decided that the settlers need not move to Pembina for the winter. They would stay put on their farms at Red River, where they would be relentlessly wooed by the Nor'Westers.

If, during the previous winter, Fort Henry had been a welcome retreat for the settlers, Fort Gibraltar was even more so. Lavish buffets were held in the Great Hall – the fine china, glassware and silver service nicely laid out. Wine and rum were freely poured. Captain Duncan Cameron presided. He was a smooth talker, welcoming the colonists warmly, remembering their names and the names of their children, chatting with them in Gaelic. When one of the settlers, Hector McDonald, jokingly offered to give Cameron lessons on the bagpipes, the captain jumped at the chance, even though he knew it would be an ordeal. He listened to all the tales, all the griping, with genuine sympathy. And he never stopped talking about freehold land in Upper Canada, about how the climate was more temperate, and how life was so much easier there. The North West Company would be delighted to assist the colonists in moving thousands of kilometres away to this Promised Land. Under company letterhead, missives were sent offering each settler free transportation, a year of free provisions, and eighty hectares in York Township.

Meanwhile Governor MacDonell seemed not to have understood the effect Cameron's campaign was having; like Don Quixote, he saw the danger in faraway places, but never under his nose. In March, word arrived that the Sioux were on the warpath and that Fort Daer was in grave danger. The governor decided to go to the rescue and, with his retinue, galloped southward to take command. He would be absent from Red River for several months, during which time Duncan Cameron successfully laid his trap.

First, frightening rumours bubbled up that Indians were planning to massacre every white person in the Red River Valley (never mind that the Saulteaux were more loyal to Lord Selkirk than anyone). Then word spread that nobody would be able to leave the area unless the cannon at Fort Douglas could somehow be disposed of. It was too dangerous, said the Nor'Westers, to leave it there, because it could be mounted on the ramparts and aimed at a point on the Red River where all convoys had to pass.

On April 4, a horse-drawn sled drove into Fort Douglas with several armed Nor'Westers aboard. They pried open the door of the munitions warehouse, loaded the cannon and other field-pieces onto the sledge, and transported it all to Fort Gibraltar. The settlers were then invited inside to celebrate with a dram of the best rum.[21]

Over the next two months, the campaign to get rid of the Selkirk Settlement intensified. Métis buffalo hunters begin to congregate at their usual meeting place, Frog Plain, ten kilometres north of Douglas Point. Marie-Anne's nights must have been filled with dread as she listened to the drumming and Indian war chants, the pounding of horses' hooves, sporadic gunfire.

At Colony Gardens, fences were torn down, horses and cattle disappeared. One night, as the settlers met to discuss the situation, they were fired on. Two were wounded, not by the Métis but by their own guns, which exploded in their hands. The community was by now thoroughly intimidated.

Jean-Baptiste must have been very worried. All his old freemen friends, Pierre Chalifoux, Philip Boudier, Jean Grou, were now all on the side of the North West Company; the heavy hand of Governor MacDonell had seen to that. How would the Lagimodières protect themselves if fighting broke out?

The tension mounted. On June 5, the three-year contracts of the Irish who came to the settlement in 1812 as its first settlers expired. To a man they set out for Fort Gibraltar, to pledge their support to the North West Company.

Oblivious to the threat to his colony, Miles MacDonell remained at Fort Daer in Pembina. The few freeman left who were sympathetic to the colony, probably including Jean-Baptiste, decided to travel south to warn him about the defections. The governor did return to Red River, but after he realized how complex and dangerous the situation was, he went into hiding. For days nobody could find him. Finally he emerged, a defeated man.

On June 1, 1815, the governor and his party were making their way across the plains towards Fort Gibraltar when they spotted dust from horses galloping in the same direction. A company of Nor'Westers was about to intercept them. Duncan Cameron, dressed in his ridiculous military uniform, announced that he held a warrant, in the king's name, for the arrest of Governor MacDonell on charges pertaining to the theft of pemmican from Fort La Souris. There was no violence. MacDonell was already convinced that if he gave himself up, bloodshed would be avoided and the colony would survive. So he did as asked. He was arrested and brought to Fort Gibraltar, where he remained under guard.

At that point the situation became truly serious. Many of the settlers, including almost all the recently arrived Sutherlanders, decided to abandon the settlement. The Lagimodières were likely standing on the banks of the Red River with the other loyal freemen families watching as one flotilla after another filled with colonists and their personal effects skimmed past on their way to the east. Sitting beside an armed guard was a shamefaced Governor Miles MacDonell.

One hundred and forty settlers, including almost all the recent arrivals, left the Red River Settlement that day, although fifty-six brave souls remained behind. They were the tough ones who had already worked hard on their farms, put down their roots. But quickly those in command at Fort Gibraltar served notice that these people too must vacate their property. Snatching up the few goods they could manage, they hurried into a bateaux and headed north on the Red River for Lake Winnipeg and the HBC's Norway House.

Colony Gardens lay in ruins. Houses and barns had burned to the ground. Fields of wheat and barley were trampled. At Fort Gibraltar red-yellow flames engulfed the governor's house, and the twenty-odd other buildings painstakingly constructed that summer were burning. In the distance, the shouts and laughter of the Métis could be heard as they continued on their destructive way.

The Lagimodières must have been perplexed, and angry. Governor MacDonell, with his high-handed manner, his disdain of anyone with mixed blood, was certainly responsible for the debacle. But the Métis had turned out to be nothing more than puppets of the Nor'Westers. They had acted with cruelty and ignorance. The Saulteaux Indians, led by Chief Peguis, were the only admirable players – kind to settlers, fair to the half-breeds. Marie-Anne and Jean-Baptiste must have lamented the death of the colony. They may also have had an inkling that the battle was far from over.

CHAPTER FOURTEEN

—

THE SELKIRK SETTLEMENT DID SURVIVE. Those courageous or perhaps foolhardy thirty-one who refused to give up returned to start over again.*

After they were driven off their land, they had loaded themselves and their cattle and sheep into small boats and made their way along the Red River to the junction of the Jack River, near the HBC's Norway House, sixty-five kilometres from the north end of Lake Winnipeg. Later they admitted they probably wouldn't have made it without the help of the Saulteaux, who guided them, helped them make camp, comforted them in their distress, encouraged them. As one settler would later report:

We parted from these friendly natives on the border of Lake Winnipic. They took leave of us with a speech expressive of their

---

* Of the twenty-five others who fled Fort Douglas, some found work at York Factory, others returned to Britain and Scotland.

affection, and told us to recruit our force and return in strength, and that they would also collect their children, and when the young ducks rose from the waters [about the middle of August] they would meet us on the lake, and bring with them all the provisions they could procure.[1]

The Indians' support of the colony continued during the trying times ahead. During the summer of 1815, Chief Peguis was summoned to the Hudson's Bay Company's Fort Douglas and told that, because the land around The Forks belonged to the Ojibwe, only the Ojibwe could demand that the settlers leave. Would he try and persuade the other side to desist with their foolishness? Peguis approached the Métis, offering them a pipe and pleading for peace. The mixed bloods were not persuaded. They replied to the Saulteaux that the colonists "will reduce you to Slavery . . . [you must] assert your Rights and secure Liberty to yourselves and your children."[2] Peguis, however, remained utterly loyal to the settlers, helping them in anyway he could. In not too many years, he would come to regret this loyalty, at least to the HBC.

By the end of August, the colonists who had fled northward were back at The Forks, having been persuaded to return by a new player on the scene, Colin Robertson, a most seasoned and savvy fur trader.

Colin Robertson arrived at Red River two weeks after the destruction, and he approached Jean-Baptiste, now considered the leader of those freemen still loyal to the HBC, to find out what was happening. He also "arranged with Logomonier who has a few excellent horses to cart home the grain and hay."[3] The two men hit it off instantly. Robertson was a redhead, nearly two metres tall, and gregarious, with chipmunk cheeks, bright blue eyes, a very long nose that seemed always to be perpetually sniffing the air, and a broad, inquisitive smile.

In his first meeting with Robertson, Jean-Baptiste told him that the Nor'Westers had offered a substantial reward if he would help drive out the settlers.[4] He had flatly refused, and he was delighted that a man of Robertson's stature was there to get the colony started again. In fact, Robertson would turn out to be the only capable leader the settlement would enjoy – perhaps because Lord Selkirk had nothing to do with selecting him.

Colin Robertson was born in 1783 in Perth, Scotland, the son of a hand weaver. He apprenticed to the trade, decided the work was too tedious, and somehow found his way to New York City. There he was hired by a grocery store manager who understood that this young man was a natural salesman. By 1804 Robertson was working as a clerk for the North West Company in posts throughout the west. Chafing at the lack of promotion, he quit five years later, and set out to join the opposition. In London, he attempted to convince the Hudson's Bay Company Committee to abandon their "slow, jog-trot manner" and take aggressive action in the Athabasca country, where the opposition was doing so well. He told them that they would be able to break the Nor'Westers' monopoly by copying them, by recruiting experienced voyageurs in Montreal, strong men who knew Indian country, and paying them well.

This bold proposal frightened the shareholders, but by 1814 they realized the company must either expand or die. Robertson was given the go-ahead. He set out from Montreal along the St. Lawrence and Ottawa rivers, with sixteen canoes, 160 paddlers and three former Nor'Westers whom he had persuaded to join him, and who knew the intricacies of the fur trade well. Along the way they ran into the dispossessed Selkirk settlers travelling in the opposite direction, who told him that the colony had been decimated and that they were on their way to Upper Canada.

Robertson sent the trading brigade on to Athabasca, and directed them to seek out the colonists at Jack River and tell them that help was imminent. Then he set out for The Forks, arriving in July 1815 to see first-hand the devastation. Shortly afterwards he travelled himself to Norway House and persuaded the thirty-one remaining settlers to return to Red River.

The Lagimodières must have been amazed at how quickly Fort Douglas was rebuilt. The usual hodge-podge of warehouses, dormitories, and large trading store seemed to go up overnight, as did the residences, not only for Robertson who was now the acting chief factor for the Hudson's Bay Company in Red River, but also for the newly appointed governor of the Selkirk Settlement, who was due to arrive in a month or so. He would replace Miles MacDonell, who was still imprisoned at Fort William. And the farms were doing remarkably well, too. The trampled fields of wheat and barley had sprouted up again. The colonists quickly got busy rebuilding their houses and the barns for the horses, sheep, and cattle that had travelled with them.

The Saulteaux continued to forge close connections with the colony. Robertson described their arrival on October 13:

Peegus arrived this morning with his Band consisting of 65 men. When they doubled Point Douglas and were in sight of the Fort they fired a volley which we returned by a three pounder. We then hoisted our flag. Peeguis immediately returned the compliment by mounting his Colours at the end of his canoe, and then the whole Squadron came in sight consisting of nearly 150 canoes, including those of women and children. It had a wild but grand appearance – their bodies painted in various colours – their heads decorated, some with branches and others with feathers. Every time we fired the cannon the woods re-echoed with that wild whoop of joy, which they gave to denote the satisfaction they received.[5]

Colin Robertson wanted peace in the community and he planned to do everything he could to win over the hearts of the Métis and Indian populations. His motto had always been "when you are among wolves, howl!"[6] and he began his howling by paying extravagant sums for the pemmican, dried meat, grease, hides, and other provisions brought into the fort by the Indians and Métis.

Not only was Robertson handing out money for supplies, but the goods, newly arrived from York Factory were going for bargain rates. Many of the freemen's wives – surely Marie-Anne was one of them – rushed over and purchased Hudson's Bay point blankets of a creamy white with stripes of red, green, yellow and indigo; yards of colourful gingham; and any other item that was going for half-price.

It turned out that Robertson's strategy had two prongs: he would woo the Métis, yes, but he would be tough with the North West Company.

On the lovely afternoon of October 15, 1815, Duncan Cameron, still dressed in his scarlet military uniform, still insisting he was the captain of the Voyageur Corps, went out for a stroll. Suddenly Robertson and a gang of loyal freemen that probably included Jean-Baptiste Lagimodière galloped up and arrested Cameron on the spot. As Robertson wrote, "I then sent over Cameron with an escort to Gibraltar where he is to be prisoner all night."

The next day, the HBC loyalists took over Fort Gibraltar. Colin Robertson once again confronted Duncan Cameron, lecturing him until the Nor'Wester's cheeks turned scarlet, insisting that if he heard of one more violent incident involving Cameron's men and the settlers he would send him to London to be tried for his crimes. Cameron muttered something about how much trouble Robertson would be in if he made a false arrest. According to Robertson, Cameron began "ardently to solicit for his liberty. Really the Heroes of last spring cut a pitiful appearance. I was as much ashamed of their meanness in adversity as [I was] shocked at their former arrogance in prosperity."[7] The Nor'Westers promised to keep the peace, so the HBC delegation left the fort. Before Robertson left, he pinched the Nor'Westers once more: "Gentlemen, you know me of old! Should you fail in any of the points you have agreed to, rest assured that I will always have it in my power to remedy the Evil."[8]

The colonists were becoming more and more agitated. Having lived through the troubles of the previous summer, they doubted that Cameron would remain tame for long. And there was bound to be trouble among the half-breeds over Cameron's arrest.

On October 16, Jean-Baptiste told Marie-Anne that Colin Robertson was going to pay them a visit the next day. She did everything she could to make her modest home presentable. She swept the floor until the packed dirt shined, nailed up the Hudson's Bay blanket over the opening that separated the main room from the children's quarters, put some wildflowers in the one glass container she had, and scrubbed her offspring until they shone. When the huge man arrived, all she could offer him was a seat on a wobbly bench and tea in a cracked cup.

Robertson explained that he had come to ask Jean-Baptiste for a very big favour, a service that would help establish the stability they all craved. Lord Selkirk had arrived in Montreal with his family, and it was imperative that he know that the colony had been re-established. Jean-Baptiste was to carry that message to him. Admittedly this mission was very dangerous. Jean-Baptiste would have to walk for over 2,200 kilometres in the dead of winter through enemy territory – the Nor'Westers would be on the lookout, and who knew what they would do if they caught him. For his service he would be paid fifty pounds. Robertson would understand if Jean-Baptiste refused, but if he and Mme Lagimodière agreed, then he must leave as soon as possible.

Jean-Baptiste instantly asked what would become of his family in the months he would be away. Robertson reassured him that they would be provided for. Marie-Anne and the children would be lodged at Fort Douglas. And if Jean-Baptiste perished while performing his duties, Marie-Anne would receive an annuity of seven pounds for ten years.[9]

On the night of Jean-Baptiste's departure, LaPrairie, LeCyprès, Benjamin, and Reine, who was holding Pauline, lined up to kiss their father goodbye. If they were good children, obedient to their mother, he told them, he would bring back a present for each one. Soon Colin Robertson and a several settlers arrived to wish him luck, and to say *au revoir*. Then the Saulteaux guide and a Métis who worked for the HBC – both names have been lost to history – and Jean-Baptiste strapped on their snowshoes, shouldered their rifles and, pulling a well-loaded sledge, disappeared into the bush.

Marie-Anne and the children quickly settled into the HBC's Fort Douglas. It was not unlike the arrangement at Fort Edmonton. Their living quarters consisted of one small, cramped room, but they took their meals in the main mess, so there was plenty of company, and the children had the entire large square to play in.

The main topic of conversation revolved around the new governor. What was he like? Supposedly he was a capable man, with enormous energy, whom Lord Selkirk absolutely trusted. But his chief qualification seemed to be that he was the author of a series of travel books with sententious titles: *Walks and sketches at the Cape of Good Hope; to which is subjoined a journey from Cape Town to Blettenberg's Bay* and *Observations on a journey through Spain and Italy to Naples; and thence to Smyrna and Constantinople: comprising a description of the principal places in that route, and remarks on the present natural and political state of those countries.*

Governor Robert Semple finally arrived at Red River on November 3. As he wrote to Lord Selkirk, "The Colours were hoisted, the guns were fired, at night we laughed, and drank and danced and now the serious Calculations of the Colony Commence."[10] But many at the fort were disappointed. He was a slight man of thirty-nine, with scant hair and round, bulging eyes reminiscent of a bullfrog. It was obvious from the start that he was as haughty as Colin Robertson was down to earth. Rules fluttered down, forbidding Indians and half-breeds entrance to the fort after dark, limiting the places they could go during the times they were permitted entrance, trying to prohibit (without much success) contact between the native people and the fort's residents.

Just a few days after Semple arrived, a contingent of Métis loyal to the HBC appeared at Fort Douglas, offering their services in the event of any trouble. The governor condescendingly dismissed them. "Mr. Robertson seems certain as to their sincerity," he wrote, "but they want only rum and tobacco."[11] His true colours were further revealed when he refused to shake hands with Seraphim Lamar, one of the Métis leaders. "One mustn't fraternize with the enemy," he told a flabbergasted Colin Robertson.

Robertson asked if he hadn't been sent with a directive to strike peace, but the governor replied that he didn't need to parley with these people, as he was not only the governor of Assiniboia, but also the chief magistrate. They must obey the law like everyone else.

Eighty settlers had accompanied Governor Semple to Red River, and these people had to be accommodated. Since supplies were once again low, the tedious journey to Fort Daer at Pembina, where hopefully the buffalo would be plentiful, had to be undertaken once again. For the first time Marie-Anne didn't go with them. She and the children remained in the relative comfort of Fort Douglas, where wood, food, and water were readily supplied. The fort was eerily quiet but everyone could sense menace in the air.

All winter messengers travelled back and forth across the snowy plains bringing news to North West Company posts of Duncan Cameron's humiliation at the hands of Colin Robertson and the racist attitudes of Governor Semple. Scores of angry Métis had made their way from outposts at Moose Lake, English (Churchill) River, and Cumberland House, to congregate at Fort Qu'Appelle. The postmaster at the HBC fort there wrote a desperate letter to Robertson: "They [the Métis] have got two of the Captain's Cannon in their War house pointed to us to prevent us from working, they are determined on Killing us all . . . perhaps this will be the last letter you will have from us."[12]

Many of Métis gathered at Qu'Appelle were famous warriors, Peter Pangman and old François Deschamps, for example, the latter formerly a devoted servant of the HBC. The poet of the New Nation, Pierre Falcon, translated the heartfelt nationalism into song. A flag was devised – a red or blue ground with a white figure that looked like an 8 – the infinity sign – placed horizontally in the middle. Cuthbert Grant, who had been promoted to captain-general, addressed the assembled Métis several times. The lands of Assiniboia were owned by their Indian ancestors, he insisted, and no one, neither Governor Semple nor Lord Selkirk himself, had title to this precious soil. The colony must be destroyed. Alexander Mcdonell, cousin of Miles and the representative of the North West Company, urged them on, quoting

Cameron, who had said, "They [the HBC] will prevent you from hunting. They will starve your families."[13]

Governor Semple had gone on an inspection tour of the various Hudson's Bay Company posts located within his domain, so Colin Robertson had to act alone on information of the Métis insurgency he had received from the Saulteaux and others. He gathered together the HBC servants and the more robust settlers, and on March 17 marched into Fort Gibraltar. Duncan Cameron was taken prisoner, his hands chained behind his back. They rifled through his correspondence – paper flew like seagulls around the fort's office. Cameron kept yelling about what a "bloody embarrassment it is." An incriminating half-written letter was found on his desk urging the half-breeds to attack the colony. "I wish that some of your *Pilleurs* [looters] who are fond of mischief and plunder would come and pay a hostile visit to these sons of Gunpowder and riot, they might make a very good booty if they went cunningly to work."[14]

But something else other than the fomenting of a Métis revolt devastated Robertson. One of the documents outlined the tragedy of the Hudson's Bay Company's Athabasca brigade, which Robertson had organized and led as far as Red River. No fewer than sixteen of his men had starved to death. Adequate rations had not been provided, and the Nor'Westers were so angry about Selkirk's settlement and the dictates being handed down by its administrators that they refused to help them out.

Two days after the ransacking of Cameron's office, a crack dog team of the North West Express came jingling in through the Fort Gibraltar's gates. Robertson's men surrounded the couriers, pointed guns at their heads, and demanded that the post be handed over. The Nor'Westers were furious about the loss of the formerly sacrosanct mail.

On March 21, the colonists wintering at Pembina, emboldened by Robertson's actions at Fort Gibraltar, attacked the North West Company's Fort Henry and burned it to the ground. The few people there, mostly Métis, were taken prisoner and brought to Fort Douglas. Robertson was furious. He told the settlers that, unlike his stealing of the mail, which he claimed was legitimate, their action was totally unjustified. They had no legal right to destroy the North West Company's property. He was worried that half-breeds stationed at Pembina would now join Cuthbert Grant's forces at Fort Qu'Appelle.

After these events Marie-Anne became ever more anxious. Everyone knew that her husband had been sent with a message for Selkirk and she was therefore considered an enemy by the Métis. The fort offered protection only as long as the HBC was in possession of it, and now not only was there a threat from the North West Company, but the HBC brass were fighting among themselves.

The antagonism between Colin Robertson and Governor Semple was alarming everyone. It was apparent that the two men loathed each other. Not only were they complete opposites in character, but their strategies for dealing with the Nor'Westers and the Métis were very different. Robertson believed that decisive action was needed. After he arrested Duncan Cameron, he advised the governor to occupy Fort Gibraltar, confiscate all the weaponry, and burn the place to the ground. But Semple hesitated, frightened to provoke all-out conflict. He probably didn't realize that the Métis and freemen gathered at Fort Qu'Appelle were organized and ready for battle, and that Fort Gibraltar would serve as their stronghold.

In early May Captain-General Cuthbert Grant and his cavalry of half-breeds and Canadian freemen intercepted an HBC brigade of six canoes and twenty men on the Assiniboine River, travelling from Fort Qu'Appelle to The Forks. Peter Fidler reported that the attackers had "their faces all painted in the most horrid & terrific forms & dress like Indians and all armed with Guns, Pistols, Swords, & Spears, & several had Bows & Arrows; and made War-whoop or yell like the Natives in immediately attacking their Enemies."[15] The Métis took the leaders prisoners and seized six hundred bags of pemmican and twenty-two bales of furs. The HBC men were kept prisoners for a week, and before they were freed they were made to sign a declaration pledging that they would not bear arms against the NWC.

A few days later, Grant and his men occupied the HBC's Brandon House, on the Assiniboine River, two hundred kilometres west of Fort Gibraltar. Peter Fidler again described what happened: "A little after noon about 48 Canadians, half-Breeds, & Indians, mostly half-Breeds appeared in the plain all on horse back with the Half-Breeds flag flying, this little army marched in regular order in an oblong square; one was near the middle beating an Indian drum & accompanying it with an Indian Song, the greater part of the rest bearing Chorus."[16] Grant's party then ransacked Brandon House; rum, ammunition, tobacco, calico, and beads flew everywhere. Singing, dancing, and drinking continued for a week. The HBC people fled to the prairie, taking shelter in a Cree encampment.

When, on June 9, word of the melee reached Fort Gibraltar, Governor Semple was finally prodded into taking action. He ordered the Hudson's Bay Company's boats to block the North West Company brigades' access to Lake Winnipeg, but the Nor'Westers easily out-manoeuvred Semple's men, and continued on their voyage eastward to Fort William, thumbing their noses at Fort Douglas as they passed by.

Colin Robertson watched the conflict with growing unease. There was an armed force wearing war paint on its way and the governor was doing nothing to stop it, but the last straw for Robertson came when a settler threatened to shoot him in the head.

When the decision had been made to abandon the Red River Settlement the previous year, one of the colonists, John Bourke, the storekeeper at Fort Daer, had insisted his family stay put. But his wife had had enough and sailed off with the others to Upper Canada. Bourke, a thin, wiry man, had a terrible temper and an exaggerated understanding of his Highland mythology – boldness and warriorlike valour were necessary to achieve results, no matter how dishonourable the actions might be. He had been the leader of the posse who destroyed Fort Pembina and arrested the Nor'Westers. Colin Robertson reprimanded him, insisting that he had committed an unlawful act.

Bourke was infuriated. Why was it legitimate for Robertson to arrest their leader, Duncan Cameron, steal his letters, and threaten to burn down his fort while he, Bourke, was supposed to do nothing? Robertson pointed out that Duncan Cameron had been inciting violence. All Bourke had managed to do was to convince the half-breeds, who had remained neutral for months, to go over to the Nor'Westers' side. Bourke then pulled out his pistol and pointed it at Robertson, yelling at him to get out of his sight before he blasted his head off. When Semple returned from his tour, he refused to properly reprimand Bourke, and Colin Robertson decided right then he had had enough. It was time to leave Red River. He told the residents, most of whom pleaded for him to stay, that he no longer had any influence and that he couldn't prevent Semple from falling into his own trap.

The morning of June 11, Robertson left Red River for York Factory, taking his prisoner, Duncan Cameron, with him. That same day Governor Semple finally ordered the destruction of Fort Gibraltar. Every piece of useful wood was dismantled, carried to the river, and rafted downstream to Fort Douglas. Then a huge fireball exploded in the air as the remainder of the North West Company's premier fort was set ablaze. If anything was needed to further infuriate the Métis this was it. That night many freemen who, until that time had remained loyal to the HBC joined Cuthbert's force.

On the morning of June 16, an Indian (or possibly a Métis) named Moustache arrived at Fort Douglas, insisting that he had escaped from a half-breed camp situated at Portage La Prairie, seventy-two kilometres west. Their leader, none other than Alexander Mcdonell, had told him that the Nor'Westers intended to drive the settlers off this land, and if they resisted the prairies would be drenched with their blood. Mcdonell tried to persuade him to join them, but Moustache had refused.

At that point Chief Peguis rushed to Fort Douglas and offered the services of his warriors. Governor Semple responded bluntly by thanking him for the offer of assistance, and telling him that it wouldn't be necessary. The colonists had organized themselves into a fine fighting force and, of course, he was the chief magistrate with the rule of the law on his side. The next day Peguis returned again, begging Semple for ammunition to defend the colony in case of attack. Again Governor Semple rebuffed him.

That evening many of the settlers moved from their farms into Fort Douglas. There were now over one hundred people crowded into the garrison, including Marie-Anne and her five children.

A heavy silence hung over the fort during the next two days. No preparations for their defence were in the works, no plan of action had been devised. Everybody was nervous except, it seemed, Governor Semple. He wandered about as nonchalant and haughty as ever. He still didn't believe that the half-breeds would go against his word, especially when he explained to them that he was the sheriff. He planned to read them a document to that effect, when he got the chance.

On June 19, Cuthbert Grant and sixty men and boys set off down the Assiniboine River; they had been assigned to deliver provisions to a North West Company contingent at Lake Winnipeg. After several hours, they arrived at Catfish Creek, five kilometres from The Forks. There they anchored their canoes and transferred their pemmican to two Red River carts previously brought overland by men on horseback. After holding a council, they split in two groups and started off in a northwesterly direction across the prairie. They were supposed to be heading toward Frog Plain, where they had arranged to meet North West Company canoes at the mouth of the Red River, but they lost their bearings and wandered closer to Fort Douglas than they had planned to.

In late afternoon, a boy standing guard on the fort's palisade shouted out that he had spotted a line of riders coming from the west. He guessed there were about thirty-five, although in reality there was double that number. People spilled out of the various doorways, including Governor Semple, who climbed up the palisade and took the telescope from the boy. He yelled out that a large contingent of half-breeds and some Indians dressed in feathers and war paint were approaching. Some of the women began to cry. Marie-Anne gathered her children together and told them they must carefully follow any instructions she would give in the coming hours.

Governor Semple made a plea for volunteers, and almost every able-bodied man and boy responded. Twenty-one were chosen. No instructions were given concerning arms or ammunition; some grabbed a few rounds, a few had bayonets. John Bourke asked Semple if they shouldn't take the three-pounder cannon, but the governor said no, they didn't want to look as though they were at war.

The little troop straggled out the front gate. With the others Marie-Anne ran to the top of the palisade to watch the tragedy unfold.

A short distance from the fort, Semple's army formed into a single column and marched down Settlement Road. Ten minutes later, a sharp crack rang out; a gun had accidentally gone off. Those gathered on the palisade could see Governor Semple scolding the man responsible.

The Métis, having stopped at a grove of oak and willow trees known as Seven Oaks, were waiting on their horses. Some distance away Governor Semple and the settlers also came to a halt; suddenly one of his men turned and headed back to the fort. It had been decided that the three-pounder cannon would be needed after all.

The two groups stood still, facing each other. Then Semple and his men moved forward again. Suddenly the Métis pulled away; one group rode east toward the Red River, the other turned west into the open prairie. The colonists thought the half-breeds were retreating, but this was a tactic they often used in chasing buffalo – forming a crescent that enclosed their prey. Realizing what was happening, Semple's men retreated. They attempted to make a run for the fort, but one section of the crescent nudged them toward the river. Suddenly a lone half-breed, François Firmin Boucher, a long-time associate of Jean-Baptiste's, came forward, waving his arms.

"What do you want?" Boucher called out to Semple.

"What do you want, half-breed?" the governor demanded.

"We're carrying supplies for the brigades coming from Upper Canada. You are a damned rascal if you try to stop us."

"Scoundrel, do you dare talk to me in such a manner?" With that Semple grabbed Boucher's gun while catching hold of the reins of his horse. Then one of the governor's men (it was never ascertained who) shot off his musket. In retaliation the Métis, every one a fine marksman, opened fire. Settlers fell to the ground like so many buffalo calves.

In a few moments the terrible din stopped, but it was a while before the Métis cavalry pulled away.

John Bourke had arrived back at Seven Oaks, pushing the cannon, just as the massacre was happening. As he turned to flee he was shot and severely wounded, but he made it back to the fort. The others were not so lucky. Twenty-one of Semple's party – twelve Scots, five Irish, three English, and one Dane – died that day. Batoche Letendre was the only Métis to perish. He was the son of a good friend of Jean-Baptiste Lagimodière, a freeman who did not approve of the Métis' tactics. Another half-breed, Joseph Trottier, was wounded.

Governor Semple was murdered in the massacre. There are several accounts of how he lost his life. The Lagimodières' friend, James Bird, blamed his death on François Deschamps, an old freeman:

> The last scene of Mr. Semple's life is known only from the accounts of Boucher and some of the other Half-breeds who say that as they approached him laying wounded on the field, he asked them to spare his life and while they stood yet undetermined, an old Canadian named François Deschamps went behind him and with more than savage cruelty blew out his brains.[17]

But Nor'Wester Archibald McLeod had another version:

The Governor begged for his life after he was wounded severely, which the half breeds granted and one of them stood by to protect him, but an Indian whose child had died in the winter and to whom the governor told on the plenitude of his confidence that he lost his child for his attachment to the NWC, told the governor, "today you must follow my child as you boasted it was medicine killed him," so saying shot him. Lord Selkirk has lost a great many men in the course of last winter and spring, no fewer than 58 have paid the great debt, 30 of whom starved to death.[18]

The next morning, efficiently and quietly, the Saulteaux began to dig graves and, as prayers were uttered by friends and relatives, the dead were buried. For Governor Semple a crude wooden coffin was constructed; the rest were wrapped in Indian blankets.

Marie-Anne knew every one of the deceased men. She was fond of their wives and children. They were honest, decent folk, wanting only to escape the poverty of their homelands. She expected grief to sweep over her, but she was overwhelmed by another emotion – terror. She knew the Métis would return. What would become of her five children? How could she, a woman alone, protect them? Where was her husband?

CHAPTER FIFTEEN

—

A MESSENGER ARRIVED. Marie-Anne and the children must steal out of Fort Douglas after dark and proceed down the steep hill to the dock. Waiting were three canoes: Saulteaux warriors occupied two, the third awaited the Lagimodières. The children carefully took their seats, but just as Marie-Anne was to embark, she suddenly blacked out. She fell forward, the canoe tipped over. The children screamed as they fell into the cold water. The Indians quickly grabbed them and helped their mother ashore. No harm was done.[1] Whether it was caused by the many nights of little or no sleep, the terrible slaughter she had witnessed on the battlefield, or simply her fright, Marie-Anne was nonetheless embarrassed by the incident. It was not like her to show such signs of weakness.

The Saulteaux were camped at Netley Creek at the mouth of Red River, about fifteen kilometres from Lake Winnipeg. It took three hours by canoe to get there. The Indians were nervous; the Métis were patrolling the riverbanks and who knew what might happen if the party was spotted. Fortunately they arrived safely.

Marie-Anne and the children had fled just in time. The day after the Seven Oaks incident, a message arrived from Cuthbert Grant. Fort Douglas must be vacated, all property left intact, the settlers must leave, or else they would all be murdered. Mere intimidation or a genuine threat? Nobody knew for sure, but after the carnage of the previous day, no chances were taken.

On June 20, a settlement was negotiated allowing the colonists safe passage out of the Red River Valley. Two days later, after a full inventory of all property on the premises, the fort was turned over to Grant. He formally signed a nine-page document: "Received on account of the North West Company, by me Cuthbert Grant Clerk to the North West Company, Acting for the North West Company" which indicated to everyone that it was the fur company and not the Métis who were the strategists and instigators of the coup.

On June 23, about one hundred people, and as much baggage as could be managed, were loaded into canoes, and the bewildered colonists set off once again for York Factory. If Marie-Anne had been among them, she would have had great difficulty finding Jean-Baptiste – she might never have seen him again. The night of their arrival at the Saulteaux camp, Marie-Anne and the children were shown to a small, cone-shaped wigwam covered with birchbark. On the floor sprigs of hemlock would have been laid, and on top were beds of rabbit and fox fur. The exhausted Lagimodières fell into a deep sleep.

In the morning Marie-Anne awakened to find, in the firepit, a cup of berry tea and a bucket of water to wash herself and the children. During her entire stay at the Saulteaux camp she was treated with dignity and kindness, on orders of Jean-Baptiste's remarkable friend, Chief Peguis.

Peguis was born in 1774 near Sault Ste. Marie. Originally his name was spelt Begwa-is (he-who-cuts-into-the-beaver-house), indicating that he was a skilful fur trapper. He moved to the Netley Creek area with his family when he was a young man, already famous for his oratory, charm, and ability to settle any dispute. He was a handsome man, even though part of his nose had been bitten off in a fight. He wore his hair in two long braids studded with brass jewellery, and when it was necessary to make an impression he sported a feathered war bonnet and a fringed buckskin tunic.

The Saulteaux village consisted of dozens of scattered lodges – 250 people lived there – dogs were everywhere and never stopped barking, kids ran around with little or no clothing, slabs of buffalo meat and whole fish hung on drying lines, skeletons of large animals were strung in trees as a sign of respect to the spirits, implements used in the hunt and the fishery were strewn about. The largest structure in the Saulteaux compound sat isolated in a clearing and consisted of a series of domes covered by cattail mats. This was the *midéwigamig*, the Grand Medicine Lodge, a very holy place where the ceremonies of the Midewiwin were celebrated. Most European eyes would have seen nothing but chaos, but Marie-Anne had been around buffalo camps long enough to detect the underlying organization. In fact, the Saulteaux were a prosperous nation.

White people referred to the place as Netley Creek, but the Saulteaux called it Death River. When they first arrived they had found one lodge after another filled with corpses – all had perished from smallpox. And yet it was a kind of Garden of Eden. Maples yielded plenty of sap every spring from which syrup and sugar were made. There was every kind of berry – raspberries, huckleberries, cranberries, bearberries. The river was full of sturgeon and other delicious fish. In the fall, wild rice was harvested in streams nearby. The marshes were home for many of the wildfowl that the

Saulteaux loved to eat. And there was still some muskrat and otter left that they trapped and traded at the forts for the white man's goods. And they farmed.

When the Saulteaux first arrived at Netley Creek, a band of Ottawa Indians were already there. These Ottawa were used to living in villages where they fished, grew corn, harvested rice. So when Alexander Henry gave them some corn seed, they knew what to do with it. They taught the Saulteaux how to plant corn, squash and potatoes, and how to harvest in the fall.

The North West Company traders thought that the Indians wouldn't bother trapping furs and trading them if they had enough food, and they began to harass the Saulteaux and Ottawa, riding into their camp and taunting them: "Who do you think you are – white men? You'll never be farmers. Stick to what you know – trapping." They tried to bribe them by giving them rum.

In 1810, while the Saulteaux and Ottawa were sleeping, war cries rang out in the surrounding woods. They ran for their guns, thinking that the Dakota Sioux were attacking, and they were surprised to find that the attackers were Blackfoot. The North West Company had paid them to come all that way from the west to teach the farming Indians a lesson. They were so drunk that the Saulteaux were able to defend their women and children, although three young warriors were killed. The Ottawa were not so lucky. Four families were wiped out and many braves died. They decided right then to leave the place. They moved to Plantation Island in Lake of the Woods, where they could follow their old-style ways in peace. The Saulteaux remained behind, trying to remember the agricultural practices the Ottawa had taught them.

At the time of Marie-Anne's visit, Peguis had four wives, three of whom were sisters. The oldest was Peguis's number one wife, whom he married very young and always loved dearly. The husbands of the other two had died during a Sioux attack many years before, and the chief had taken them in. But number four, the youngest, prettiest one, he chose for himself, During the meal that evening, she served everyone else – the guests, the four sisters, and the seven children – before she took a bite. All the wives had been ordered by Chief Peguis to be pleasant to Marie-Anne, and they were solicitous toward her. They probably asked her where her husband was, a question she never stopped asking herself: it had been almost eight months since Jean-Baptiste had taken off for Montreal, yet she had received no word from him.

After he had said goodbye to his family, Jean-Baptiste and his two guides made their way eastward, battling a truly ferocious winter. On Lake Superior, the ice broke and all three were thrown into the frigid water. The Saulteaux perished, but as biographer Z. M. Hamilton writes, "By almost superhuman effort [Jean-] Baptiste succeeded in saving [himself and] his Halfbreed. "[2]

The Nor'Westers knew of Jean-Baptiste's mission and badly wanted to capture him and his documents; he and his companions were constantly on the lookout for kidnappers. As they neared Fort William their provisions gave out; they were desperate for food. After they made a cold camp in the woods, not far from the North West Company post, a large fat dog came sniffing around. Jean-Baptiste killed it and the two men enjoyed a meal that night. Then, giving Fort William a wide berth, they pushed on eastward. The rigours of the trail were too much for the half-breed, and somewhere along the road Jean-Baptiste lost him."[3]

Finally on March 10, 1816, Jean-Baptiste arrived in Montreal and hurried directly to Lord Selkirk's residence. There is a colourful painting by Adam Sheriff Scott, shown often in Canadian rotogravures of the 1920s, that captures the drama of the encounter. A grand ball is underway at Selkirk's elegant home. The women are decked out in low-cut pastel-coloured gowns, The gentlemen are attired in formal evening wear or elegant military dress. Jean-Baptiste has just burst in. The servants have obviously tried to prevent the wild-looking woodsman from entering the ballroom: one has been harshly brushed aside and has fallen on his behind, another is trying to restrain the intruder without success. Jean-Baptiste is dressed pure native – antelope-skin leggings and coat, *l'Assomption* sash, a red cap. A heavy black beard makes him appear even more the barbarian. Lord Selkirk stands in the centre of the room looking alarmed and very effete, his beautiful wife at his side. Jean-Baptiste is about to hand him the leather sack containing the precious dispatches he has carried over two thousand kilometres. Although the scene is surely exaggerated, some rendition certainly occurred.

Selkirk had been in Lower Canada for some months. In September 1815, he and Lady Selkirk and their retinue had sailed from Liverpool to New York (among the mountain of baggage was a grand piano and harp). In New York he had learned about the destruction of the colony the previous June. This news had infuriated him, of course – "It is necessary that I should obtain justice for those who have thrown themselves on my protection,"[4] he pompously wrote – but it didn't exactly propel him into action. There followed a leisurely trip to Montreal in November, where the aristocratic couple threw themselves into a lively season of social engagements.

Lord Selkirk had written a letter to Sir Gordon Drummond, the lieutenant-governor of Lower Canada, asking that an armed force be sent to Red River. "It would surely be most disgraceful to the British government, if these lawless ruffians should be suffered to make open war upon their fellow subjects."[5] But Drummond always believed that this was a war between two feuding fur trading companies, and had declined to assist. With Jean-Baptiste Lagimodière's news of the resurrection of the colony, Selkirk decided to take matters into his own hands. He hired a small private army of four officers and seventy soldiers. This was a contingent of foreign mercenaries called de Meurons – Germans, French, Italians, and Swiss – who had fought for Britain during the Napoleonic Wars, and who had been brought to Canada during the War of 1812. On arriving at Red River, they were to be granted parcels of land for their service. (They were, however, old soldiers, not farmers, and few evolved into the model settlers envisaged by Lord Selkirk.) Selkirk and his army set out for Red River.

Before he left, Selkirk asked Jean-Baptiste Lagimodière to perform yet another dangerous, exhausting mission. He was to carry warrants for the arrest of the Métis ringleaders as well as other instructions back to Red River. Before he left Montreal, Jean-Baptiste indulged in a few weeks of rest and a shopping spree, buying clothes for himself and his family, and toys for the kids, probably with the fifty pounds he received for his services. Whether he returned to Maskinongé to visit his family and in-laws is not known, but probably he didn't have enough time.

By early April, he had set out again for Red River. He was advised to travel lightly until he reached York (present-day Toronto) in Upper Canada, where he would be outfitted for the trip west. According to the merchant who was to supply him, Alexander Wood, Jean-Baptiste had a hard time forcing himself to get on with his trip.[6] Wood kept urging him to leave, but he kept procrastinating; the taverns were so comfortable and inviting. He had always been gregarious, and with grog in his belly he couldn't help but brag to his fellow tipplers about his mission, how serious and important it was. Word soon reached North West Company officials.

Finally, he was on his way. For the next month and half, he trekked west without incident. But as he was passing the Nor'Westers' post at Fond du Lac (near the present-day city of Superior, Wisconsin), he and his travelling companions were ambushed by ten natives in the pay of the North West Company and taken at gunpoint to the Fond du Lac Fort where they was kept in irons in a storehouse for many weeks. Jean-Baptiste was regularly beaten. When they were finally released, they were stripped of everything they had – food, knives, guns and powder, tents, even personal belongings, capotes, *ceintures fléchées*, rum – and all the gifts that he had bought in Montreal for his family. With no provisions, they almost starved to death. Fortunately, a freeman named Pierre-Paul Lacroix found them at Rainy River and provided them with food and clothing.[7] The Nor'Westers, of course, had confiscated his leather pouch and had read Selkirk's documents with great interest.

Meanwhile, the warm summer days passed peaceably at the Saulteaux encampment at Netley Creek. Every morning fresh fish, duck, rice, and berries were brought to Marie-Anne's lodge. Her only tasks were to cook the meals, keep the bark house clean, and look after the children. The last would not have been much of a job. The three oldest bonded instantly with the Indian children, and were usually gone for the entire day. Marie-Anne caught sight of them every now and then, naked as little pigs, running in packs. Everyone in the camp looked after them. If there was trouble, a fight perhaps, it was the job of the adults close by to scold the children responsible. If a knee was scraped or a finger cut, someone applied a balm and gave a word of comfort. As for the two youngest – Benjamin was now four and Pauline three – the older girls vied to take care of them.

At the beginning of August, some voyageurs told Marie-Anne

that Jean-Baptiste had arrived in Montreal the previous March, that he had rested there for a month before heading for York – and that nobody had seen or heard of him since.

Meanwhile, two expeditions, under the auspices of Lord Selkirk, were on their way to Red River. The first, which consisted of potential settlers and livestock, was led by none other than former governor Miles MacDonell, who was still out on bail from charges filed against him in Lower Canada by the North West Company. Utterly mortified that he had given himself up so easily the previous year, he had volunteered to lead the group to Red River. Selkirk had agreed, primarily because MacDonell was still the governor, in name at least, of the colony, The other force consisted of the sixty demobbed de Meuron soldiers, well-armed and dressed in uniforms that would become shabbier as the journey proceeded. It would take both groups a long time to finally arrive at their destination – Fort Gibraltar.

Marie-Anne and the children moved back to their crude cabin in mid-October. Things had calmed down; she was no longer afraid of being attacked by the Métis and she didn't want to impose on Chief Peguis's hospitality any longer.

As the cold, dark winter closed in, her neighbours, particularly the Bellegardes, tried to assist her as much as they could. But everyone was busy hunting buffalo for food for their own children. Marie-Anne would have found herself chopping wood until her arms ached. The pemmican she had been able to buy and the bannock she made were barely enough to feed the children. One morning she found a huge sack of potatoes and squash on her doorstep, but she had no idea who'd left it there. By mid-December these supplies were used up and she was becoming desperate. After the New Year, she decided that she would have to somehow get to Pembina, where bison meat would be more easily obtained.

Despite her worries, she attempted to make Christmas special. At Netley Creek she had woven little reed dolls and horses that she coloured with plant dyes, and each of the children received one of these as a present. Luckily she spotted a rabbit near the shack, which she shot and made into a fine stew. The family were sitting around, for once feeling a lighthearted, laughing, when they heard a loud bang at the door. In walked Jean-Baptiste. He had many, many stories to tell them – but unfortunately no gifts.

On January 10, 1817, at six on a very cold morning, Lord Selkirk's men scaled the walls of Fort Gibraltar. They found almost no supplies and few people inside – everyone including Cuthbert Grant was out on the plains hunting buffalo. Nevertheless, the occupation established Selkirk's authority in Assiniboia.

Meanwhile Selkirk and his entourage were slowly winding their way to their destination. According to Chief Peguis, Selkirk was almost assassinated on the way.

> The year he [Lord Selkirk] came here, Cuthbert Grant, with 116 warriors, had assembled at White Horse Plans, intending to waylay him somewhere on the Red River. I no sooner heard of this than I went to Cuthbert Grant and told him, if he came out of the White-horse Plain where his warriors were assembled, I should meet him at Surgeon Creek with my entire tribe . . . and stand and fall between him and the Silver Chief [Selkirk]. This had the desired effect, and Mr. Grant did not make the attempt to harm the Silver Chief, who came as he went, in peace and safety.[8]

On June 21, 1817, to the salute of cannons and loud cheers, the "Silver Chief" finally made it to Red River. By this time he was showing signs of advanced tuberculosis, exultant one minute, depressed the next – and all the time coughing blood into his handkerchief. (He would die three years later from the disease in Pau, France.) Nonetheless, he remained in the settlement for three months, once again attempting to forge the utopia of his dreams. He drew up plans for bridges, roads, and churches, and promised a well-stocked store. This time, he was sure, the community would thrive.

A surveyor was set to work imposing order on the colony's physical contours, and soon about 150 of the settlers who had fled after Seven Oaks returned. Some of the mercenary soldiers who had come west with Selkirk's party stayed and built houses, thirty-one of them, on the settlement's first main road, German Street.

Eventually the community evolved into the shape of a cross, with the Red River forming the stem and the Assiniboine and little Seine, the arms. Scattered along its length were small villages, clusters of distinct religious and ethnic groups – Scots, English, Americans, Canadians, Germans, French, Métis – a society very much segregated by language and ancestry. St. Boniface, on the east side of the Red, became the heart of the French and Métis world. Here in 1833 an enormous and expensive project was undertaken, a cathedral built of stone, boasting two soaring twin towers from which three bells clanged all day. St. Boniface Cathedral would come to symbolize religious authority in the Canadian west and to dominate the lives of the Catholics in the Red River Settlement. It must have reminded the Lagimodières of the church of St. Joseph in Maskinongé.

The Lagimodières benefited from Lord Selkirk's largesse. As a token of his gratitude, he presented Jean-Baptiste with a fine ceremonial sword; for generations it was proudly displayed in the Lagimodière household. Ironically, this symbol of deference to authority was hung near the casket of grandson Louis Riel as he lay in state in the family home after he had been hanged for treason.

Of more immediate practical advantage was the grant of land bestowed on the Lagimodières. Wedged between the Red and Seine rivers, the triangular tract would eventually become prime Red River property.* Jean-Baptiste spent the winter of 1817–18 cutting logs. A comfortable house was built, with large windows, a real door, and a roof of thatch, the couple's first permanent house since their marriage eleven years earlier. During the summer the Lagimodières, all seven of them, moved in. Marie-Anne marked the occasion by planting a field of corn.

---

* In 1881, one of the Lagimodières' sons sold this land, and other parcels he had acquired in the area, for $100,000 – a fortune in those days.

EPILOGUE

—

AT FIRST THERE WAS GREAT OPTIMISM among the Red River people. On July 16, 1818, the first Catholic missionaries to take up permanent residence finally reached Red River. Marie-Anne would later tell her grandchildren that she cried for joy when Father Joseph Provencher and Father Sévère Dumoulin stepped from their canoe. Only days later, over one hundred Métis and Indian children were baptized. Because the priests considered Aboriginals to be unsuitable godparents, Marie-Anne served as godmother to them all. Only three of the Lagimodière children were baptized right away; Reine, now eleven, and LaPrairie, nine, had to be taught Catholic catechism first. No schools were built; the clergy felt that saving the souls of the *sauvages* was a greater priority. Although Marie-Anne was literate, none of her children learned to read and write, a situation that saddened her for her entire life.

The Saulteaux remained faithful to the settlement – they took to calling Selkirk "Father" – and, for an annual payment of " 100 pounds of goods and merchantable tobacco," they ceded three kilometres of land on either side of the Red River, from Pembina to the Great Forks, along the Assiniboine River as far as Muskrat Creek, and ten kilometres from Fort Douglas on every side. But according to Chief Peguis, the Saulteaux believed that was only the first installment:

> Those who have since held our lands, not only pay us only the same small quantity of ammunition and tobacco, which was first paid to us as a preliminary to a final bargain, but they now claim all the lands between the Assiniboin and the Lake Winipeg, a quantity of land nearly double of what was first asked from us. We hope our Great Mother [Queen Victoria] will not allow our lands to be taken from us in this way.[1]

By the late 1850s, the tribe would be nearly destitute; they blamed their sad situation on their once-close allies, the Hudson's Bay Company. "They pay us little for our furs, and when we are old are left to shift for ourselves. We could name many old men who have starved to death in sight of many of the Company's principal forts."[2]

But it wasn't only the Saulteaux who suffered. Like Job, the settlers faced many tribulations. For four consecutive summers, the grasshoppers arrived in clouds so thick the sky was black. Crops, gardens, every piece of greenery were destroyed by these ravenous insects within hours. In 1822, a decent amount of wheat was finally harvested, and there was more of the same the following two years. The colonists were suddenly more optimistic; Selkirk's dream was coming true. Then came the savage winter of 1824–25. A blizzard descended and lasted for days. One family, a husband, wife, and three children, were buried under a shelter of snow for five days without food or water before they were finally dug out. The woman and two of her children survived the ordeal, but the others perished. Another thirty-three people lost their lives. Corpses of horses and cattle littered the prairies. The buffalo mysteriously disappeared.

And that was only the beginning of that tragic year. In the spring came the great flood. By May 5, fifty houses along the riverbank, including the Lagimodières', were first battered by huge ice blocks and then swallowed by the surge; trees were torn up and cattle swept away. After all the years of danger and hardship, Marie-Anne finally gave up. She pleaded with Jean-Baptiste to join what was quickly becoming a mass exodus from the colony to Lower Canada – almost all the de Meurons had left that spring. He replied that if the priests were brave enough to stay – and they had made no sign of leaving – they too must screw up their courage and remain at Red River.

Eighteen twenty-five proved to be the nadir of the colony's miseries. The fall of 1828 produced a bumper crop, and after that, although hard times still now and then befell the settlement, the threat of starvation eased. During the 1830s, prosperity was in the air and the Lagimodière family was one of the most successful.

Jean-Baptiste continued to hunt buffalo and produce pemmican and, to a lesser degree, trap furs. Gradually, though, these activities were replaced by agriculture. By 1832 he had established his farm, with eleven hectares planted; by 1849 he was seeding thirty hectares, the largest farm in St. Boniface, the town that had sprung up on the land assigned by Lord Selkirk to Fathers Provencher and Dumoulin. And he kept one hundred head of cattle. He started a transportation business, and by 1843 owned forty Red River carts and oxen. And he ran a successful grist mill.

Marie-Anne gave birth to three more children, Roman in 1819; Julie, Louis Riel's mother, in 1822; and Joseph in 1825. At a time of high mortality rates, and despite the hardships they endured, all of the Lagimodière offspring lived to adulthood. All four sons, LaPairie (Jean-Baptiste Jr.), Benjamin, Roman, and Joseph joined their father in his various thriving businesses. Marie-Anne's greatest regret involved her beloved first child, Reine. She was married in 1824, at age sixteen, to a French-Canadian settler, Joseph Lamer. After the terrible flood of 1922, the Lamers and their two children fled to the United States. It would be forty-two years before mother and daughter would be reunited.

For all his life Jean-Baptiste would stay out of the politics that bubbled under the surface of the community, now and then erupting into conflict, mostly involving the Métis and the Hudson's Bay Company. There is no way of knowing what he thought of his famous revolutionary grandson Louis Riel, but it is probable that he wouldn't have approved. Jean-Baptiste Lagimodière died in 1850, at the age of seventy-four, but Marie-Anne lived to see her grandson's triumph. Louis was one of her favourite grandchildren, and she was still alive, when, at the age of twenty-four, he instigated the Red River Rebellion and led Manitoba into Confederation. (There is a strong movement today in favour of officially naming Louis Riel as a Father of Confederation.) She probably applauded him long and hard.

Marie-Anne Gaboury died in 1878, at the remarkable age of ninety-six. It was said she was healthy and wise right up until the end, spending hours mesmerizing her grandchildren with stories of the old west. They weren't fairy tales; she had lived them, each and every one.

BIBLIOGRAPHY

—

Archives and Manscripts

Hudson's Bay Company Archives:

Edmonton House Journals, 1808–1814

Edmonton House Account Books: 1808–1814.

Edmonton House Annual Report, 1816

Journal of the Red River Settlement, 1814–1815

Pembina Post Journal 1812–1813

Pembina Account Book, 1811–1812

Peter Fidler's list of free Canadians, 1814.

Select Committee on the Hudson's Bay Company, 1858

Library and Archives Canada

Alexander Mcdonell Papers

Miles MacDonell Papers

Selkirk Papers

Université de Montréal, Programme de recherches en démographie historique
  Parish records, baptisms, marriage and deaths, for Maskinongé
  and St-Antoine-sur-Richelieu

In Private Hands
  Clément Plante: The will of Father Ignace Prudent Vinet, June 8, 1818

Articles and Books

Amos, A. (ed.). *Report of the Trials in the Courts of Canada Relative to the Destruction of the Earl of Selkirk's Settlement of the Red River with Observations* (London, 1820).

Barron, F.L. "Victimizing His Lordship: Lord Selkirk and the Upper Canadian Courts," *Manitoba History*, 7, 1984.

Beaudoin, Marie-Louis. *Les premières et les filles du roi à Ville-Marie* (Montreal: Maison Saint-Gabriel, 1996).

Binnema, Theodore. *Common & Contested Ground: A Human and Environmental History of the Northwestern Plains* (Norman: University of Oklahoma Press, 2001).

——. "Old Swan, Big Man, and the Siksika Bands," *Canadian Historical Review*, 77, 1996.

Bishop, Charles A. *The Northern Ojibwa and the Fur Trade: An Historical and Ecological Study* (Toronto: Holt, Rinehart and Winston, 1974).

Black, Arthur. *Old Fort William* (Thunder Bay: Old Fort William Volunteer Association, 1985).

Blackfoot Gallery Committee. *Nitsitapiisinni: The Story of the Blackfoot People* (Toronto: Key Porter Books, 2001).

Brown, Jennifer S.H. "'A Colony of very Useful Hands'" *The Beaver*, 307(4), 1977.

Brown, Jennifer S.H. ——. *Strangers in Blood: Fur Trade Company Families in Indian Country* (Vancouver: University of British Columbia Press, 1980).

Bryce, George. *The Romantic Settlement of Lord Selkirk's Colonists* (Toronto: Musson, 1909).

Bumsted, J.M. *Fur Trade Wars: The Founding of Western Canada* (Winnipeg: Great Plains Publications, 1999).

——. "Lord Selkirk's Highland Regiment and the Kildonan Settlers," *The Beaver* 309(2), 1978.

——, ed. *The Collected Writing of Lord Selkirk 1810–1820*, (Winnipeg: Manitoba Record Society, 1987).

Burt, Alfred Leroy, *The Province of Old Quebec* (St. Paul: University of Minnesota Press, 1933).

Buteau, Hélène and Daniel Chevrier. *D'audace en mémoire: Le lieu dit Lachine, un regard archéologique* (Montreal: Collection in situ, 2001).

Campbell, Claire Elizabeth. *Shaped by the West Wind: Nature and History in Georgian Bay* (Vancouver: UBC Press, 2005).

Campbell, Marjorie Wilkins, *The North West Company* (Toronto: Macmillan, 1957).

Campbell, William A. *Northeastern Georgian Bay and Its People* (Subury: William A. Campbell, n.d.).

Campey, Lucille H. *The Silver Chief: Lord Selkirk and the Scottish Pioneers of Belfast, Baldoon and Red River* (Toronto: Natural Heritage Books, 2003).

Careless, J.M.S. *Canada A Story of Challenge* (Cambridge: Cambridge University Press, 1953).

Carlos, Ann M. and Frank D. Lewis. "Marketing in the Land of Hudson Bay: Indian Consumers and the Hudson's Bay Company, 1670–1770" *Enterprise & Society*, 3, June 2002.

Chalmers, J.W. *Red River Adventure: The Story of the Selkirk Settlers* (Toronto: Macmillan, 1956).

Christensen, Deanna, *Cumberland House Historic Park* (Regina: Department of Tourism and Renewable Resources, 1974).

The Clio Collective. *Quebec Women: A History*, trans. by Roger Gannon and Rosalind Gill (Toronto: Women's Press, 1987).

Coues, Elliott. *Manuscript Journals of Alexander Henry and David Thompson, 1799–1814* (Minneapolis: Ross & Haines, 1897).

Coutts, Robert. "The Forks of the Red and Assiniboine: A Thematic History, 1734–1850," Report #383 (Winnipeg: Parks Canada, n.d.).

Coutts, Robert and Richard Stuart, eds. *The Forks and the Battle of Seven Oaks in Manitoba History* (Winnipeg: Manitoba Historical Society, 1994).

Jennifer S.H. Brown. "Commentary"

J.M. Bumsted. "Lord Selkirk and His Agents"

Joe Martin. "Conflict at Red River: Collision at Seven Oaks"

Laura Peers. "The Ojibwa, Red River and the Forks, 1770–1870"

Fred J. Shore. "The Origins of Métis Nationalism and the Pemmican Wars, 1780–1821"

Danziger, Edmund Jefferson, Jr. *The Chippewas of Lake Superior* (Oklahoma: University of Oklahoma Press, 1979).

Dick, Lyle. "The Seven Oaks Incident and the Construction of a Historical Tradition, 1816 to 1970," *Journal of the Canadian Historical Association*, 2, 1978.

Dickinson, John A. and Brian Young. *A Short History of Quebec* (Montreal: McGill University Press, 2003).

Duckworth, Harry W. "The Last Coureurs de Bois," *The Beaver,* 314(4), Spring 1984.

Dugast, Georges. *The First Canadian Woman in the Northwest or the Story of Marie Anne Gaboury, Wife of John Baptiste Lajimoniere, Who arrived in the Northwest in 1807, and Died at St. Boniface at the Age of 96 Years* (Winnipeg: The Manitoba Free Press Company, 1902).

Epstein, Clarence. "The Quebec that Never Was" *The Beaver,* December 1, 1996.

Fleming, Patricia Lockhart. "Cultural Crossroads: Print and Reading in Eighteenth- and Nineteenth-Century English-Speaking Montreal," *American Antiquarian Society*, 112, 2002.

Foster, John E. "Wintering: the Outsider Adult Male and the Ethnogenesis of the Western Plain," *Prairie Forum*, 19(1), 1994.

Friesen, Gerald. *The Canadian Prairies: A History* (Toronto: University of Toronto Press, 1987).

Germain, Georges-Hébert. *Adventurers in the New World: The Saga of the Coureurs des Bois* (Hull: Canadian Museum of Civilization, 2003).

Giraud, Marcel. *The Métis in the Canadian West*, 2 vols., trans. George Woodcock (Edmonton: University of Alberta Press, 1986).

Gosman, Robert. *The Riel and Lagimodière Families in Métis Society, 1840–1860*, Parks Canada, Manuscript Report no. 171, Ottawa, 1977.

Gough, Barry M. *The Journal of Alexander Henry the Younger, 1799–1814* (Toronto: Champlain Society, 1988).

Goulet, Agnès. *Marie-Anne Gaboury : Un femme dépareillée* (Saint-Boniface: Éditions des Plaines, 1989).

Gousse, Suzanne & André. *Costume in New France from 1740 to 1760: A Visual Dictionary* (Chambly: La Fleur de Lyse, 1997).

Grant, Peter. "The Saulteux Indians" in L.R. Masson, *Les bourgeois de la compagnie du Nord-Ouest : Récits de voyages, lettres et rapports inédits relatifs au nord-ouest canadien* (New York : Antiquarian Press, 1960).

Gray, John Morgan. *Lord Selkirk of Red River* (Toronto: Macmillan, 1963).

Hamilton, Z.M. "The Story of the Beautiful Marie Gaboury," Saskatchewan Archives Board, SHS 31, date unknown,

Hannon, Leslie F. *Forts of Canada: The Conflicts, Sieges, and Battles that Forged a Great Nation* (Toronto: McClelland & Stewart, 1969).

Hardy, René and Normand Séguin. *Histoire de la Mauricie* (Laval: Les Presses de l'Université Laval, 2004).

Harris, Richard Colebrook. *The Seigneurial System in Canada: A Geographical Study* (Kingston: McGill-Queen's University Press, 1966).

Healy, W.J. *Women of Red River* (Winnipeg: Women's Canadian Club, 1923).

Heidenreich, Virginia, ed. *The Fur Trade in North Dakota* (Bismarck: State Historical Society of North Dakota, 1990).

Hickerson, Harold. "Charles Jean Baptiste Chaboillez," *Ethnohistory*, 6(3), 1959; 6(4), 1959.

———. "The Genesis of a Trading Post Band: The Pembina Chippewa" *Ethnohistory*, 3(4), 1956.

Hilger, M. Inez. *Chippewa Child Life and its Cultural Background* (St. Paul: Minnesota Historical Society Press, 1992).

———. *Chippewa Families: A Social Study of White Earth Reservation, 1938* (St. Paul: Minnesota Historical Society Press, 1998).

Huck, Barbara. *Exploring the Fur Trade Routes of North America* (Winnipeg: Heartland, 2000).

Hungrywolf, Adolf. *Traditional Dress: Knowledge & Methods of Old-Time Clothing* (Summertown: Book Publishing Company, 2003).

Jackson, John G. *The Piikani Blackfeet: A Culture Under Siege* (Missoula, Mountain Press Publishing, 2000).

Kaplan, David H. "'*Maîtres Chez Nous*': The Evolution of French-Canadian Spatial Identity," *American Review of Canadian Studies*, 19(4), 1989.

Kaye, Barry, "The Red River Settlement: Lord Selkirk's Isolated Colony in the Wilderness," *Prairie Forum*, 11(1), 1986.

Kostash Myrna. *Reading the River: A Traveller's Companion to the North Saskatchewan River* (Regina: Coteau Books, 2005).

Lamonde, Yvan. "Cultural Crossroads: Print and Reading in Eighteenth- and Nineteenth-Century French-Speaking Montreal," *American Antiquarian Society*, 2004.

Landry, Yves, and Rénald Lessard. "Causes of Death in Seventeenth- and Eighteenth Century Quebec as Recorded in the Parish Registers, *Historical Methods*, 29(2), 1996.

Legget, Robert. *Ottawa Waterway: Gateway to a Continent* (Toronto: University of Toronto, 1975).

Losey, Elizabeth Browne. *Let Them Be Remembered: The Story of the Fur Trade Posts* (New York: Vantage Press, 1999).

MacEwan, Grant. *Cornerstone Colony: Selkirk's Contribution to the Canadian West* (Saskatoon: Western Producer Prairie Books, 1977).

——. *Marie Anne: The Frontier Spirit of Marie-Anne Lagimodière* (Saskatoon: Western Producer Prairie Books, 1984).

Martin, Chester. *Lord Selkirk's Work in Canada* (London: Oxford University Press, 1916).

McCulloch, J.H. *The Men of Kildonan: A Romance of the Selkirk Settlers* (Toronto, McClelland & Stewart, 1926).

Mcdonell, Alexander. *A Narrative of Transactions in the Red River Country; From the Operations of the Earl of Selkirk, till the Summer of the Year 1816* (London: B. McMillan, 1819).

Morrison, Jean, ed. *Lake Superior to Rainy Lake: Three Centuries of Fur Trade History* (Thunder Bay: Thunder Bay Historical Museum Society, 2003).

——. *Superior Rendezvous Place: Fort William in the Canadian Fur Trade* (Toronto: Natural Heritage Books, 2001).

Morse, Eric W. *Canoe Routes of the Voyageurs: The Geography and Logistics of the Canadian Fur Trade* (Quetico Foundation of Ontario and the Minnesota Historical Society, 1961).

Mount, Graeme S., John Abbott, and Michael J. Mulloy. *The Border at Sault Ste. Marie* (Toronto: Dundurn Press, 1995).

Munro, William Bennett. *The Seigneurs of Old Canada: A Chronicle of New-World Feudalism* (Toronto: Glasgow, Brook, 1915).

Murray, Laura J. "Fur Traders in Conversation," *Ethnohistory*, 50(2), 2003.

Neatby, Hilda. *Quebec: The Revolutionary Age, 1760–1791* (Toronto: McClelland & Stewart, 1966).

Nute, Grace Lee. *The Voyageur's Highway: Minnesota's Border Lake Land* (St. Paul: Minnesota Historical Society Press, 1941, 2002).

Pannekoek, Frits. *The Fur Trade and Western Canadian Society 1670–1870*, Canadian Historical Association, Historical Booklet No. 43, 1987.

Parker, Bruce A. "Thomas Clark: His Business Relationship with Lord Selkirk," *The Beaver*, Autumn 1979.

Payne, Michael. *The Most Respectable Place in the Territory: Everyday Life in Hudson's Bay Company Service York Factory, 1788 to 1870*, Studies in Archaeology Architecture and History, Environment Canada, 1989.

Peers, Laura. *The Ojibwa of Western Canada 1780 to 1870* (Winnipeg: University of Manitoba Press, 1994).

Peterson, Jacqueline, and Jennifer S.H. Brown, eds. *The New Peoples: Being and Becoming Métis in North America* (Winnipeg: University of Manitoba, 1985).

Ray, Arthur J. *Indians in the Fur Trade: Their Role as Hunters, Trappers and Middlemen in the Lands Southwest of Hudson Bay 1660–1870* (Toronto: University of Toronto Press, 1974).

Rich, E.E., ed. *Colin Robertson's Correspondence Book, September 1817 to September 1822* (Toronto: Hudson's Bay Record Society, 1938).

Ross, Alexander. *Red River Settlement: Its Rise, Progress and Present State* (Minneapolis: Ross and Haines, 1957).

Ruddel, David T. *Quebec City, 1765–1832: The Evolution of a Colonial Town* (Ottawa: Canadian Museum of Civilization, 1987).

Russell, Dale R. *Eighteenth-Century Western Cree and Their Neighbours*, Archaeological Survey of Canada, Mercury Series Paper 143, Canadian Museum of Civilization.

Schenck, Theresa M. "Against All Odds . . . and with the Help of Our Friends: The Native Role in Establishing the Red River Colony, 1812–1817," *North Dakota Quarterly*, 6S(4), 1998.

Siggins, Maggie. *Riel: A Life of Revolution* (Toronto: HarperCollins, 1996).

Silversides, Brock. *Fort de Prairies The Story of Edmonton House* (Victoria: Heritage House Publishing Company, 2005).

Sleeper-Smith, Susan. *Indian Women and French Men: Rethinking Cultural Encounter in the Western Great Lakes* (Amherst: University of Massachusetts Press, 2001).

Sprague, D.N., and R.P. Frye. *Genealogy of the First Métis Nation* (Winnipeg: Pemmican Publications, 1983).

Swan, Ruth, and Edward A. Jerome. "The Collin Family at Thunder Bay: A Case Study of Métissage," from *Lake Superior to Rainy Lake: Three Centuries of Fur Trade History*, ed. Jean Morrison (Thunder Bay: Thunder Bay Historical Museum Society, 2003).

Tanner, John. *The Falcon: A Narrative of Captivity & Adventures of John Tanner During Thirty Years Residence Among the Indians in the Interior of North America* (New York: Penguin Books, 1994).

Taylor, A.M. "Fort William: Structures and Space," unpublished manuscript, Fort William Archaeological Project, Thunder Bay, 1976.

Thistle, Paul C. *Indian-European Trade Relations in the Lower Saskatchewan River Region to 1840* (Winnipeg: University of Manitoba Press, 1986).

Thompson, Albert Edward. *Chief Peguis and His Descendants* (Winnipeg: Peguis Publishers, 1973).

Tomczyszyn, Pat. "Sifting Through the Papers of the Past: Using Archival Documents for Costume Research in Seventeenth- and Eighteenth-Century Quebec," *Material History Review*, 55, Spring 2002.

Van Kirk, Sylvia. *Many Tender Ties Women in Fur-Trade Society, 1670–1870* (Oklahoma: University of Oklahoma Press, 1980).

Voyageurs National Park Special History: The Environment and the Fur Trade Experience in Voyageurs National Park, 1730–1870.

Warren, William W. *History of the Ojibway People* (St. Paul: Minnesota Historical Society Press, 1984).

Waters, Thomas F. *The Superior North Shore: A Natural History of Lake Superior's Northern Lands and Waters* (Minneapolis: University of Minnesota Press, 1987).

White, Richard. *The Middle Ground: Indians, Empires, and Republic in the Great Lakes Region, 1650–1815* (Cambridge: Cambridge University Press, 1991).

Whiteley, David H. "Letters Home: Correspondence to and from the Red River Settlement 1812–1870," *Manitoba History* (26), 1993.

Theses

Hamilton, James Scott. Fur Trade Social Inequality and the Role of Non-Verbal Communication, PhD thesis, Simon Fraser University, 1990.

Little, Bruce Pennoyer. People of the Red Path: An Ethnohistory of the Dakota Fur Trade, 1760–1851, PhD thesis, University of Pennsylvania, 1984.

Mann, Rob. Colonizing the Colonizers: Canadien Fur Traders and Fur Trade Society in the Great Lakes Region, 1763–1850, PhD thesis, Binghamton University, State University of New York, 2003.

Podruchny, Carolyn. 'Sons of the Wilderness': Work, Culture and Identity among Voyageurs in the Montreal Fur Trade, 1780–1821, PhD thesis, University of Toronto, 1999.

Smyth, David. The Niitsitapi Trade: Euroamericans and the Blackfoot-Speaking Peoples, to the mid-1830s, PhD thesis, Carleton University, 2002.

Swan, Ruth. The Crucible: Pembina and the Origins of the Red River Valley Métis, PhD thesis, University of Manitoba, 2003.

Internet Sources

Excerpts from the Journal of Colin Robertson, Manitoba Historical Society, www.mhs.mb.ca/does/pageant/08/robertsonjournal.shtml.

Through the Bay: The Arrival of the Hector McDonald Family in Canada, July 12, 1999, www.telusplanet.net/public/cfdun/hectornav.htm

NOTES

—

CHAPTER ONE

1. Université de Montréal, parish records for Maskinongé.

2. Clio Collective, *Quebec Women: A History*, trans. Roger Gannon and Rosalind Gill (Toronto: Women's Press, 1987), p. 47.

3. John A Dickinson and Brian Young, *A Short History of Quebec* (Montreal: McGill University Press, 2003), p. 71.

4. Clio Collective, *Quebec Women*, p. 43.

5. David H. Kaplan, "' Maîtres Chez Nous': The Evolution of French-Canadian Spatial Identity," *American Review of Canadian Studies* 19, 1989, p. 407.

6. René Hardy, and Normand Séguin, *Histoire de la Mauricie* (Laval: Les Presses de l'Université Laval, 2004) pp. 56, 60.

7. David T. Ruddel, *Quebec City, 1765–1832: The Evolution of a Colonial Town* (Ottawa: Canadian Museum of Civilization, 1987), p. 56.

8. Ruddel, *Quebec City*, p. 28.

9. Clément Plante to Maggie Siggins, November 2, 2004.

10. Clio Collective, *Quebec Women*, pp. 49–50.

11. Patricia Lockhart Fleming, "Cultural Crossroads: Print and Reading in Eighteenth- and Nineteenth-Century English-Speaking Montreal," *American Antiquarian Society* (112), 2002, p. 239.

12. Dickinson and Young, *A Short History of Quebec*, p. 72.

13. Georges Dugast, *The First Canadian Woman in the Northwest, or the Story of Marie Anne Gaboury, Wife of John Baptiste Lajimoniere, Who arrived in the Northwest in 1807, and Died at St. Boniface at the Age of 96 Years* (Winnipeg: The Manitoba Free Press Company, 1902), p. 1.

14. Clio Collective, *Quebec Women*, p. 107.

15. Ibid., pp. 69–70.

16. Pat Tomczyszyn, "Sifting Through the Papers of the Past: Using Archival Documents for Costume Research in Seventeenth- and Eighteenth-Century Quebec," *Material History Review* 55 (Spring 2002), p. 7.

17. Clio Collective, *Quebec Women*, pp. 68–69.

18. Dickinson and Young, *A Short History of Quebec*, p. 61.

19. Quoted in Clio Collective, *Quebec Women*, pp. 103–104.

CHAPTER TWO

1. Robert Gosman, *The Riel and Lagimodière Families in Métis Society, 1840–1860*, Parks Canada, Manuscript Report no. 171, Ottawa, 1997.

2. Clio Collective, *Quebec Women: A History*, trans. by Roger Gannon and Rosalind Gill (Toronto: Women's Press, 1987), p. 73.

3. Maggie Siggins, *Riel: A Life of Revolution* (Toronto: HarperCollins, 1996), p. 33.

4. John A. Dickinson and Brian Young, *A Short History of Quebec* (Montreal: McGill University Press, 2003), p. 86.

5. Ibid., p. 73.

6. George Frederick Burns to Maggie Siggins, January 14, 2006.

7. Georges Dugast, *The First Canadian Woman in the Northwest, or the Story of Marie Anne Gaboury, Wife of John Baptiste Lajimoniere, Who arrived in the Northwest in 1807, and Died at St. Boniface at the Age of 96 Years* (Winnipeg: The Manitoba Free Press Company, 1902), p. 2.

8. Ibid.

9. Ibid., pp. 2–3.

10. Robert Legget, *Ottawa Waterway: Gateway to a Continent* (Toronto: University of Toronto, 1975), p. 37.

11. Frits Pannekoek, *The Fur Trade and Western Canadian Society 1670–1870*, The Canadian Historical Assoc., Historical Booklet No. 43, 1987, p. 171.

12. J.M.S. Careless, *Canada: A Story of Challenge* (Cambridge: Cambridge University Press, 1953), p. 28.

13. Dickinson and Young, *A Short History of Quebec*, p. 20.

14. Georges-Hébert Germain, *Adventurers in the New World: The Saga of the Coureurs des Bois* (Hull: Canadian Museum of Civilization, 2003), p. 59.

15. James Scott Hamilton, Fur Trade Social Inequality and the Role of Non-Verbal Communication, PhD thesis, Simon Fraser University, 1990, p. 45.

16. Ibid., pp. 17–18.

17. Dickinson and Young, *A Short History of Quebec*, p. 76

18. Ruth Swan, The Crucible: Pembina and the Origins of the Red River Valley Métis, PhD thesis, University of Manitoba, 2003, p. 171.

19. Marcel Giraud, *The Métis in the Canadian West*, trans. George Woodcock (Edmonton: University of Alberta Press, 1986), vol. 1, p. 584.

CHAPTER THREE

1. Georges-Hébert Germain, *Adventurers in the New World: The Saga of the Coureurs des Bois* (Hull: Canadian Museum of Civilization, 2003), p. 71.

2. Carolyn Podruchny, 'Sons of the Wilderness': Work, Culture and Identity Among Voyageurs in the Montreal Fur Trade, 1780–1821, PhD thesis, University of Toronto, 1999, p. 100.

3. Ibid.

4. Quoted in James Hamilton, Fur Trade Social Inequality and the Role of Non-Verbal Communication, PhD thesis, Simon Fraser University, 1990, p. 177.

5. Eric W. Morse, *Canoe Routes of the Voyageurs: The Geography and Logistics of the Canadian Fur Trade* (Quetico Foundation of Ontario and the Minnesota Historical Society, 1961,) p. 16.

6. Marjorie Wilkins Campbell, *The North West Company* (Toronto: Macmillan Company of Canada, 1957), p. 25.

7. Robert Legget, *Ottawa Waterway: Gateway to a Continent* (Toronto, University of Toronto Press, 1975), p. 61.

8. Ibid., p. 61

9. Ibid., p. 36

10. Ibid., p. 61

11. Edmund Jefferson Danziger, Jr., *The Chippewas of Lake Superior* (Norman: University of Oklahoma Press, 1979), p. 7.

12. Legget, *Ottawa Waterway*, p. 84.

13. Ibid., p. 257.

14. Morse, *Canoes Routes of the Voyageurs*, p. 74.

15. Colonel George Thomas, Landmann, *Adventures and Recollections* (London: 1852), vol. II, p. 168.

16. Morse, *Canoes Routes of the Voyageurs*, pp. 75–76.

17. Ibid., pp. 28–29.

18. Ibid., p. 259.

19. Ibid., p. 15.

20. Ibid., p. 16.

21. Claire Elizabeth Campbell, *Shaped by the West Wind: Nature and History in Georgian Bay.* (Vancouver: UBC Press, 2005), p. 31.

22. Elizabeth Browne Losey, *Let Them Be Remembered: The Story of the Fur Trade Forts* (New York: Vantage Press, 1999), p. 77.

23. Ibid.

24. Georges Dugast, *The First Canadian Woman in the Northwest, or the Story of Marie Anne Gaboury, Wife of John Baptiste Lajimoniere, Who arrived in the Northwest in 1807, and Died at St. Boniface at the Age of 96 Years* (Winnipeg: The Manitoba Free Press Company, 1902), p. 4.

CHAPTER FOUR

1. A.M. Taylor, Fort William: Structures and Space, unpublished manuscript, Fort William Archaeological Project, Thunder Bay, 1976, p. 136.

2. James Scott Hamilton, "Fur Trade Social Inequality and the Role of Non-Verbal Communication," PhD thesis, 1990, p. iii.

3. Ibid., p. 177.

4. Ibid., p. 164.

5. Ibid. , p. 157.

6. Ruth Swan and Edward A. Jerome, "The Collin Family at Thunder Bay: A Case Study of Métissage," from *Lake Superior to Rainy Lake: Three Centuries of Fur Trade History*, ed. Jean Morrison (Thunder Bay: Thunder Bay Historical Museum Society, 2003), p. 112. Also Ruth Swan, The Crucible: Pembina and the Origins of the Red River Valley Métis, PhD thesis, University of Manitoba, 2003, p. 111.

7. Quoted in Elizabeth Browne Losey, *Let Them Be Remembered: The Story of the Fur Trade Posts*, (New Yiork: Vantage Press, 1999), pp. 90–91.

8. Voyageurs National Park, Binder 2, Chapter 3: Material Culture, Transportation, p. 6.

9. Ibid., p. 317.

10. Morrison, *Superior Rendezvous Place: Fort William in the Canadian Fur Trade* (Toronto: Natural Heritage Books, 2001), p. 35. Also Hamilton, Fur Trade Social Inequality, p. 66.

11. Jean Morrison, *Superior Rendezvous Place*, p. 35.

12. Maggie Siggins, *Riel: A Life of Revolution* (Toronto: HarperCollins, 1994), p. 8.

13. Voyageurs National Park, Binder 2, Chapter 3: Material Culture, Transportation, p. 2.

14. Losey, *Let Them Be Remembered*, p. 87.

15. Ibid., p. 177.

16. Voyageurs National Park Special History: The Environment and the Fur Trade Experience in Voyageurs National Park, 1730–1870, p. 7.

17. Elliott, Coues. *Manuscript Journals of Alexander Henry and David Thompson, 1799–1814* (Minneapolis: Ross & Haines, 1897), November 25, 1805.

CHAPTER FIVE

1. Ruth Swan, The Crucible: Pembina and the Origins of the Red River Valley Métis, PhD thesis, University of Manitoba, 2003, p. 166.

2. Coues, Alexander Henry's Journals, May , 1801

3. Ibid., May 17, 1801.

4. Ibid. April 8, 1803.

5. Ibid., May 7, 1801.

6. Ibid. Sept. 23, 1804.

7. Ibid. April 2, 1804.

8. Swan, The Crucible, p. 177.

9. Ibid., p. 184.

10. John E. Foster, "Wintering: the Outsider Adult Male and the Ethnogenesis of the Western Plain," *Prairie Forum*, vol. 1, No. 1, Spring, 1994, p. 2.

11. Coues, Alexander Henry's Journals, November 1, 1801.

12. Marcel Giraud, *The Métis in the Canadian West*, trans. George Woodcock, (Edmonton: University of Alberta Press, 1986), vol. 1, pp. 215–216.

13. Peter Grant, "The Saulteux Indians," in L.R. Masson, *Les bourgeois de la compagnie du Nord-Ouest : Récits de voyages, lettres et rapports inédits relatifs au nord-ouest canadien* (New York : Antiquarian Press, 1960), vol. 2, p. 320.

14. John Tanner, *The Falcon: A Narrative of Captivity & Adventures of John Tanner During Thirty Years Residence Among the Indians in the Interior of North America* (New York: Penguin Books, 1994), p. 84.

15. Swan, The Crucible, p. 230.

16. Ibid.

17. Grant MacEwan, *Marie Anne The Frontier Spirit of Marie Anne Lagimodière* (Saskatoon: Western Producer Prairie Books, 1984), p. 45.

18. Sylvia Van Kirk, *Many Tender Ties: Women in Fur-Trade Society, 1670–1870* (Oklahoma: University of Oklahoma Press, 1980), p. 79.

19. Coues, Alexander Henry's Journals, September 6, 1804

20. Swan, The Crucible, p.221.

21. Coues, Alexander Henry's Journals, October 3, 1803.

CHAPTER SIX

1. Sylvia Van Kirk, *Many Tender Ties: Women in Fur-Trade Society, 1670–1870,* (Oklahoma: University of Oklahoma Press, 1980), pp. 37–38.

2. M. Inez Hilger, *Chippewa Child Life and Its Cultural Background* (St. Paul: Minnesota Historical Society Press, 1992), p. 13.

3. Ibid., p. 15.

4. Ibid.

5. Ibid., p. 12.

6. Ibid., p. 13.

7. Agnès Goulet, *Marie-Anne Gaboury : Un femme dépareillée* (Saint-Boniface: Éditions des Plaines, 1989), p. 23.

8. Coues, Alexander Henry's Journals, December 29, 1807.

9. Hilger, *Chippewa Child Life*, p. 23.

10. Ibid., p. 26.

11. Ibid., p. 21.

12. Ibid., pp. 130–31.

13. Quoted in Laura Peers, *The Ojibwe of Western Canada 1780 to 1870* (Winnipeg: University of Manitoba Press, 1994), p. 46.

14. Coues, Alexander Henry's Journals, May 15, 1801.

15. Bruce Pennoyer Little, "People of the Red Path": An Ethnohistory of the Dakota Fur Trade, 1760–1851, PhD thesis, University of Pennsylvania, 1984, p. 108.

16. Harold Hickerson, "The Genesis of a Trading Post Band: The Pembina Chippewa" *Ethnohistory*, vol. 3 (4), Autumn 1956, p. 307.

17. Coues, Alexander Henry's Journals, August 2, 1805.

18. Ibid.

19. Ibid., December 29, 1807.

20. Ibid., March 4, 1808.

21. Ibid.

22. Ibid.

CHAPTER SEVEN

1. Harold Hickerson, "The Genesis of a Trading Post Band: The Pembina Chippewa" *Ethnohistory*, vol. 3, (4), Autumn 1956, p. 320.

2. Peter Fidler's list of free Canadians, Hudson's Bay Company Archives, B. 235/a/3 (IM153), 1814.

3. Coues, Alexander Henry's Journals, September 2, 1808.

4. Ibid., August 13, 1808.

5. Ibid., August 19, 1808.

6. David Smyth, The Niitsitapi Trade: Euroamericans and the Blackfoot-Speaking Peoples, to the Mid-1830s, PhD thesis, Carleton University, 2002, p. 147.

7. Quoted in Deanna Christensen, *Cumberland House Historic Park* (Regina: Deptartment of Tourism and Renewable Resources, 1974), p. 6.

8. Ibid., p. 14.

9. Ibid., p. 16.

10. Elizabeth Browne Losey, *Let Them Be Remembered: The Story of the Fur Trade Forts* (New York: Vantage Press, 1999), p. 86.

11. Paul C. Thistle, *Indian-European Trade Relations in the Lower Saskatchewan River Region to 1840,* (Winnipeg: University of Manitoba Press, 1986) p. 65.

12. Georges Dugast, *The First Canadian Woman in the Northwest or the Story of Marie Anne Gaboury, Wife of John Baptiste Lajimoniere, Who arrived in the Northwest in 1807, and Died at St. Boniface at the Age of 96 Years* (Winnipeg: The Manitoba Free Press Company, 1902), p. 7.

13. Quoted in Myrna Kostash, *Reading the River: A Traveller's Companion to the North Saskatchewan River,* (Regina: Coteau Books, 2005), p. 280.

14. Coues, Alexander Henry's Journals, September 2, 1808.

15. Dugast, *The First Canadian Woman,* p. 7.

CHAPTER EIGHT

1. Marcel Giraud, *The Métis in the Canadian West,* trans. George Woodcock (Edmonton: University of Alberta Press, 1986), vol. 1, p. 382.

2. Ibid., p. 383.

3. Theodore Binnema, *Common & Contested Ground: A Human and Environmental History of the Northwestern Plains* (Norman: University of Oklahoma Press, 2001), p. 118.

4. Brock Silversides, *Fort de Prairies: The Story of Edmonton House* (Victoria: Heritage House Publishing Company, 2005), p. 8.

5. David Smyth, The Niitsitapi Trade: Euroamericans and the Blackfoot-Speaking Peoples, to the Mid-1830s, PhD thesis, Carleton University, 2002, p. 203.

6. Elizabeth Browne Losey, *Let Them Be Remembered: The Story of the Fur Trade Forts* (New York: Vantage Press, 1999), p. 222.

7. Leslie F. Hannon, *Forts of Canada: The Conflicts, Sieges, and Battles that Forged a Great Nation* (Toronto: McClelland & Stewart, 1969), p. 214.

8. Silversides, *Fort de Prairies*, p. 6.

9. Coues, Alexander Henry's Journals, Sept. 13, 1808.

10. Ibid. Sept. 15, 1809.

11. Sylvia Van Kirk, *Many Tender Ties: Women in Fur-Trade Society, 1670–1870*, (Oklahoma: University of Oklahoma Press, 1980), p. 93.

12. Giraud, *The Métis in the Canadian West*, vol. 1, p. 292.

13. Kirk, *Many Tender Ties*, p. 125.

14. Observations at Fort Edmonton Park, Edmonton.

15. Losey, *Let Them Be Remembered*, p. 226.

16. Smyth, The Niitsitapi Trade, p. 19.

17. Binnema, *Common & Contested Ground*, p. 74.

18. Ibid., p. 61

19. Ibid., p. 91.

20. Arthur J. Ray, *Indians in the Fur Trade: Their Role as Hunters, Trappers and Middlemen in the Lands Southwest of Hudson Bay 1660–1870*, (Toronto: University of Toronto Press, 1974), p. 12.

21. Binnema, *Common & Contested Ground*, p. 77.

22. Ibid., p. 193.

23. HBC Journals: Edmonton House, May 4, 1809.

24. Binnema, *Common & Contested Ground*, p. 72.

25. Smyth, The Niitsitapi Trade, p. 23.

26. HBC Journals, Edmonton House, March 12, 1809.

27. Ibid. March 18, 1809.

28. Ibid. March 22, 1809.

29. Ibid. April 24, 1809.

30. Binnema, *Common & Contested Ground*, p. 40.

31. Ibid., p. 42.

32. Coues, Alexander Henry's Journals, August, 1800.

CHAPTER NINE

1. Theodore Binnema, *Common & Contested Ground: A Human and Environmental History of the Northwestern Plains* (Norman: University of Oklahoma Press, 2001), p. 149.

2. Edmonton House Journals, September 22, 1806.

3. Binnema, *Common & Contested Ground*, p.156.

4. Ibid.

5. Ibid., p. 158.

6. Ibid., p. 186.

7. Ibid.

8. Smyth, The Niitsitapi Trade, p. 203.

9. Ibid., pp. 203–204.

10. Coues, Alexander Henry's Journals, September 13, 1809.

11. Ibid., October 9, 1809.

12. Ibid., October 11, 1809.

13. Ibid., November 7, 1809.

14. Edmonton House Journals, November 13, 1809.

15. Edmonton House Journals, January 2, 1810.

16. Binnema, *Common & Contested Ground* p. 196. Also Dugast, *The First Canadian Woman*, p. 17.

17. Michael Payne, *The Most Respectable Place in the Territory: Everyday Life in Hudson's Bay Company Service York Factory, 1788 to 1870*, Studies in Archaeology Architecture and History, Environment Canada, 1989, p. 99.

18. Edmonton House Journals, June 14, 1809.

19. Ibid.

20. Ibid.

21. Dugast, *The First Canadian Woman*, pp. 14, 15.

22. Ibid., p. 17.

23. Ibid., pp. 13, 14.

CHAPTER TEN

1. Coues, Alexander Henry's Journals, February 13, 1811.

2. Ibid., June 3, 1811.

3. Edmonton House Journals, October 31, 1810.

4. Thoedore Binnema, *Common & Contested Ground: A Human and Environmental History of the Northwestern Plains* (Norman: University of Oklahoma Press, 2001), pp. 34, 35.

5. Edmonton House Journals, April 17, 1807.

6. Georges Dugast, *The First Canadian Woman in the Northwest or the Story of Marie Anne Gaboury, Wife of John Baptiste Lajimoniere, Who arrived in the Northwest in 1807, and Died at St. Boniface at the Age of 96 Years* (Winnipeg: The Manitoba Free Press Company, 1902), p. 18.

7. Binnema, *Common & Contested Ground*, p.26

CHAPTER ELEVEN

1. Alice E. Brown, ed. *Excerpts for the Journal of Colin Robertson*, Manitoba Historical Society, August, 24, 1815.

2. Bruce A. Parker, "Thomas Clark His Business Relationship with Lord Selkirk," *The Beaver*, Autumn 1979, p. 50.

3. Lucille H. Campey, *The Silver Chief: Lord Selkirk and the Scottish Pioneers of Belfast, Baldoon and Red River* (Toronto: Natural Heritage Books, 2003), p. 9.

4. Ibid., p. 71.

5. Barry Kaye, "The Red River Settlement: Lord Selkirk's Isolated Colony in the Wilderness," *Prairie Forum*, 11(1), 1986, p. 6.

6. Thomas Douglas Selkirk, *The Collected Writings of Lord Selkirk, 1810–1812*, ed. J.M. Bumsted (Winnipeg: Manitoba Record Society, 1988), p. 165.

7. J.M. Bumsted, *Fur Trade Wars: The Founding of Western Canada* (Winnipeg: Great Plains Publications, 1999), p. 54.

8. Ruth Swan, The Crucible: Pembina and the Origins of the Red River Valley Métis, PhD thesis, University of Manitoba, 2003, p. 249.

9. Ibid., p. 25.

10. D.N. Sprague and R.P. Frye, *Genealogy of the First Métis Nation* (Winnipeg: Pemmican Publications, 1983), p. 28.

11. Fred J. Shore, "The Origins of Métis Nationalism and the Pemmican Wars, 1780–1821, in Robert Coutts and Richard Stuart, eds., *The Forks and the Battle of Seven Oaks in Manitoba History* (Winnipeg: Manitoba Historical Society, 1994) p. 79.

12. Bumsted, *Fur Trade Wars*, p. 130

13. George Bryce, *The Romantic Settlement of Lord Selkirk's Colonists* (Toronto: Musson, 1909), p. 41.

CHAPTER TWELVE

1. Theresa M. Schenck, "Against All Odds . . . and with the Help of Our Friends: The Native Role in Establishing the Red River Colony, 1812–1817," *North Dakota Quarterly*, 6S(4), 1998, p. 37. Also John Morgan Gray, *Lord Selkirk of Red River* (Toronto: Macmillan, 1963), p.72.

2. Marcel Giraud, *Métis in the Canadian West*, trans. George Woodcock (Edmonton: University of Alberta Press, 1986), vol. 1. p. 442.

3. Thomas Douglas Selkirk, *The Collected Writings of Lord Selkirk, 1810–1820*, ed. J.M. Bumsted (Winnipeg: Manitoba Record Society, 1988), p. 143.

4. Barry Kaye, "The Red River Settlement: Lord Selkirk's Isolated Colony in the Wilderness," *Prairie Forum*, 11(1), 1986, p. 17.

5. Gray, *Lord Selkirk*, p. 83; Lucille H. Campey, *The Silver Chief: Lord Selkirk and the Scottish Pioneers of Belfast, Baldoon and Red River* (Toronto: Natural Heritage Books, 2003), p. 86; J.M. Bumsted, *Fur Trade Wars: The Founding of Western Canada* (Winnipeg: Great Plains Publications, 1999), pp. 71, 72.

6. Alexander Mcdonell, *A Narrative of Transactions in the Red River Country; From the Operations of the Earl of Selkirk, till the Summer of the Year 1816*, (London: B. McMillan, 1819), p. 263.

7. J.W. Chalmers, *Red River Adventure: The Story of the Selkirk Settlers* (Toronto: Macmillan, 1956), p. 46. Also Albert Edward Thompson, *Chief Peguis and his Descendants* (Winnipeg: Peguis Publishers, 1973), p.10.

8. Mcdonell, *A Narrative of Transactions*, p.3.

9. Chalmers, *Red River Adventure*, p. 48.

10. Mcdonell, *A Narrative of Transactions*, p. 4.

11. Ibid.

12. Ibid.

13. Quoted in Ruth Swan, The Crucible: Pembina and the Origins of the Red River Valley Metis, PhD thesis, University of Manitoba, 2003, p. 265.

14. Ibid., footnote, p.265.

15. Mcdonell, *A Narrative of Transactions*, p. 4.

16. Ibid.

17. Schenck, "Against All Odds," p. 45.

18. Laura Peers, "The Ojibwa, Red River and the Forks, 1770–1870" in Robert Coutts and Robert Stuart, eds., *The Forks and the Battle of Seven Oaks in Manitoba History* (Winnipeg: Manitoba Historical Society, 1994), p. 4.

19. Ibid.

20. Alexander Ross, *Red River Settlement: Its Rise, Progress and Present State* (Minneapolis: Ross and Haines, 1957), first published in 1856, p. 23.

21. Chalmers, *Red River Adventure*, p. 52.

22. Bumsted, *Fur Trade Wars*, p. 94.

23. Selkirk Papers, Library and Archives Canada, C16, p. 34.

CHAPTER THIRTEEN

1. Quoted in J.W. Bumsted, *Fur Trade Wars, The Founding of Western Canada* (Winnipeg: Great Plains Publications, 1999), p. 116.

2. Marcel Giraud, *Métis in the Canadian West*, trans. George Woodcock (Edmonton: University of Alberta Press, 1986), vol. 1, p. 442.

3. Selkirk Papers, Library and Archives Canada, 63: 16869.

4. Ibid.

5. Hudson's Bay Company Archives, Pembina House, Hugh Heney's Journal, January 1, 1813.

6. Quoted in John Morgan Gray, *Lord Selkirk of Red River* (Toronto: Macmillan, 1963), p. 93.

7. Giraud, *Métis in the Canadian West*, vol. 1, p. 385.

8. Quoted in Bumsted, *Fur Trade Wars*, p. 103

9. Alexander Mcdonell, *A Narrative of Transactions in the Red River Country; From the Operations of the Earl of Selkirk, till the Summer of the Year 1816*, (London: B. McMillan, 1819), p. 5.

10. Gray, *Lord Selkirk*, p. 96.; Theresa M. Schenck, "Against All Odds . . . and with the Help of Our Friends: The Native Role in Establishing the Red River Colony, 1812–1817," *North Dakota Quarterly*, 6S(4), 1998, p. 40.

11. J.H. McCulloch, *The Men of Kildonan A Romance of the Selkirk Settlers* (Toronto, McClelland & Stewart, 1926), pp. 45–47; Gray, *Lord Selkirk*, p. 16.

12. Gray, *Lord Selkirk*, p. 16.

13. Quoted in Schenck, "Against All Odds," p. 41.

14. Bumsted, *Fur Trade Wars*, pp. 121–23.

15. Schenck, "Against All Odds," p. 41.

16. Bumsted, *Fur Trade Wars*, p. 116.

17. Selkirk, *Collected Writings of Lord Selkirk*, vol. 2, pp. 1504–05.

18. Ibid.

19. Bumsted, *Fur Trade Wars*, p.106, Gray, *Lord Selkirk*, p. 106.

20. Selkirk, *Collected Writings of Lord Selkirk*, vol. 2, p. 1506.

21. Bumsted, *Fur Trade Wars*, p. 114.

CHAPTER FOURTEEN

1. Hudson's Bay Company Archives E/8/5:139.

2. Affidavit of Joseph Baudre, or Musquau, Selkirk Papers 60:16029.

3. Alice E. Brown, *Excerpts from the Journal of Colin Robertson*, Manitoba Historical Society, September 3, 1815.

4. J.W. Bumsted, *Fur Trade Wars: The Founding of Western Canada*, (Winnipeg: Great Plains Publications, 1999), p. 125.

5. E.E. Rich, ed. *Colin Robertson's Correspondence Book, September 1817 to September 1822*, (Toronto: Hudson's Bay Record Society, 1938).

6. George Woodcock, *Dictionary of Canadian Biography*, "Colin Robertson," p. 2.

7. Journal of Colin Robertson, October 16, 1815.

8. Ibid.

9. Maggie Siggins, *Riel: A Life of Revolution*, (Toronto: HarperCollins, 1994), p. 21.

10. Quoted in Bumsted, *Fur Trade Wars*, p. 127.

11. Ruth Swan, The Crucible: Pembina and the Origins of the Red River Valley Métis, PhD thesis, University of Manitoba, 2003. p. 288.

12. Quoted in Bumsted, *Fur Trade Wars*, p. 127.

13. Quoted in Grant MacEwan, *Cornerstone Colony: Selkirk's Contribution to the Canadian West* (Saskatoon: Western Producer Prairie Books, 1977), p. 96.

14. Quoted in Chester Martin, *Lord Selkirk's Work in Canada* (London: Oxford University Press, 1916), p. 39.

15. Quoted in Bumsted, *Fur Trade Wars*, p. 145.

16. Ibid., p. 146.

17. Hudson's Bay Company Archives: Edmonton House Annual Report, 1816.

18. Ibid., A.N. McLeod, Fort William to Justice Reed, July 29, 1816.

CHAPTER FIFTEEN

1. Georges Dugast, *The First Canadian Woman in the Northwest or the Story of Marie Anne Gaboury, Wife of John Baptiste Lajimoniere, Who arrived in the Northwest in 1807, and Died at St. Boniface at the Age of 96 Years* (Winnipeg: The Manitoba Free Press Company, 1902), p. 24.

2. Z.M. Hamilton, "The Story of the Beautiful Marie Gaboury," Saskatchewan Archives Board, SHS 31 date unknown, p. 5.

3. Ibid.

4. Quoted in J.W. Bumsted, *Fur Trade Wars: The Founding of Western Canada*, (Winnipeg: Great Plains Publications, 1999), p.130.

5. Quoted in Bumsted, *Fur Trade Wars*, p.130.

6. Alexander Wood Letter Book: Toronto Public Library.

7. Statement of James Grant on stopping of Lagimodière, October 5, 1816, Selkirk Papers, 3169.

8. Report from the Select Committee on the Hudson's Bay Company, 1858, p. 445.

EPILOGUE

1. Select Committee on the Hudson's Bay Company, p. 445.

2. Ibid.

INDEX

—

aboriginals: access to guns by, 104, 140; co-habitation with Europeans by (*see* Europeans, cohabitation with aboriginals by); contempt for Europeans by, 133, 151–53, 155–56, 166, 210; European diseases affecting, 33, 104, 118, 124, 209, 251; as objects of fear, 11, 26, 30; skills of, 83–84; trading interests of, 32; wars among, 104–9, 138, 150, 156–58, 168, 209–10, 252. *See also specific groups of,* e.g. Algonquin people; Assiniboine people

accounting, the fur trade and, 62

Acton House, 141, 174

alcohol, abuses of, 63, 69, 80, 87, 160, 252

Algonquin people, 11, 33, 45

Arapaho people, 143

Assiniboia, 179; claimed for Selkirk's settlers, 199; Métis claims to, 239

Assiniboine people, 81, 104, 131, 140, 153, 156, 168, 177–78, 209

Assiniboine River, 117, 218, 241, 259, 261

Athabasca (region), 190, 217, 233–34

Athabasca Brigade (HBC), starvation of, 240

Athabasca District, 71

Athabasca River, 132

Athapaskan linguistic group, 142

Auguemance (Ojibwe chief), 107–8

Aulneau, Father, 72

Ballantyne, Robert M., 73–74

Barnard, Father, *xv*

Battle River, 139, 144, 177

Battle River House, 165

bears, 86; as food, 38, 80; grizzly, 127–28

beaver: disappearance of, 176, 196; near extinction of, 51–52, 115, 132; pelts as objects of trade, 34, 65–66, 153 (*see also* the fur trade); wool (felt), 31–32

the Beaver Club (Montreal), 16–17

Bellegarde, Charles, 116, 124, 158, 162, 194, 257

Bertrand, Father, 3

Bérube, M. (suitor of Marie-Anne), 12

Binnema, Theodore, 140, 170

Bird, James (HBC chief factor), 130–31, 134, 136, 141, 143–44, 150, 155, 157, 159–61, 167–68, 171, 175–76, 185, 247

Blackfoot people, 137–41, 149–54, 157, 167–68, 173, 177, 252. *See also* Siksika people

Blood people, 138, 140, 142, 150, 153

Bois-Brûlés. *See* Métis

Bonga, Pierre, 86–87

Boucher, François Frimin, 246

Boucher, Pierre, 6

Boudier, Philip, 228

Bourgeoys, Marguerite, 29

Bourke, Father Charles, 192

Bourke, John, 243, 245, 247

Bouvier (the freeman attacked in camp), 125, 127–29

Brandon House, 219, 242

Brébeuf, Jean de), 11

Buckingham House, 151

buffalo: "chips," 95; controlling the movements of, 170, 174, 206, 246; disappearance of, 173–74, 176, 263; hunting of, 31, 36, 80, 82, 88–89, 93–94, 142, 144–47, 179, 194, 216, 224–25, 257–58; meat, 21, 85, 128, 132, 136, 147, 149, 157, 164, 168, 208, 213, 226, 251 (*see also* pemmican); skins and robes, 84, 95, 100, 132, 135, 147, 149, 167, 205; stampedes, 147–48; tanning the hides of, 100 101

Bumsted, J.M., 224

Cameron, Duncan: arrested by Robertson, 235–36, 239; arrests Governor MacDonell, 229; background of, 223; takes command at Fort Gibraltar, 224–26; woos the Selkirk Settlers, 226–27

canot de maître, 21; capsized, 56–57; described, 39; steering of, 52

canot du nord, 69–70

Careless, J.M.S., 31

Cartier, Jacques, 11, 13, 32, 120

the Catholic Church: authoritarian nature of in Quebec, 8, 25, 28; importance of in New France, 7, 9–11; land grants to, 6; tithes,

ACKNOWLEDGEMENTS

I'm indebted to several people who have helped me with this project. Clément Plante was generous in the information he provided about the Gaboury and Lagimodière families in Maskinongé. My researcher, Rachel Knudsen, as usual, did an amazing job of digging up everything, including the kitchen sink. I thank my brother-in-law Steven Sperling, who travelled in Marie-Anne's footsteps with me, although by motor boat, not canoe. I appreciate the encouragement of McClelland & Stewart's Susan Renouf, who was able to see the possibilities of this amazing woman's life. And finally, it is my husband, Gerry Sperling, who always makes it possible.